HONEY, I
BOUGHT AN
AIRPLANE

Stories, Histories and Recollections of
597 flights in the Midwest

Bob Hechlinski

BOB HECHLINSKI
And
Piper Cherokee 180C N8369W

authorHOUSE®

AuthorHouse™
1663 Liberty Drive
Bloomington, IN 47403
www.authorhouse.com
Phone: 1-800-839-8640

Published by AuthorHouse 7/20/2012

ISBN: 978-1-4634-3992-7 (sc)
ISBN: 978-1-4634-3993-4 (hc)
ISBN: 978-1-4634-3991-0 (e)

Library of Congress Control Number: 2011913955

Any people depicted in stock imagery provided by Thinkstock are models,
and such images are being used for illustrative purposes only.
Certain stock imagery © Thinkstock.

This book is printed on acid-free paper.

Credits
Editing by R.E. Schingoethe
Cover design by the author and AuthorHouse
Book Design by AuthorHouse
Front Cover "General Aviation Aircraft On The Moon" Copyrighted by the author
Back Cover courtesy of R.E. Schingoethe
Quotes courtesy of R. W. Smith and Ben Bloede

TO 'HONEY' READERS AND CONTRIBUTORS:

WHILE MY INITIAL *pilot mission was simply to visit air fields, over a 14-years period I discovered much, much more. Enough for an entire book. This book.*

Here I recount literally hundreds of people, events, locales, anecdotes and conversations along the way — some from notes and records, others as best I can recall them. If I have misstated or omitted details, misquoted anyone or otherwise erred within these pages, I sincerely apologize and assure you it was unintentional.

As for you pilots or pilot wannabes, please note that the well-known admonition, "Don't try this at home, boys and girls!"... could apply to some of my aerial antics. While I always flew safely and rather conservatively, sometimes weather or other factors prompted me to make judgment calls that were not necessarily "by the book."

With a sincere "thank you" to all who contributed, directly and indirectly, I bid you "Godspeed" on your journey through these pages with me.

TO MY FELLOW PILOTS AND FLYERS

BEING BORN IN 1941 positioned me squarely in the era of phenomenal growth in aviation speed and capability. Factually, we have seen the curtain drop on that scene which lasted for 30 to 50 years.

Arguably, the aircraft that opened this phase was the Japanese Zero-Sen A6M2 built by Mitsubishi Heavy Industries. It was equally adept in its roles as a fighter-interceptor and in ground support. It was extremely well engineered with excellent speed and extraordinary range. Built light to be quick in the turns and devilishly maneuverable, it was far in advance of any Allied fighter-bomber in either the European or the Pacific theater. Equally contestable would be my selection of Lockheed's SR-71 as the hallmark plane in the final chapter. The Blackbird, designed and built by Kelly Johnson's Skunk Works, continues its service career operating at speeds faster than a bullet fired from the highest powered rifle known to man, at altitudes foreign to all other aircraft and flying temperatures that would soften aluminum. It occupies a distinct technological position without peer.

During the first five years of this marked half century (1940 to 1945) the world entered into a fight to the death with biplanes made of steel tubes and doped fabric and exited with jet propulsion at the very threshold of exceeding the sound barrier. Opponents initiated combat with conventional bombs and bullets; we finished with German rockets and American atomic weapons. Clearly, in terms of speed and capability, we used World War II, Sir Winston Churchill's 'Gee Whiz War,' as an accelerant for flight technology. This accelerator, in turn, became the platform for further development until the speed of sound was no longer a target but a means of measurement for other aircraft that routinely flew at two and three times the speed of sound.

The era of incredible technological aerospace advances is now over. In the succeeding years since the end of the war, we have commercial aircraft rolling off the production line which have a cruising speed not significantly different than the Boeing 707-100 or the Douglas DC-8-20 when introduced into service in the late 1950's and early '60's. Airliners are bigger and more efficient but there is no wholesale abandonment of airliners due to faster planes on the horizon with which the current fleet can compete. The Concorde has proven that speed past Mach1 will be desirable to only a few and affordable to even fewer. Therefore, there is no market demand to pursue more and more velocity in our commercial aircraft.

There has been a remarkable change in the military mind set as well. The most recent history shows that there remains a special, well defined space for air superiority aircraft and we will continue to refine the accepted aircraft and their subsequent replacements as time goes on. But this is a very small and limited portion of military aircraft technology.

The wider based development is for military planes that do not (or cannot) go above the speed of sound. The incredible longevity of the B-52 with a top speed of 550 miles per hour is a lingering reminder of this thought. Rather, we look for planes that typically fly below the speed of sound, perform their job quietly and do it at night. These are the desired winged craft of today's wars. Now the race for speed is done, the ability to lift more and more payload has ebbed, and the quest for efficiency goes forward.

Another case in point is the A-10 Warthog by Fairchild Republic. With a cruising speed of 335 mph and a top speed of 450 mph, it is fast enough to dart into and out of harm's way as the pilot desires. Using abrupt maneuvers to stay a bullet width ahead of enemy gunfire, it can ease itself inside the death zone of its incredible weapons inventory. Three hundred and thirty five miles per hour and there is nothing on the developmental horizon to replace it.

So then, what is the presence of aviation for folks like us? We, the unwashed in that little theater of general aviation, GA or "sport aviation" as the Experimental Aircraft Association prefers to call our pastime.

The growth to-date has taken place mostly in military aircraft, but that culture has bequeathed its wealth to the progeny of sport aviators. It is with us that aviation has continued to progress. When WW II ended, Taylorcraft, Piper and Cessna, Beech and Bellanca and all the others went right back to tube and fabric aircraft and that is all that was on the fare for sport aviators.

But today the general aviation fleet is much different than it was in the late 1940's. GA aircraft are more varied and diversified than ever before. Two-engine aircraft, for example, abound in such variety that there are separate categories. There are light and heavy twins, twins with turbine engines and business twins. There still remains a single category of the Cessna 337; the in-line twin. Anyone who can fly a complex single will have no difficulty in progressing to a light twin. Migrations into more and more complicated aircraft are a way of life with corporate pilots.

It does not stop there, either. The home built plane has advanced far beyond everyone's imagination. The material used on the leading edge of technology and the techniques incorporated into their build is equal (if not superior) to any other aircraft on earth. Today's homemade aircraft can easily have retractable gear, a constant speed propeller and cabin pressurization enabling altitude capability. These planes rival the very best to come off the Beech or Cessna production lines in Wichita, Kansas, or Vero Beach, Florida based Piper Aircraft, or any other established manufacturers for that matter.

And there is still more. Whole populations of baby boomers are aging past their ability to pass an FAA physical. It is a daily event to see an advertisement for a used airplane for sale that starts with the words "Lost physical, must sell." These people increasingly populate the ranks of the Ultra-Light Revolution. They pursue the epitome of cheap and easy flying. We kill 1,000 people a week on our nation's highways, but our government only tightens and increases its control of our pilots which, at most, comprise less than one-tenth of one percent of America. The feds concoct and connive more ways to infest our last bastion against Big Brother almost to the point of unlawful harassment. The Ultra-Lights, exempt from all federal control, are a safe haven for the graying American population. Point A-to-Point B speed is not the objective. Rather, the trip between Point A and a very nearby Point B is the anticipated adventure.

The general aviation factory built planes are all aluminum now. Unlike so many fabric aircraft of the past, they will last forever, given a modicum of maintenance. Our airplane is a great example of what can be expected. When we bought N8369W, she was 26 years old. She sold for $12,500 when she was new and we paid more for her than that. As soon as we bought her, we immediately invested more than we paid for her with new avionics, a new interior and new instrumentation. N8369W is good as new and performs every bit as well now as she did in June of 1965 when she rolled out the north door of the Vero Beach plant. These planes do not die. Their fabric does not rot off and hang from their bones. They age begrudgingly, tending to show their years while remaining airworthy. Those that aren't airworthy can easily be brought back into flying condition. This is my arena and this is my mount.

These aircraft, personified and characterized by one plane in particular, N8369W, is my attachment to that great group of achievers in a sport unique to a few, a handful of sportsmen. Proudly, this small minority of Americans gathers at the airports of the United States and looks to the skies. Only the fields that I visited with the little Cherokee are enumerated in this these pages. Whatever flying that I did in Alaska, Florida, California and other places I have lived is not recounted here.

Hundreds of pilots and aviators (maybe even thousands) were met in my many-year adventure. If forced to provide the common denominator that binds them together, it may be buried in one obscure comment. Spoken many years ago, a man whose name is lost to me summed it all up when he said, "Hell, sometimes I go to the airport and just sit in the damn thing!"

It is from this assembly of men and women that I derive my urge to visit other airports and to engage with other pilots. Every field is a new set of circumstances to behold. If there were six or seven fields visited each day, I looked forward to each one with the anticipation of a youngster in a candy store or a teenager on a date... to be satisfied only by the understanding that, at the end of the day, there are still more airports to visit and more pilots to befriend. After almost 600 airports, I still look forward to the next one.

Some of the stories that follow are simple remembrances of pleasant experiences. Others are a little more profound or are memories of a lifetime. Most of them fit somewhere in between. With polite respect and admiration, I offer these reminiscences to my fellow pilots, aviators, and those who love to fly.

PROLOGUE

OUR FAMILY, LIKE so many others coming out of the depression, was always short of cash. Twelve years of hard times had reduced the entire country (in fact, the entire world) to a bare subsistence economy. People just got by as best they could. It was especially grim for families with immigrant names. They never had a chance to get ahead to begin with. So they started out in poor position when bad times came. The best they could hope for was a job as a factory laborer. Otherwise, it would be a dirt poor mill job or farm work. The bad times never seemed to end. A generation grew up knowing only poverty and hunger.

My Dad and Mom, born in 1909 and 1919, respectively, had limited schooling. Dad dropped out of school at the 5th grade to get a job the South Bend Toy Company. By the time he was 11, he ran a wood lathe and made baseball bats 12 hours a day, six days a week. Mom, although somewhat younger, still did not make it through high school. She took full time work in a shoe factory a few weeks before her 16th birthday. This doesn't mean that they didn't have grit, however.

When they married, Dad drove a milk truck as an independent milk broker for the early years of my life. He had his own route and bought milk directly from the dairy to service his customer base. With dad's encouragement and backing, Mom got additional schooling to learn her trade as a beautician. They both worked very hard and very long hours. Over the years they managed to get ahead little by little. They watched their pennies and kept close scrutiny over expenses. Flying an airplane clearly had no part in their lives.

Regardless, they saw the adventure in flight and made it a point to get their youngest son into a Piper Cub for his first airplane ride at the age of eight. It took place at a grass strip in LaPorte, Indiana. The pilot sat in the back seat, Dad was in the front seat and I was on his lap. I don't recall a seat belt being used during that flight.

For the little boy, the ride was claustrophobic. With the prop wash rhythmically banging against the thin plastic window and the sun with all its brightness and withering heat, the little boy on daddy's lap did the expected: he vomited all over the place. The pronouncement was made right then and there that little Bobbie would never be able to fly in an airplane or, Heaven forbid, be a pilot.

When I was a pre-teenager, a youngster by the name of Eddie Minczewski became a childhood friend. Eddie's dad, a World War II Army Air Corps veteran, flew B-24s and B-17s in the European theater. A graduate of Notre Dame's School of Law, he was a good family friend. He also owned a light airplane and flew it as a hobby. The airplane, a Stinson Voyager, was beautiful. It was much larger than the only other vehicle I had been in, the family car, and it got off the ground. The nose was upswept, giving it a snooty look. The tail assembly started immediately after the rear seat resulting in a very full profile. I vividly recall my first ride in the Stinson.

We emerged from its T-hangar on Bendix Field in South Bend and flew to Michigan City. South Bend was a very lovely airport with paved runways and taxiways. Michigan City, being privately owned by Joe Phillips, was a large, square sod field reminiscent of old WW II training fields. A pilot could land with a favorable wind every time. The Stinson is flown from the front seat. Eddie and I sat in the back. At Michigan City, we enjoyed a 6-ounce bottle of Coke-A-Cola. (These were the bottles that had the city of the bottling company molded into the bottom.) I don't recall what we did there but I sure thought it a great way to live: flying anywhere, whenever, to do whatever could be done was a form of true freedom. And I liked it.

I wouldn't fly again until after high school. It was 1958 and, again, times were tough. It was hard to get a job and further education was not an option; there wasn't that kind of money in the house. I found my immediate future in the military. Specifically, I joined the Air Force. My overseas assignment was Elmendorf Air Force base in Anchorage, Alaska. For the next 24 months, my home would be addressed only as APO 942. My outfit was the 1727th Support Squadron. Our job was to tend to the C-124s, both "A" and "C" models, that kept our DEW LINE sites stocked and equipped. While my work was that of an aircraft and engine mechanic, I did a lot of flying as an in-flight mechanic. It was the best job I could expect in the service.

But it wasn't until I returned stateside that the idea of flying lessons came to mind. I was stationed with the 62nd Troop Carrier Wing at Travis Air Force Base near Fairfield, California. There was a little grass strip in nearby Vacaville that had a couple of training airplanes. One was a Piper J-3 Cub and the other was a Taylorcraft DCO-65. The instructors, who came and went with the wind, treated these aircraft as interchangeable parts. It was hard to tell which I would be flying from week to week.

There were no flight manuals; we were expected to write our own based upon the verbal lessons and discussions. There were no radios or electrical systems; we had to first learn how to prop an engine. There was no ground school; we were to buy some books on aviation and hoped we could learn enough to pass the eventual written examination. The curriculum was straight-forward. Fly with an instructor for six hours or so and then solo. When it seemed appropriate, there would be a cross country flight to Nut Tree Resort which had an east - west runway and was conveniently located about 40 or 50 miles to the east. Equally convenient would be the fact that the Vacaville airport was also on the northern shoulder of Route 40 and so was the Nut Tree. Getting lost was not even considered a possibility. After that, I'm not so sure what they had in mind.

The cost was $8 per flight hour: $2 for the instructor and $6 for the airplane with gas included. This is cheap by today's standards. In 1961, eight dollars was also 15% of my monthly take home pay.

The aircraft were unforgettable. The Cub, tail number 32503 (serial number 5398, built in 1940) seemed to be my favorite if only because it was the first airplane that I would actually manipulate and the one in which I accumulated the most flight time.

Upon checking current FAA registration, I see that she is still flying under the loving ownership and tender care of Dr. Steve

Holifield, an Endodontic in California who keeps the restored Cub at the Sonoma Skypark Airport. Steve tells me that he does not feel he truly owns Piper Cub 32503. Rather, he assumes he is the interim caretaker. As such, he will only be allowed to pass along his charge to the next flyer.

The other, a Taylorcraft with tail number 68907 started life as a 3 place, military glider. Built in 1942, she was one of the 250 Taylorcraft TG-6 gliders procured for training purposes. A frontal nose assembly was installed in the normal engine position. Added, then, was an odd looking, glassed-over nose which also held the third seat. It looked too bulky and too ugly to fly. It was relatively easy to remove the bulbous nose and re-install a Continental 65 horsepower engine. Many of these were converted into DCO-65 powered tandem ships after the war by Taylorcraft dealers across the USA. Only a few remain today, but it is a nice flying plane. It had the same performance speeds as the Cub but it seemed to be much roomier in the front seat where most folks flew her.

On the day of my solo, the Cub was gone on a cross country trip and wouldn't be back for several hours. So, the instructor scheduled me for the Taylorcraft. I waited and waited in the little bar/café that the airport owner ran to provide his primary income. The plane's return was long overdue. A TWA pilot had it out for some aerobatic flying and should have been back in time for my solo. That expected time of return passed and everyone was worried. Then the Highway Patrol came in and told the owner about the crash in an onion field about 10 miles away. The pilot was hurt but he would fully recover.

The aircraft owner and I got into the airport flatbed truck and went to get what was left of 68907. We found it with its butt stuck up in the air and the landing gear folded up behind the pilot's seat. She was a mess. Both wings were ripped off and the engine was stuck in the autumn mud. The prop was in splinters, and the interior was splattered with blood. The aircraft would have to be scrapped. I would not solo on this day. In fact, I would not solo for another nine years!

During the following year my enlistment was briefly extended for the Berlin Wall crisis which presented a distinct danger. I was married, separated from the service, re-located to northern Indiana, and brought back into the service for the Cuban missile crisis. Still, there was no time for flying. Like other folks, we were too busy establishing ourselves. This load became heavier when the newly enacted Vietnam GI Bill enabled me to go to college.

My job in Florida was that of a technical service representative for my company back in South Bend, the Bendix Aerospace Corporation. I had three distinct duties, or responsibilities. First of all, I provided technical service for the commercial wheel and brake business. That is, I took care of Eastern, Pan Am, National and all the South American airlines with their Bendix wheels and brakes. That kept me busy in Miami on a day-to-day basis.

The other two assignments kept me on the road quite a bit. One was jet fuel control work with military installations and the other concerned fuel injection systems in the general aviation arena. These included the Jet Ranger helicopter fleet at Pensacola, and Fort Rucker near Dothan, Alabama. Also included was the Piper Aircraft facility at Vero Beach and its sister division, Cavalier Aircraft on the west coast. Beyond that, I had to provide field service to all the fixed base operators who handled aircraft equipped with Bendix fuel injection systems. These are the IO series of Lycoming engines such as IO-360's and IO-540's.

Typically, I would leave home before sunrise on Monday morning to arrive at my first stop around opening time. Each night, I dragged myself into a hotel at about 7 or 8 PM. If I was lucky, there would still be one more steak in the hotel kitchen. The trip would continue until Friday when I would usually return home after dark. It was grueling, but I was young, and enthused.

Travel in Florida is extremely favorable for general aviation flying under Visual Flight Rules. The skies are usually clear and the only cloud formations are cumulus at about 4,000 feet MSL. And, don't forget, MSL and AGL in Florida are less than 100 feet apart no matter where you go! It rained occasionally, but it cleared up instantly afterwards. The hurricane season or rainy season was different. That stopped a lot of flying time.

It was clear that a pilot's license could ease my travel burden. After all, I was driving from one Fixed Base Operator (FBO) to another. What took a full five days could be done in three. And it would be easier traveling.

Surprisingly enough, the idea got very little support from the home office. In fact, general aviation flying for business purposes was discouraged. The old salts knew from past experience that airplanes are not considered in the same emotional vein as automobiles. To a road man, a car is a car no matter what. If one breaks down, a rental car is substituted and the work goes on. But when an airplane is grounded, well, that's a different story. The emotional attachment, the home-based supervisors and managers have learned, renders a pilot out of service at the same time. The owner wants to stay with the airplane until it is airworthy again. A private airplane in company use was more disruptive than what it was worth.

In talking about the use of airplanes in company work, the older tech reps, (who had been business flying for years,) showed us younger men how to pull it off. First of all, don't raise any red flags, don't tell the home office about flying from call to call. They will find out in due time, so don't lie about it either. Cover the expenses as if the airplane were a car. At that time, we got ten cents a mile for our personal car. Aircraft rental ran about $10 per hour (gasoline included) and we could count on an air speed of 100 mph or a little better. At 10 cents per mile, the expense account would cover most if not all the costs. If a breakdown should occur or if the weather is below your capabilities, leave the plane and get right into a rental car to finish the job. These were reasonable guidelines. The task was feasible and appeared to be practical. It was decided: I would get a private pilot's license.

In early 1970, I showed up at Tamiami airport exactly on the weekend that they were closing the field. It seems that the five mile control zones around Miami International and Tamiami overlapped by a few hundred feet. Tamiami was dead east of the international field. With the prevailing west to east winds, that put Tamiami square in the sights of departing commercial DC-8s and 707s. The airspace over Tamiami was known by the airline pilots as "Indian Country" because that is where the Cherokees, Navajos and Comanche's flew.

The plan was to relocate Tamiami south by about 15 miles to

Kendall, Florida in two days! Not only did I learn the initial steps required in becoming a pilot, I was pressed into service loading trucks and vans. The new airport was spacious. There were two east-west runways of 5,000 feet each and a diagonal 4,000 foot runway laid out with 13/31 headings. The diagonal would be rarely used. Helping with the move gave me a good feeling. It was as if I were an immediate friend and a real part of the sport-aviation community in south Florida. It also enabled me to make good friends that would be helpful during my learning experience.

My training was in a Cessna 150 type aircraft. They were all 100 horsepower then, but my favorite was the Cessna Aerobat. It had the tail number of 8419M. It was actually a 150K model. The plane was built in 1969 with serial number 15000119. It is still in service. When I last checked, it was registered to Cumberland Aero Service in Bronston, Kentucky. With its orange, white and black starburst paint scheme and higher stressed components, it was the best choice of the available aircraft. It would be the one in which I would solo and eventually earn my private ticket.

I split my time between the Aerobat and another Cessna 150, a "J" model numbered 51106. Like the Aerobat, it is still in service, registered to Alan Drury of Blackshear, Georgia. Of course, both of these were good airplanes even though the presence of a passenger and a full tank of gas would typically put the airplane over its weight limit.

Afterward, I substituted the little Cessna in my work whenever I could. It was adventurous and exciting travel. At the end of each trip my wife would be subjected to endless tales of what happened during my business trips. More than half of those stories were related to flying.

But soon, the flying days would come to an end. In 1972, I was brought back to the home office. We again would uproot our lives and follow the career. A lot of friends were left behind. While I certainly enjoyed flying all over the state of Florida, the flying life style had to be stopped for the time being. The whole tumultuous process of moving to a new town again would put any thoughts of flying into abeyance for a long time. There would be no more flying until 1989, in fact.

WHAT ARE YOU GOING TO DO
WITH AN AIRPLANE?

IT ALL BEGAN as a random thought that I said aloud one night in late 1988 or early '89 while having dinner with my wife. Recalling that we were at Briar Ridge Country Club, I casually mentioned that I wanted to get back into private flying. The comment barely raised a reaction. This was only dinner conversation and thinking aloud started conversations. We did not have an issue to resolve. This was not a key family decision. It was just another thought that the two of us could share with each another. However, I had mulled the thought of re-entering general aviation around in my mind for several months. It was just now that I would share the ideas with my wife.

The dinner conversation became more specific than Nancy had anticipated. In developing my thought, she became aware that we were about to own an airplane. What we were discussing was not simply a trip or two to the airport and then this whim of mine would be satisfied. Somewhere in the back of my mind was an idea of buying our own airplane. Should we decide to buy an airplane, my feelings were that it should be a used plane because it would be more affordable. More than likely, it would be a Piper Cherokee, although I had not decided if it should be any specific horsepower. As I went on, Nancy began to realize that I had come to a conclusion on the matter. My mind was firmly made-up.

She began to listen more intently to what I was saying. Now we had an issue to address. Soon, she stopped eating and listened carefully to every word I said. Finally, she asked the question: "What are you going to do with this airplane once you get it?"

Through our 48 years of marriage, Nancy has been the stabilizing factor. These are the moments when she looks into my dreaming to see if it needs to be turned back to sensibility. If she didn't take this time to help me see where some of my ideas were going to take us, then it wouldn't be done.

She needed to understand the justification for this sizable expenditure. For me, it was typical male shock. I had covered all the bases except this one. I had no specific reason to buy it. To merely say that I would have fun with an airplane seemed totally inadequate and if it were even muttered, the idea would be scuttled. The business need for aircraft ownership was no longer there.

Nancy did not like flying in a small airplane. With that realization went the thought that a family that flies together, stays together. I had already used the argument about an investment that grows. The last time that I used that reason was for a sail boat. The story on the boat is that we paid a lot of money for it, spent a lot of money putting little goodies in it and on it - then we ended up selling it for a lot less than we had in it. No, the 'return on investment' angle wasn't going to work.

So, I grabbed the first viable thought that came to mind. In a split second, all the useless and hackneyed reasons had been considered and discarded. The only neutral rationalization that I could come up with should never have even been uttered. I spurted out my objective for the airplane: I would fly to all the airports in Indiana!

Where that idea came from, I will never know. But there it was, out in the open. I said it. Now I had to defend it. Nancy and I have lived all over the United States. On innumerable occasions, we had discussed the pros and cons of all the different areas of the country. After everything was weighed, we knew our hearts belonged in the Midwest. In fact, we had determined that Indiana was the place where we wanted to spend our remaining years. We had fallen in love with Indiana, so my idea about visiting all the airports in the state was not totally absurd. Nancy was not yet satisfied, but she seemed willing to be convinced.

We left the restaurant that night with far different thoughts. I had a heart full of anticipation. The adventure lay ahead. I had the green light to actively look for an airplane. For Nancy, it was yet another case of "What is he getting us into this time?"

THE PLANE

THE SEARCH DIDN'T take long. As soon as I mentioned the fact that I was in the market for a Cherokee, a friend immediately volunteered that he had an acquaintance who had been trying to sell his plane for some time. The principal reason it hadn't been sold yet is that the owner, Jon Hussey, the last remaining member of a three-way partnership, was not aggressively trying to find a buyer. There was no real need for the airplane in the family, but it was hard to get rid of an old friend. We met at the Gary Regional Airport one cold Saturday in December.

The airplane was a Cherokee 180. Since it was a "C" model built in 1965, it was still the short version Cherokee. The extra seven inches in fuselage length was still to come at Vero Beach. The paint and interior were original. The avionics dated back to the times of the apostles. The airplane had no added value since the time she rolled out of Piper on June 16th, 1965.

The engine was in its first one-third life of an overhaul and the airframe only had 2,500 hours. That is relatively little time for a 25-year-old airplane. The price was fair, but more assuring, the airplane would be sold as it came out of its annual inspection. The owner was well aware of what he had. The little Cherokee had seen sparing service in the last five years. In fact, it only had three tachometer hours in the last two years. The engine would have to be watched closely. The owner was reluctant to fly the airplane as it was already a year out of date from its last annual inspection. Jon insisted that the annual inspection would have to be done at the Gary airport; the airplane should not be flown until it was thoroughly inspected and serviced.

It took the fixed base operation (FBO) at the Gary airport (Gary - Millionaire) more than two months to get the airplane through its annual inspection. The folks at Millionaire didn't care to work on general aviation aircraft when there were corporate jets to look after. Some days they would do something on the airplane. Then, they would ignore it for a week or more. Little people like us didn't make a lot of profit and loss sense to them. No matter what the owner said or did, Gary - Millionaire could not be motivated to move along faster on the inspection. It was aggravating and irritating. Regardless, the weeks of anticipation were over and the airplane was handed over to Nancy and me. We were airplane owners for the first time.

From now on it was going to be different. No more would I show up on a beautiful Saturday morning to rent an airplane only to find out that all the planes had been scheduled well in advance and there were no airplanes to fly. No more would I schedule a rental airplane only to find out that the day that I so carefully planned was the one where ground fog ruled the morning and thunderstorms were moving in for the afternoon.

This was my plane. This is where the term "Pride of Ownership" aptly applies. It was the product of a grown man realizing that he finally owned his own airplane. Never mind that the hourly cost of ownership exceeds the equivalent rental time. Never mind that taxes, insurance, maintenance and avionics upgrades couldn't be paid for on an hourly basis. No sir. This was my airplane. I could fly it whenever I wanted. I would not have problems with availability either. There would be no overdue renters or inconvenient schedule. It would just be 8369W and me. This was a match made in heaven. But there were things to tend to before we got serious.

As a Cessna trained and reared pilot, there was a transition to take place and it had to be an orderly one. It would not do for me to get into a strange plane and splash it in during a take-off or landing. A little time with a certified flight instructor was the more prudent move. After an hour of full-stop landings and take-offs, he judged me a 'non-dangerous pilot'. He did not pronounce me a good one; rather, one that was rusty but not likely to hurt myself. The prescription was to practice touch and go's and other simple maneuvers. He felt I should stay in the area of the airport for about three or four hours.

Yeah, sure.

The very next morning was Saturday, the weather was seriously clear and there was fifty gallons of gas in the airplane. Certainly, that would be enough to get me through the initial training with this new mount. The radio work with Ground Control and the Tower came back easily. Thank goodness that I was trained at Tamiami airport where intensive radio training was an integral part of my flight education. The first take-off was an exhilarating experience. With just me on board, she climbed like the proverbial homesick angel. This was a good airplane and we could easily grow into each other.

The first solo circuit was nothing to write home about, but a relationship was growing. The first landing was a little heavy handed and there was some slight swerving of the Cherokee. Slowing to just less than 50 MPH and reconfiguring the plane for takeoff, we were ready for nose up. I pushed in the throttle a little too quickly. The fast application of power quickly reminded me about prop torque. That was another lesson remembered. From that point on, power increases would be slower and smoother to avoid abusing the airplane. As instructed by the tower, I reported left base for Runway 12. Something was taking place within me. This airplane and I began to fit together.

It was not clear at the time, but this was not just a relationship; it was a partnership or maybe some sort of marriage. From now on, N8369W was to become an equal partner in my flying exploits. It would never be correct to think of the airplane as a tool or just a vehicle. From this point forward, the little Cherokee and I would be teammates in one adventure after another.

Furthermore, we would pledge ourselves to each other. There would be mutual promises of Trust, Respect, Faithfulness and Honesty made between us. These were not idle agreements, but solemn vows - vows taken with at least as much sincerity as a couple during their marriage ceremony or a priest upon entering the religious order.

Over time, we found that we remained faithful to each other. I never asked the airplane to do more than it could and the little Cherokee never gave less that it was able. We were good for each other.

THE PLAN

TO SAY THAT the approach to visiting all the airports in Indiana was 'unstructured' is an understatement. At first, there was some apprehension. Each trip was tentative and was draped with extreme caution. It can be seen that the first cities visited consisted of a fast dash in and then a quick trip home. The rate would be one airport per day. Finally, at airports six and seven, I dared to visit two towns in one day: Warsaw and Wabash.

And I was learning. The airplane became very predictable, as Cherokees often are. The equipment was reliable and trustworthy. Especially, the Loran C exhibited extreme accuracy, and I began to be totally dependent upon it. Only occasionally did the VOR system play a part in air navigation. The Non Directional Beacon never did work reliably and I wondered if it should even remain in the airplane. Remarkably enough, it managed to function through my instrument training. Soon after the FAA gave me the instrument rating, the NDB failed and has not worked since. Nonetheless, the airplane and the equipment were dependable and enduring.

Finally, about the third or fourth month into the adventure, four or more air field visits per day became the norm. Along with more airports came longer legs. As a matter of fact, I would over-fly some fields to get to others. The next time out, I would stop at cities between the ones that I visited earlier. It was more a rapid accumulation of flying hours than a growth in the number of cities visited. Obviously, confidence was growing.

Another hallmark of trust was the time when the first guests were taken along. Even that was cautiously measured. The first to fly with me were other pilots! As time went on, non-flying adults and finally children were to be my company. My favorite passengers were my wife, my parents, and young children, in that order. My wife because I love her so much, my parents because I wanted to share my joy with them, and young children because it was a thrill to see their faces light up when they realized that they could fly an airplane.

In all cases with children, they were immediately enamored with the airplane and flight. Their senses took in everything they saw and they missed nothing that I did. What really caught and kept their attention was the extra 'steering wheel' in front of them. This wasn't present in daddy's mini-van. I would set up the airplane to fly straight and level without being attended. When the kids were accustomed to being aloft, I would simply ease back and my hands would slowly leave the control column. Then, with my arms folded, I would point out to my young guest that one of us should be flying the airplane. In every case, the youngster would react, mostly as an expression of fright, and grab the wheel. They were flying the airplane. They didn't even think about it. Once they realized that they were indeed providing primary input to the control of the plane, they would look at me for approval. Maybe the broad smile across my face provided them with the endorsement they sought.

Let's fly

THE AIRPORTS OF INDIANA

#1   Gary, Indiana   Gary Municipal Airport
Type: Class D Identifier: GYY   March 25, 1990

#2   Plymouth, Indiana   Plymouth Municipal Airport
Type: Paved Identifier: C65   May 6, 1990

THE FIRST VISIT

GARY IS MY home field so it is really the first airport on my list. But Plymouth was the first field visited. The first visit was a mistake. It wasn't supposed to happen on that May 6th; it just evolved that way!

The pre-flight inspection took about half an hour. Nothing went unnoticed. Once in the airplane, the settling in process took another half hour or so. Finally, I was about as ready as I was going to be. It was time to follow the flight examiner's instructions and make touch and go's for a few hours. I announced my intentions to Gary Tower and they cleared me onto Runway 12. Like most airplanes with minimal load and one person, the airplane literally jumped off the ground.

The first take-off and landing were good, better than expected. As I came around the left side for the second landing, my eyes began to look further and further out into the horizon. The second landing was about as good as the first, but the climb out was different. Doing touch and go's for two hours was going to become very boring. In fact, it was becoming too boring to continue. My mind focused in on Plymouth, Indiana. It was only 70 miles away and, for goodness sake, climbing out on a heading of 120 degrees, the plane was pointed right at Plymouth! What the heck! At the next radio reporting point, I requested a straight away departure and that was that.

This was the first cross country in our new (to us) airplane. The plane was everything I expected. It seemed solid and predictable. While it had some years on it, the total number of hours was lower than could be expected. The plane was 25 years old but only had twenty six hundred flying hours on the tachometer. While this was positive, the fact that it had only accumulated four or five hours in the past three years was troublesome. Furthermore, we bought the airplane out of annual inspection. During the annual, the mechanics found some corrosion. It seems that little animals had nested in the plane. The urine and waste matter combined with condensation took its toll on the bottom skin. While it was fixed in the inspection process, this condition still added to my concern. The interior was in terrible condition. The avionics were vintage 1965 coffee grinder Narco's and the FAA was ready to outlaw them in favor of narrower band width models. All this and I paid more for the airplane than what it sold for when it was new. While I wouldn't turn back, there were some concerns.

Frank Kish was the manager at the Plymouth FBO. He said something nice about the Cherokee and I told him that we just bought it. He wanted a closer look. Frank spent the better part of an hour going over the whole airplane. He paused at several places to point out areas of concern. He was impressive with his intimate knowledge of Piper Cherokees. Frank found nothing wrong or in need of urgent attention. He felt that we would get years of reliable service from this airplane. A warm feeling came over me because two things were resolved that morning. First of all, we had a good airplane. The people who conducted the annual inspection pronounced it airworthy, and now the independent opinion of a person without a vested interest deemed it trustworthy and reliable. The flight back to Gary was a good one. Frank's opinion was very important and well received. He would be doing our annual inspections from now on!

A SECOND STORY ABOUT PLYMOUTH!

I WENT TO PLYMOUTH every so often because it was an easy and relaxing flight. It was also reassuring to chit-chat with Frank about the condition of the plane and flying in general. This was the case on September 17, 1990.

The parking ramp at Plymouth will hold about 15 or 20 airplanes but, usually, there are only four or five planes at the most. On this day, there was only one but it was distinctive. As I taxied up, this

Piper Cherokee 235 was visually the exact twin of my airplane. Same year, same color, same paint scheme; everything was the same except the 235 model was a little bigger.

Walking into the front office, Frank Kish was standing behind the counter and taking care of a couple of other pilots. He appeared to be filling out some sort of paperwork - a receipt, perhaps. He noticed that someone walked in, so he glanced up to see who it was. Recognizing me, he looked up again and said "Hello" and went back to his task. Then the surprise came.

Almost immediately, he looked up again and asked "Bob, what would you say if I told you that three of the four people in this room have the same last name?"

He made me think a little. 'Kish' is not an unusual name but it is not common either. Having been in the steel business, I knew that there was such a thing as "Kish iron" and we had some family friends with the name of Kish. I told Frank that this was certainly ironic. Then he responded:

"What if I told you that you were one of them?"

With a knowing smile across his face, he introduced me to the two other men in the room. "Bob Hechlinski, meet Bill Hecklinski and Dave Hecklinski."

I could have been knocked over with a feather! Bill Hecklinski is my second cousin. Dave is his son. His grandfather and my grandfather were brothers. Bill's grandfather was the first to change the spelling of the family name from Hechlinski to Hecklinski. My family was not too close. It had been decades since we had last seen each other. In fact, I had probably contributed to the gap between our families by making no effort toward cohesiveness. The mirror image Cherokee parked next to mine was their airplane. What a small world!

From that point on, we became great friends and frequently communicated. Bill may have had the same regrets about our casual attitude of family ties. For years afterward, we worked very hard at contributing to the genealogical tree with two others in our family.

#3 LaPorte, Indiana   LaPorte Municipal Airport
Type: Paved Identifier: PPO May 18, 1990

#4 Knox, Indiana   Starke County Airport
Type: Paved Identifier: OXI May 27, 1990

THE MOST UNFRIENDLY AIRPORT

L ANDING AT KNOX's airport was one of the most disappointing events of my quest. The excitement of my goal to land at all of Indiana's airports caught up with me. I happily shared this with everyone I met. The exhilaration was contagious! Folks usually wished me good luck and expressed a desire to do the same thing or something similar.

Not in Knox. Those folks wanted nothing to do with me. They didn't even acknowledge my presence when I showed up. Whether I stayed or moved on made no difference to them. This behavior had to be an aberration. Certainly, this couldn't be the normal reaction to a new and unfamiliar face showing up at Knox County. Sure enough, each and every time that I went to Knox, everyone ignored me. This never changed no matter how many times I landed there over the next several years. I never found out why they were so cold to visitors.

On my list, Knox was deemed the most unfriendly airport visited.

#5 Kentland, Indiana   Kentland Municipal Airport
Type: Paved Identifier: 50I May 27, 1990

KENTLAND'S STRANGE HOLE

FLYING IN INDIANA, and adjoining states as well, is a reassuring sport. Engine stoppage or any other catastrophe that would force an airplane to the ground is rarely deadly. Indiana is so flat and so clear that a landing site can be made with a minimum of altitude. As a matter of record, my airplane has made a forced landing due to fuel exhaustion. No bent metal, just red faces. The most expensive damage was done to the crops. The pilot and then owner, was liable to pay the farmer for all the soy beans he ruined with the landing and the subsequent destruction caused by the equipment used to extract the airplane.

In fact, with 111 public access airports and several hundred farm fields, the chance of an 'off-field' landing is minimal. That is why the strange hole off the end of Runway 27 at Kentland is so intriguing.

Kentland and the rest of Newton County is as plain and featureless as it was when it was scraped flat by the last glacier that scrubbed across it some 11,000 years ago. The hole at the end of the runway, called "The Kentland Disturbance" by geologists, is about 4 miles in diameter and was discovered by local farmers around 1880. The farmers found a large area of crushed rocks on the surface and began to quarry the stones. After all, this is black dirt country and rocky terrain anywhere is an odd occurrence. Larger quarry operations after 1900 exposed more of the structure that became known as 'disturbed' as it was a different rock structure and composition than that to which they had been accustomed. Geologists quickly concluded that the disturbed area was the result of volcanic action.

What? We have a volcano in Indiana? And I thought volcanoes were the sole provinces of the Pacific Ocean and areas around the Mediterranean Sea: Surely not Indiana.

Subsequent scientific thought prevailed. Evidence in the hole indicated that an enormous blast had occurred - far larger than what could be affected by dynamite being used in the day to day mining operations. Furthermore, the blast came from dead overhead. By the late 1960's, it seemed clear that the Kentland structure had been formed by the violent impact of a meteorite. It probably was large. Experts calculate that it was probably on scale with the great Meteor Crater in Winslow, Arizona, except that it has been eroded so much. Some still cling to the volcano theory. Although many discredit the volcano idea, contending that a volcano has not been explained thoroughly, the meteor theory has not been demonstrated conclusively, either.[1]

Maybe, just maybe, this meteor hole is somehow akin to that big hole in the bottom of Lake Michigan. You know, right in the middle of the lake; the hole that is 20 to 30 miles in diameter and exceedingly deep. This is the hole where all the alien spaceships come and go at night. You know about that, don't you?

#6 Warsaw, Indiana	Warsaw Municipal Airport
Type: Paved Identifier: ASW	May 28, 1990

Flying into the Warsaw airport is a very pleasant adventure. Given our flat topography and clear summer visibility, the distinctive "L" shaped layout and the epicenter of activity being at the juncture of the two runways is easy to locate. The airport serves a community of only 10,000 people, but the city of Warsaw is very proud of its airport. This little farming community is unique in its cooperative effort to build, develop and maintain a good municipal airport. The beginning of the field belongs to the memory of forward sighted citizens in the mid 1940's. Most pronounced of these are three men; Thomas Mitchell, John Stevens and John Teghtmeyer.

Viewing aviation accessibility as a very desirable community resource, they contributed over 116 adjacent acres to the Warsaw Chamber of Commerce in 1945. The deed of gift intended the land's use to be for construction of an airport on the property. Also appreciating the importance of aviation to Warsaw's economic development, the City Council, passed Ordinance No.170 on February 18, 1946 which established the first Board of Aviation Commissioners. This was done in compliance with the Federal Aviation Act of 1945, which enabled and encouraged communities to form airport authorities, increase civil flying activity and to petition for Federal funds for the growth and enhancement of

1 Roadside Geology of Indiana 1999. Mark J. Camp and Graham T. Richardson

civilian air fields. In 1947, the Chamber of Commerce deeded the above-mentioned parcels of land to the City of Warsaw, creating what was then known as the Warsaw Memorial Airport.

By 1948, a 2400-foot North and South paved runway replete with taxiway was constructed. This was completed in conjunction with the Federal Aviation Administration Program. In 1951, with the help of Federal funds, an aircraft apron and automobile parking areas were added to the airport. Subsequent grants in 1959 allowed for extension of the existing runway to 3600 feet and widening the taxiway to 30 feet.

More citizen involvement provided a homemade lighting system for aircraft desiring to use the airport at night. This did the job until 1969 when the hand-made system was replaced with a modern Medium Intensity Runway Lighting System that is a 36-inch diameter rotating beacon on a 51-foot tower. A constant work in progress, continuing airport improvements saw the runway (and the parallel taxiway) extended to an eventual length of 4,020 feet. In the 1960's, an administration building was constructed and additional land was acquired to buffer the field. A Remote Relay Site was installed, allowing pilots radio communication with Fort Wayne approach\departure control while still on the ground. The second runway added has headings of 90 and 270 degrees. It is 6,000 feet long, grooved and 100 feet wide and is an ILS \ DME precision approach runway. It also has a parallel taxiway.

In many instances today, airports are put out of business by encroaching urban sprawl. This field is a treasure that is guarded by law. The city council wisely protected their aviation jewel with ordinances that prevented non-conforming land use or hazards to safe flying operation of the airport within specified approach zones.

The Warsaw Municipal Airport is unusual in the large amounts of local improvements done entirely by the community--a fact indicating the willingness and desire that Warsaw had to see its airport improve. The city recognized these community efforts by naming the airport Parker Field to honor Earl W. Parker, a citizen who was tireless in his efforts to promote an airport for Warsaw. It has been renamed since then.

Our gratitude to Warsaw, Indiana website; warsawcity.net

#7   Wabash, Indiana   Wabash Municipal Airport
Type: Paved Identifier: IWH   May 28, 1990

#8   Angola, Indiana   Tri-State Airport
Type: Paved Identifier: ANQ   June 10, 1990

#9   Valparaiso, Indiana   Porter County Airport
Type: Paved Identifier: VPZ   June 26, 1990

#10   Michigan City, Indiana   Michigan City Municipal
Type: Paved   Identifier: MGC   July 4, 1990

HERE'S ONE FOR THE RECORD BOOK!

MICHIGAN CITY HAD been blessed with two fine general aviation airports. One, on the south side of town, was the municipal field, while the other, Joe Phillip's field, was immediately to the east of the city. By far, Philip's was a more utilized and better favored airport by sport pilots. The municipal airport would eventually be abandoned. In the late 1990's the strip would be yellow X'd and all the buildings would be demolished. By 1978, the property was sold off to developers with retail outlet zoning. Today, a Lowe's Home Improvement sits on that site with the south-east corner of the building sitting squarely on what used to be middle of the east-west runway.

In the years that followed, I would visit Michigan City quite often as I took a job there while still living in Dyer, Indiana. As weather and schedule would permit, I would fly the Cherokee to work. For this reason, I kept a bicycle at the Michigan City Airport. The manager was kind enough to give me a key to the storage shed and the bike was perfectly safe while it was in his care. This is rather rare in a location such as northwest Indiana which has fabled inconsistent weather. It was about a 50-mile jaunt or a 1 1/2 hour commute by car between Dyer and Michigan City.

This story begins on the morning of June 3rd, 1994. It was an absolutely gorgeous day. There wasn't a cloud in the sky, and the softest hint of a breeze. Ground haze was totally absent, which is rare in northwest Indiana where there are six iron and steel making companies and where some of the largest oil refineries call home. Faced with fighting traffic on Interstate 94 during rush hour, I concluded this was a good day for air travel. It was a 21 minute flight.

Once at MGC, the bike ride to the railroad maintenance yard was brisk. I rode the three miles in about 20 minutes. Once at the office, there were only routine faxes and voice messages to handle. These were all dispatched in a few minutes. Things changed upon entering the car maintenance barn. The first item on their agenda was an out-of-order wheel slip system on a car now parked in the Chicago loop. The train would be there all day but had to be ready for rush hour service starting at 3:00 PM. I got a spare wheel slip controller from Stores and caught the 10:35 AM departure from the Michigan City station. There would be plenty of time to make the repairs needed.

Now then, most of the track work on the South Shore line is done during daylight hours starting immediately after the last rush hour train in the morning and picking up immediately before the first rush hour train in the afternoon. This day was one of those instances. All day time train traffic was stopped at about the half-way point to Chicago for track repair. This work was localized and we got around it easily by using buses. The railroad always provided ad hoc patch jitney transportation in cases like this. On the other side of the repair site, another train was waiting to shuttle us to the Loop.

The station officer was waiting for me at the Randolph Street station. The car was ready as well. It didn't take long to justify the corrective action and we would have to replace the bad unit with the spare from Stores. The work would have to be done outdoors at track level. The cool morning temperatures and cloudless sunshine made for excellent working conditions. In about 45 minutes my work was done, just in time for a great lunch at one of the super Chicago Loop restaurants.

As luck would have it, the train that I took back to Indiana would have the same car in the train that I worked on. The trip eastward was uneventful. I got off the train at Dunes Park, which is the railroad's headquarters. I saw Dan Gornstein, the railroad's engineer, and told him what had transpired. After our small chat concluded, I found out that the next train would not arrive for over an hour. One of the railroad employees, Agnes Simmons, offered to give me a ride. She lived in Michigan City and, in fact, very close to the railroad shops. She could easily drop me off. It was a great offer and it would get me home on time. Let's see if I have it now. There was travel:

1. by car,
2. then by an airplane,
3. then by a bicycle,
4. followed by a train,
5. a bus ride and ended up with a
6. hitchhiked ride.

That should be a record of some sort. All that was missing was a boat ride or something with water!

Coincidently, Joe Phillip's field is the very first landing that I remember. A very dear friend of mine was Eddy Minczewski Jr. His father, a more proper Edward V. Minczewski Sr., was a pilot from World War II. While Ed senior flew many types of multi-engine aircraft in the European theater, he seemed to be recognized mostly as a B-24 Liberator pilot. Now he was a Notre Dame educated lawyer and he had the bearing and presence to go along with that pedigree. He remains quite the gentleman and a pillar of his church and community.

His love for flying carried on after his release from the military. I recall that Edward V. had a maroon 1953 Studebaker station wagon and he had a decal on the back window of a funny looking set of wings. This decal identified him as a member of Aircraft Owners and Pilots Association. It would be years later that I saw Edward V. Sr. on the cover of AOPA Pilot magazine in a group of 10 or 12 other men. They represented what remained of the charter members of AOPA at the time of AOPA's 50th anniversary. High distinction, that.

Mr. Minczewski owned a series of small airplanes after the war. The one we flew on the occasion of our trip to Michigan City was a Stinson Voyager, one of the nicest Stinsons ever built. It was a typical arrangement on that summer day, young Eddie and I would be side by side in the back seat while Edward the Dad would fly. Our flight would be the 20 or so miles to Michigan City. The appearance of the field is still vivid in my mind, as it was all grass with a well-worn landing gear tracks. Wherever an airplane taxied, a cloud of dust was right behind. Edward Sr. sprung for Cokes before we returned to Bendix Field in South Bend. (You remember the 8 ounce bottles that had the name of the bottling city on the bottom, don't you?) Afterward, we flew back to South Bend to wash the airplane. That is how we "paid" for our free flight. And it was my first time washing an airplane!

#11	Winimac, Indiana	Arens Field
Type:	Paved Identifier: RWN	July 4, 1990

It was a beautiful Wednesday morning with the softest of breezes to ruffle the trees. It was a good day for a change of view with a short flight to Winimac. There was some holiday activity at the airport but it was more important to get away for a few hours or so. Winimac is but 45 minutes away and seemed to be the perfect destination for the relaxed mood I was in.

The little Cherokee was the only transient airplane at RWN. Once in the office, I got into a little bit of chit-chat with the FBO manager, Woody Barnes. Woody was retired for more than ten years and chose to take on the job at the airport to spend as much time as possible with his true loves, pilots and flying. He was a steel man by occupation, having worked at US Steel in Gary all his life. According to Woody, he was either making steel at the Gary Works or flying. He laughed and commented that while the steel mills paid well, the overtime is what allowed for his flying. The more OT he worked, the more hours he flew. He had the log books to back up his claim, too.

After a little while, we were joined by his lovely wife Bertha. She was soft and mellow with a comforting tone. Her presence in the conversation suited me fine. She asked about my intention to fly to all the Indiana airports and listened with serious attention to my explanation. She asked to see my plane, so the three of us sauntered onto the ramp. Bertha seems to prefer low wing airplanes and winked her approval of mine.

Instead of going back into the office, we walked into the strip of open-air hangars. It was full with 12 or 14 planes. Bertha could not hold back her feelings. She spoke mostly with a degree of sadness since the Winimac pilots, for whom she obviously cared a great deal, had been drifting away from sport aviation. She missed them terribly. She commented about most of the planes; "This one went through bad weather and a rough landing and the pilot has never been back to fly the plane again."

> "We don't see this fellow very much since his wife died."

> "This flyer moved to Michigan. He told us that he would be back for his plane but hasn't been here in over a year."

> "The owner of this plane thought he could do a good job and cheaper if he painted his airplane himself. He picked a fluorescent color that really did not weather well. He flew it more before he painted it."

Afterward, Bertha asked more about my plans and seemed genuinely thrilled. She encouraged me and asked that I stop back every so often or write to keep them apprised of the progress. As I walked back to the Cherokee, I looked over my shoulder and saw Woody and Bertha standing side by side watching for my taxi out. We waved at each other.

In a few days, I received a kind letter from Bertha. She wanted a picture of my airplane for the FBO office. That was easy to accommodate. I wrote every so often and she responded quickly. Truly, these were great friends. Her answering letters stopped after a few months. I don't recall exactly when it was, but I landed at Winimac to say hello. The news was not good. Bertha had died a few months back and Woody was not feeling well. Age was taking its due. I looked around the office and saw the photos that Bertha requested. They were prominently pinned to the wall with the dozens of other pictures. Emotion came in a wave. It was time to go home.

I started out to the Piper and glanced to the right toward the open-air hangar. The memories were too much. I wept.

#12   Lafayette, Indiana   Purdue University Airport
Type: Class D Identifier: LAF   July 4, 1990

LEADERSHIP IN AVIATION; PAR EXCELLENCE

PURDUE UNIVERSITY HAS long maintained a strong commitment to the advancement of aviation. Following World War I, Purdue established a Department of Aeronautics to meet the growing demands for an aviation curriculum. In 1930, development began on the airport, the nation's first to be owned by a state-supported university.

Envisioned as a field laboratory for aeronautical education and research, the airport initially consisted of 360 acres donated by Purdue Trustee David Ross. Development began with an emergency landing field, opening in November 1930. Paved runways were added in the late 1930s, and student flight instruction began in 1938.

Aviation pioneer Amelia Earhart served on Purdue's faculty from 1935 to 1937 as a women's career consultant. At the time, she had already earned her place in history as the first woman to fly solo across the Atlantic in 1932, and the first person to fly solo from Hawaii to California in 1935. In 1937, Earhart would embark on her ill-fated journey around the world in a Lockheed Electra, a flight made possible with funds provided by the Purdue Research Foundation.

But, there is more. Purdue has produced 22 astronauts, more than any other school in the nation. These include Neil Armstrong, the first to walk on the moon, and Gene Cernan, the last astronaut to do so. Gus Grissom, the first person to return to space, is also a Purdue alumnus.

Today the airport encompasses over 500 acres southwest of Campus. It is the second busiest airport in Indiana, with 176,000 takeoffs and landings in 2000, including commercial, private, and University usage, which should provide some indication of its popularity. While LAF is a great field, it remains strongly in my heart because of their controllers who stepped up for me when the weather went to 0-0 on a couple of occasions.

| #13 | Rochester, Indiana | Fulton County Airport |
| Type: | Paved Identifier: RCR | July 7, 1990 |

FLYING WITH AN OLD FRIEND

ROBERT W. SMITH was my boss when I was employed at Bendix Energy Controls Division in South Bend, Indiana. He was instrumental in my professional development. While he would not want to be identified as my mentor, he would certainly understand that it is with the deepest devotion that I look upon him as such.

We have kept in touch even though it has been decades since we worked together. He often remarked how similar our interests have been over the years. At one time or another, we both enjoyed sports cars and flying. My wife and I sailed cruising sailboats before we met Bob Smith and continued to do so after I began to work with him. Bob was ex-Navy (with a tour of duty in World War II and a call back to active duty during the Korean conflict) and an excellent sailor.

Bob and his wife Dorothy had a boat similar to ours. We competed against each other in weekly trap and skeet shooting. We were two of a kind. Bob had to know that we now had an airplane.

Bob was excited and suggested that we fly off somewhere the following weekend in our two airplanes. He would bring a couple of the guys that we worked with years ago and we would decide where to go later, a pair per plane.

July 7th, 1991 was a Saturday and Bob showed up at Gary Regional right on-time. He was alone. For different reasons, the other two men couldn't make it. One had a doctor's appointment and the other had a family commitment that arose unexpectedly. We were on our own. Bob recommended that we have lunch in Rochester, Indiana. We could talk over old times. That was a great idea. I had not been to Rochester as of yet.

On the way to Rochester, I told Bob about my quest to fly to all the airports of Indiana. He thought it was interesting and exciting. At least for Rochester, he would be a small part of Indiana history.

The trip and the reunion with Bob was great. We laughed a lot and enjoyed each other's company. He reminded me of some funny things that happened while we were both at Bendix. We also talked about some of the successes when we worked together. I was fortunate to have worked with Bob during those formative years.

Rochester lay ahead of us after some 30 or 40 minutes of flying time. With no traffic in sight and no activity on the radio, we opted for a straight-in approach. Rochester has a taxiway alongside the runway. Bob motioned that we should proceed all the way to the end. Once there, Bob instructed me to turn left, past the refueling area. I kept going past the hangars and Bob didn't say much. I started to brake the airplane as we approached the edge of the ramp. It was thick with high weeds, but Bob told me to keep going straight ahead. He motioned with his index finger as he did so. We seemed to be on some sort of beaten path. But we were still knee deep in weeds.

Turning left where the path indicated, we passed two people who were on foot. And we kept going through the weeds. Finally, after about a half mile or so of keeping up a little power and holding back on the control column, we saw three airplanes parked ahead. Civilization at last! I lined-up with the other planes and shut off the engine. We had arrived in Rochester. Bob was already on his way over the property fence and had started across the highway. Looking past him, I could see where he was going. The restaurant was called "Karen's."

A description of the flight would be incomplete without raves for the food at Karen's. Everything was exceptional. The food was tasty. There was plenty of it and it was reasonably priced. Testimony to this is the fact that we have returned several times to enjoy the food at Karen's. As I was to learn, Karen's is one of the favorite stops for pilots.

The trip back was as much fun as the flight into Rochester, the major difference being our promise to each other to keep closer in touch and not to let so much time pass between our contacts with each other. It was a promise that we would keep.

| #14 | Rensselaer, Indiana | Jasper County Airport |
| Type: | Paved Identifier: RZL | July 21, 1990 |

| #15 | Monticello, Indiana | White County Airport |
| Type: | Paved Identifier: MCX | July 24, 1990 |

| #16 | Griffith, Indiana | Griffith-Merrillville Airport |
| Type: | Paved Identifier: 05C | August 2, 1990 |

THE FRENCH CONNECTION

ON THE FOLLOWING weekend, Gary Airport was going to have an air show. This was going to be a big affair with a lot of big name acts. As a result, security was going to be tight. The airport would be closed to incoming and out-going traffic and they were not allowing anyone to visit the private hangars. Because we wanted to spend the weekend in Bloomington, the Cherokee had to be moved out of Gary before the weekend. We would move the plane to Griffith, which was only a few miles south, on Friday and leave from there Saturday morning.

On the Friday morning before the air show, I was second (or third) for take-off from Gary behind the famous French Connection aerobatic team. This was the remarkable man and woman team of Daniel Helicon and Montan Mallet who flew CAP planes in flawless tandem air ballets at almost every air show in the US. They were poised to take-off in tandem on Runway 30 and do a little practicing before the show. Their practice area would be northbound a few miles over Lake Michigan. I asked for permission to take-off with them and everyone agreed. Naturally, they were faster and climbed better than I so they pulled away from me easily. Nonetheless, it was a moment to remember as it was my only time in aviation show business - such as it was!

| #17 | Lowell, Indiana | Lowell Municipal Airport |
| Type: | Grass Identifier: C97 | August 3, 1990 |

| #18 | Crawfordsville, Indiana | Crawfordsville Municipal |
| Type: | Paved Identifier: CFJ | August 3, 1990 |

| #19 | Bloomington, Indiana | Monroe County Airport |
| Type: | Class D Identifier: BMG | August 3, 1990 |

BLOOMINGTON #1

SEVERAL STORIES ABOUT Bloomington come to mind. Either with my wife or alone, I probably flew into BMG about 50 or 60 times. It is a great airport and well managed. The principal FBO there is Cook Aviation. This operation was founded by Cook Industries, which was founded by William Cook and developed into an extremely successful adjunct of his vast business network. William Cook continues to run the firm which has become widely international in scope.

Upon landing, pilots are treated like favored customers. Assistance is offered from the time a plane taxies onto their ramp. Ramp attendants chock the plane and take orders for fuel and oil service. The desk attendants are willing to make motel and restaurant reservations and provide a courtesy Cadillac sedan. Flyers can choose from a whole fleet of these, and they are not junk cars. Rather, they are cars that had been executive driven to about 40,000 or 50,000 miles and are ready for a trade-in. They have been impeccably maintained and are a pleasure to drive. I have never flown into BMG when there wasn't a Caddy waiting for me. Returning to the field, without fail, the cockpit windows had been cleaned!

Upon arrival home, I could always expect a letter from the FBO manager, Rex G. Hinkle, telling me how nice it was to see me again and how important my business is to them. Rex is anxious to hear from me if they can improve their service in any way. Rex knows how to run an FBO; truly a class act!

BLOOMINGTON #2

BMG IS A controlled field although there really isn't the volume of traffic to warrant the expense. I suspect that it is the corporate traffic that drives the idea. One day, in beautiful VFR weather, I came in from the north and reported for landing 12 miles north of the field. The controller gave me instructions to enter a right-hand pattern for 35 and be careful of helicopters working in and near the normal pattern altitudes and proximity. I gave him an abbreviated repeat of his instructions and altered my course ever so slightly eastward. Within a minute or two, he returned with an amended clearance. Now he wanted me to change to a left hand pattern to keep me clear of the chopper traffic. I "rogered" that request then adjusted my course westward. I eventually reported on left downwind without a reply from my friend in the tower.

Just as I was about to touch down, the tower operator requested that I state my position. He was really surprised and a bit irritated when I told him I was over the threshold for 35. During rollout, he instructed me to exit the runway to the east. On the taxiway, I was to stop and call him. I did, and he admonished me for not following his right hand pattern instructions, which he took time to repeat to me in razor sharp crispness. This was demeaning and more of a scolding than anything else. He ended up with a series of "next time" warnings and threats.

I felt that something must have gone wrong on his end. I replied to him that my recollection of his instructions consisted of two separate conversations and in the second one my clearance was amended to a more standard left hand pattern. I added some of his actual sentences and phrases that he used in his communication. He came back with a substantially subdued tone, actually contrite, and acknowledged that I was probably right, as he now recalled that second set of instructions. "Proceed to the ramp" was his last comment. The next broadcast on the frequency was biting. From somewhere, from someone who was not identified, there was a final terse comment: "And that is why you didn't get the O'Hare job!"

BLOOMINGTON #3

MY WORST WEATHER-RELATED flying experience happened later on our way back from Bloomington, Indiana, one afternoon. I frightened both my wife and myself (almost to death!)

We called weather and found out that a lazy system was hanging over BMG for most of the morning. The visibility was down to two and a half miles and showed very little interest in moving or dissipating. BMG reported less than three mile visibility for most of the morning. The good news is that the northern limit of the visibility problem only went to about 5 miles north of the airport and the rest of the state reported CAVU conditions. This was clearly the makings of 'get-home-itis.' We went to the airport for the flight home and called weather again. There was absolutely no change in the conditions or the forecast. The part about the five miles and then clear was still being reported and was very appealing to me. That meant I could get a Special VFR off the field, turn north onto our course of 350 degrees and slip through all the bad stuff. That is, at most, three or four minutes in the air until we were clear. Visually, the conditions over the field looked reasonably good. The FAA weather was verifiable and still made sense.

Nancy and I had coffee and waited. I called 1 800-WX BRIEF for the third time and heard the same prognostication as before. There was neither improvement nor deterioration. That's it. We'll file special VFR, get past the MVFR visibility and scoot home. It was apparent that there was no need to wait. Nothing was going to change for hours. With VFR weather a few minutes to the north and only marginal VFR weather between us, we could go.

Upon starting, we requested our Special VFR clearance and inquired about the conditions to the north. The tower had no current information to give us. We had to assume that the same promise of clear weather five miles north had not changed. We rolled down runway 17 and made a right-hand departure to our 350-degree heading. We flew into a cloud bank immediately. I told the tower that we were in IFR conditions already and asked for a clear runway. He said that Runway 17 was open. In fact, any runway we could see would be fine with him. Just as he gave us a clearance, the sky opened - just as the FAA said it would. The clear visibility must have drifted a little more southward. We told the tower that we would continue on. He wished us good luck.

With our eyes glued onto the Loran, we watched the miles click off. When five miles north, we cleared ourselves with the tower, but the visibility was not improving like we expected. The edge couldn't be far away so we pushed on. Do you see how it happens? One little mistake after another compounding each other until they make a big mistake. Still, we were convinced that clear air was near. Surely, it was only a matter of minutes.

At 10 or 12 miles north, we were reduced to keeping track of the ground instead of looking ahead. Nancy watched the ground on the right side and me on the left. Then, that was gone. Our eyes came back into the cockpit. While the weather outside the plane was stagnant, the cockpit pressure was steadily rising. The air temperature was increasing as well. Nancy felt it, too. She didn't know much about flying, but she certainly understood the Artificial Horizon instrument, and it spoke volumes to her. Calmly, she asked, "We are in trouble, aren't we?" Nothing outside the plane told me what was going on. I scanned the instrument panel. From the seat of my pants, I felt we were in a shallow dive to the right. Looking at the AH, it was shouting to me that we were actually in a shallow dive to the left. It was then I realized that had I corrected for what I felt, I would have exacerbated the real condition and we probably would have spun over on our back. We were very close to the ground. This was as serious as it gets. The next words out of my mouth were "we're going on instruments, Nancy." Oh, where in the world was that clear weather?

We were not far off the ground, only about 2,500 feet AGL. We would not hit anything on the ground in the next few minutes and we shouldn't interfere with any IFR traffic above. We continued ahead because that is where the clear weather was. By this time, we were 20 miles north of Bloomington. At any minute, we would be CAVU. But it never came. How could this be? We had three solid reports of clear weather only a few minutes above BMG and we were still in the clouds looking for it after 15 minutes. The good weather was most certainly a minute or two away. Being on instruments vastly improved the quality of flying and stiffened my backbone to face the uncertainty of zero-zero weather. My blood pressure and heart rate most certainly came down nearer to normal, and Nancy's confidence rose proportionately.

An hour later, somewhere over Mongo, Indiana, we 'broke out.' It was just as the FAA said it would be only it was 95 miles farther north than they thought! My grip on the control column eased substantially and we both breathed a little easier. We began to talk about the harrowing event that was the previous 60 minutes. We both agreed it was scary and I was poorly prepared for it. More than anything else, it was this incident that caused me to start instrument lessons. I got my ticket about six months later.

Since then, I have religiously kept up my currency. All pilots agree that an instrument ticket makes for better pilots. I am very happy that I took the time and effort to get the training. Surprisingly enough, I don't use it. The airplane is well equipped and has excellent instrumentation and avionics but it is almost 40 years old. More significantly, the pilot is well into his fifties. Those two iron-hard facts combined with the pure VFR nature of the flying that I do does not make for a rigid need for any instrument flying. It feels good to be able to fly IFR with confidence and professionalism, however. It is a nice ability to have in the flight bag. Moreover, I am proud to be an IFR pilot.

#20   Washington, Indiana   Daviess County Airport
Type: Paved Identifier: DCY   August 7, 1990

DAVIESS COUNTY'S EARLY BIRD PILOT

THERE IS AN organization called Early Birds of Aviation. Actually, it is incorporated. Its members are those men and women (mostly men) who flew solo between 1903 and 1916. The membership roll was fixed at 599 members. The membership is maintained by the Smithsonian Institution's National Air and Space Museum in Washington. Indiana's contribution to this elite membership is Roderick M. Wright. He was born in Daviess County on March 24th, 1887. Born and raised on a farm, he was expected to carry on with the family business. With that obligation, Roderick Wright enrolled at Purdue University in an agriculture curriculum.

As a young man of 24, he had become thoroughly enamored with the accomplishments of Wilbur and Orville Wright. (By the way, there is no familial connection between Rod Wright and the Wright brothers.)

In June of 1911 he attended an air show in Evansville, Indiana and that convinced him to take flying lessons. He went to Dayton, Ohio and enrolled in the Wright Brothers flying school. On June 26, 1913, he was presented with his pilot's license. It was number 254 which was awarded by the Federation Aeronautique Internationale. Rod Wright became Indiana's first licensed pilot.

Things were never the same on the farm after that. Returning to Washington in 1933, Rod bought an airplane and built an airstrip complete with a hangar on the family farm. He commenced to teach flying to many in his family. Through the 1930's Rod used flying as his main business. When World War II came, he tested parachutes in Washington.

Wright went on to become a representative in the Indiana General Assembly in 1953, an office which he held for four years. In 1954, he flew a jet aircraft for the first time. Roderick M. Wright died on October 13, 1960. His remains are buried on the family farm.

#21   French Lick, Indiana   French Lick Municipal Airport
Type: Paved   Identifier: FRH   August 7, 1990

#22   Paoli, Indiana   Paoli Municipal Airport
Type: Paved Identifier: I42   August 7, 1990

#23   Bedford, Indiana   Grissom Municipal Airport
Type: Paved Identifier: BFR   August 7, 1990

| #24 | Madison, Indiana | Madison Municipal Airport |
| Type: | Paved Identifier: IMS | August 8, 1990 |

| #25 | Salem, Indiana | Salem Municipal Airport |
| Type: | Paved Identifier: I83 | August 8, 1990 |

| #26 | Tell City, Indiana | Perry County Airport |
| Type: | Paved Identifier: TEL | August 8, 1990 |

| #27 | Huntingburg, Indiana | Huntingburg Airport |
| Type: | Paved Identifier: HNB | August 8, 1990 |

| #28 | Orleans, Indiana | Orleans Airport |
| Type: | Paved Identifier: 7I4 | August 8, 1990 |

VISITS WITH DAD

MY STEPFATHER, EDWARD Kazmierczak, has long had an aversion to flying. This was not unusual or unexpected. Dad grew-up in the golden age of flying. Flyers during the thirties did daring things every day and they made the headlines on a daily basis. Unfortunately, the headlines they made were because so many pilots died in their daring-do. He went flying once with a neighbor. However, prior to going to the airport, he claims to have had several stiff drinks. "Just to loosen up a little," he said. Whenever he was invited to go with me, he claimed that there wasn't enough booze in the house!

The folks spent a long weekend with us in Bloomington, Indiana in early August 1990. On the 7th of August, I visited several airports in southern Indiana. During dinner that night, the highlights of the trip were discussed in some detail. The weather was good for the balance of the weekend, and I looked forward to another great day of flying.

The following morning we all discussed what we were going to during the day. Mom and Nancy were going to do some decorating around the place, and I was going to do more flying around the southern tip of the state. Dad had earlier said that he wanted to go fishing; but when it came to him, he simply said, "I'm going with Bob." What a shock! After all the refusals, now he decides to go flying without any prompting. Will wonders never cease?

The trip was a five-airport tour in perfect VFR weather. All the flights were direct from one airport to another by way of LORAN C. Dad had a hard time spotting airports at five or so miles away. I showed Dad how the LORAN worked and what to look for, and before long he was picking the fields out of the ground clutter very well. We met some nice people - especially in Orleans, where two pilots (again, names are forgotten) who were also fishermen, became acquaintances. These fellows flew from one fishing spot to another all over Indiana and Kentucky. Now they were talking Dad's language! My father instantly became aware of the magical lure of flying and the advantage of sport aviation. It changed his whole outlook on flying.

#29   Greencastle, Indiana   Putnam County Airport
Type: Paved Identifier: 4I7   August 12, 1990

#30   Mentone, Indiana   Mentone Municipal Airport
Type: Paved Identifier: C92   August 25, 1990

BIOGRAPHICAL SKETCH OF
LAWRENCE DALE BELL

(Courtesy of Lawrence D. Bell Museum Mentone, Indiana)

LAWRENCE DALE BELL was born in Mentone, on April 5, 1894, the youngest son of Isaac and Harriet Sarber Bell. He was known to everyone as Larry, and attended school in Mentone until 1907, when his family moved to Santa Monica, California.

In January, 1910, Larry and his older brother, Grover, attended the first major U.S. Air Show at Dominguez Field near Los Angeles. Immensely impressed, they returned home and built a plane of their own. It was only a model, but it flew and it changed the lives of both Bell brothers.

In 1912, a month before Larry was to graduate from high school, Grover, who had recently learned to fly, asked him to join the great stunt pilot Lincoln Beachey and himself as a mechanic. Larry easily passed the final examination that ended his formal education and joined the pilots, completely enjoying his work. Beachey temporarily quit, but the Bell brothers continued attending air shows. Grover was killed in a crash in 1913, and Larry vowed to quit aviation. In a short time, however, friends convinced him to return to the field and he went to work for Glenn L. Martin.

At age 20, Larry was shop foreman, and within a few years he became vice-president and general manager of the Martin Co. In 1928, he left to join Consolidated Aircraft in Buffalo, New York.

Consolidated Aircraft moved to California in 1935. Larry, then, decided to form his own corporation. The company, Bell Aircraft Corporation, had a slow beginning. Its undaunted engineers continued to perfect new designs. In the first 20 years of its existence, the company recorded 20 firsts. For these firsts, Larry was honored with the Daniel Guggenheim Medal, the Collier Trophy, a presidential citation, the French Legion of Honor, honorary degrees and many other honors, in addition to having schools and parks named after him.

At his death in 1956, Larry Bell was the dean of American aviation, having served the industry 44 years.

#31	Nappanee, Indiana		Nappanee Municipal Airport
Type:	Paved Identifier: C03		August 26, 1990
#32	Goshen, Indiana		Goshen Municipal Airport
Type:	Paved Identifier: GSH		August 26, 1990
#33	Kendallville, Indiana		Kendallville Municipal Airport
Type:	Paved Identifier: C62		August 26, 1990
#34	Auburn, Indiana		DeKalb County Airport
Type:	Paved Identifier: 07C		August 26, 1990
#35	Lake Village, Indiana		Lake Village Airport
Type:	Grass Identifier: C98		August 29, 1990

Lake Village airport started out as private field, a grass strip on the edge of the southbound portion of Route 41 where it intersects with Indiana Route 10. It was founded by Stanley Davis, who was a glider pilot in World War II. He flew Waco CG-4A gliders.

The most common recollections of gliders from WWII are of the CG-4A. These were designed to be towed behind a DC-3. The Wacos carried 13 (or more) armed and combat equipped soldiers. Their size and flimsiness, combined with the brief and anemic training that the pilots received, probably caused more combat fatalities than the treacherous conditions into which they flew. But these were not the only gliders used in the war. There were smaller versions – three place gliders such as the one I first learned to fly.

Lake Village airport, as an ad hoc glider center for this rural community, attracted more glider pilots than the average post-war airfield.

I wish that I had met Stanley Davis, because my flight training back in 1961 was in a three place trainer.

Lake Village is a field of many stories and I am compelled to tell the three of which I am aware.

First and foremost, a lot of antique airplanes are here. In terms of the field's activity, there are probably more old airplanes per active pilot than any other field. Now, 50 - 60 years after its founding, the field remains a magnet for older pilots and equally older planes. With other strips, planes come and go whereas at Lake Village, the older aircraft come and stay. At any given time, there were a dozen noteworthy aircraft on the field.

The "airport historian" at Lake Village is Dan Vermeulen. Dan is not a pilot except for the radio controlled models he builds and flies. He is a regular at Lake Village and is a pilot in every sense of the word - except for the FAA certificate. He loves aviation and is as much a part of the Lake Village culture as any of the other flyers. We toured the field's hangars and tie-downs with his loving comments and our collective caressing eyes.

The first aircraft we saw was a 1930 Brunner-Winkle Bird with a Kinner K-5,100 HP, tail number N789Y. The plane was made by the Brunner Winkle Aircraft Co. which was very quickly reorganized as the Bird Aircraft Company, in Queens, New York. The owner is Nick Kucki, who is also the current owner of the airport. This aircraft was probably re-engined. If not, then it was probably built in 1929 and sold in 1930. The 1930 aircraft were powered by either a 110 HP Warner-Scarab or 165 HP Wright J-5 engines. (By the way, Charles Lindbergh taught Anne Morrow Lindbergh to fly in a Bird CK at the Long Island Aviation Country Club in Hicksville.)

Next, we saw a 1989 Waco YMF-S. This aircraft is a new reproduction of the original YMF which was considered to be the finest sport aviation aircraft ever built. They may be right! With a huge number of upgrades and modern improvements, it is now a $250,000 airplane. The comfort and appointments of this aircraft surely provide pride of ownership to Nick Kucki.

Also on the field is a 1942 Stearman in Navy colors with a 220 HP Jacobs engine, N43YP. The owner is Ernie Mislich. Everyone loves a Stearman, and this one will not disappoint the most discerning aficionado.

We moved on to another highlight: a magnificent 1942 Waco UPF7, N39714 owned by Bud Hayes. This aircraft was a basket case when Bud bought it. After untold hours of work at a cost enumerated only by the wink of an eye, owner Bud Hayes produced a historic aircraft which was awarded the 1995 EAA Outstanding WW II aircraft prize. Nicely done, Bud!

Bud Hayes also owns a 1939 Deneen Sparrowhawk, N441Y. This airplane was originally a Heath parasol with a Henderson 28 HP motorcycle engine; a standard configuration. The prototype for the Heath Parasol was finished in 1926.The Heath Parasol was designed and built by Claire Linstead and Edward Heath. The idea to build the Heath came from Weston Farmer. Mr. Farmer not only made the suggestion, he also provided a Henderson engine and wings for the prototype. After the plans were published, more than a thousand Heath Parasols were constructed and flown in the late 1920s and 1930s. Bud Hayes took this base and turned it into a biplane. The Sparrowhawk is cute because it is small (it only weighs 600 pounds) and it is sexy because of the very attractive tapered wings, top and bottom.

Bud Davidson of EAA wrote an impressive article on this airplane in the July, 2002 issue of Sport Aviation, a monthly publication of the Experimental Aircraft Association.

Still another aircraft of interest was a 1946 Trojan A-2 with a 90 hp Continental engine. Harold "Pops" Emigh built 58 of these, of which some 20 or 25 still exist. This is a fascinating airplane mostly because of its wings. The wings are equipped with full-length ailerons and are constructed with round head rivets that are about 1-1/2 times the diameter of usual aircraft rivets. The wings are also fitted with external stiffeners: 3/4" x 3/4" aluminum "L" extrusions. They wrap around the wings at each rib location. The oversize rivets and the external braces gave the airplane the look of a World War I tank! But there is more.

This airplane has very unique wings, to say the least: they are interchangeable from left to right and back. Well now, the wind has a constant NACA 0012-63 airfoil from root to tip. This means that they cannot have any wash-out or it would be reverse on one wing and the airplane would be prone to corkscrewing through the air. Furthermore, with a constant airfoil and no washout, I believe that the whole wing would stall at the same time. This alone would make slow flight a dicey proposition!

Secondly, the brother of the field's founder is none other than

Leeon Davis. Leeon Davis is the designer and developer of the Davis DA-2A aircraft of home-built fame. It is not as smooth as the later glass or composite home built aircraft on the market. In fact, it can best be described as angular. It has a V tail like a Bonanza. It only takes an engine in the 65 to 125 HP range, but it handles and performs a lot better than it looks. Owners say it handles like a Piper Cherokee except the control response is much quicker. In this sense, the Davis DA-2A is more like an American Yankee.

The airplane has been written-up in any number of journals, the most recent being an article by Budd Davisson in the September, 2003 issue of EAA's Sport Aviation. There is even a web site for the model.

My third story is that the field has regained some glider activity and because of it the field has started a return to its original gliding roots. The uniqueness of this activity rests in the gliding student base.

The flying instructors involved in a program have sought out disadvantaged kids from Robbins, Ford Heights, Harvey and Chicago's South Side to give them an opportunity to obtain their glider pilot's license, or even a private pilot's set of wings.

Teachers in several community high schools announced that any students interested in flying should stay after school. These students were told of the heretofore unexpected opportunity to fly, but there were some conditions. They had to be willing to devote their Saturdays to the program, and they must keep their grades in the "B" range. In other words, they had to make a commitment.

Enter into this picture Patrick Carron. Pat Carron is the founder of the Aviation Scholarship Foundation which conducts this program. Carron learned to fly before he learned to drive and decided he wanted to give other teens that chance. He formed the foundation in 1995 to give promising youths who otherwise might not have the opportunity the chance to earn their wings. Carron's group has awarded more than $50,000 in scholarships since its inception.

Instructors first teach students to fly on gliders then move them up to powered planes when they are ready. The increase in the level of self-confidence as the students' progress through the program is amazing.

The youngsters all had eager looks on their faces whenever I saw them. I am of the opinion that they learned lessons for life.

Lake Village is an airport without fences or gates. I guess there is no real need for security guards, metal detector wands and under-paid, under educated and overly sarcastic inspectors. They do just fine with their 1940s approach to aviation.

#36	Knox, Indiana	Wheeler Airport
Type:	Grass Identifier: 3C5	August 30, 1990

SO THAT IS 'DENSITY ALTITUDE'

BILL WHITE JOINED me in trying to find the Westville Airport one evening. Once again, there was no luck in spotting the field. The landing strip at Westville runs north and south. All the section lines run north and south. Half of the county roads in Indiana run north and south as well as all the tree lines. It is a heck of a lot easier spotting a grass strip when it runs other than with a cardinal compass heading. A landing at Westville would have to be put off once again.

It did not matter. Although it was a very hot and humid evening, it was still a good night for flying and the company was great. Bill and I have known each other for several years. It was the Knights of Columbus that brought us together. While Bill was in a different Council as a 3rd Degree Knight, we were both in the same 4th Degree Assembly. Often, we would don our fancy regalia and stand honor guard for a special religious occasion or a more somber affair, a funeral for one of our brother Sir Knights. We both relished being Knights of Columbus.

Bill was a pilot in training. He had a late start. His flight training began after his retirement from the postal service. At age 65, learning to fly was regrettably difficult for Bill. Whenever an opportunity arose, we would fly together to expand his education. I had no idea that we would learn about Density Altitude this day.

After failing to locate Westville airport, we diverted to Wheeler's Field near Knox. Upon landing, we met up with some young folks also in training. We chatted about flying and airplanes. Some of our tales of flight were true. All were entertaining. But it was time to go; the sun was getting low on the horizon.

A quick run-up and a casual taxi to the end of the field and we started our take-off roll. I didn't bother to go to the end of the runway. Instead, I took an angular entrance to the westbound runway and lackadaisically applied take-off power.

We bumped along the field and slowly gained speed. The huge stand of trees at the end of the runway was imposing. I wish there was a little breeze to help us get off. I brought some back pressure against the control column, but the Cherokee showed no inclination towards lifting her nose. We continued to bounce slowly along, with air speed building up excruciatingly slowly. The trees were looming larger. A decision had to be made. The plane would lift off but could it clear the trees? It seemed to be stupid to continue with the take-off. I chopped the power and we trundled to taxi speed.

Bill accepted my explanation and he agreed with the decision to abort. This time we taxied to the end of the runway. I turned west and applied full power while I held the brakes. Ten degrees of flaps and then brake release. Yes, the laws of physics work all the time. We climbed slowly in the hot, wet air and began a climbing turn to the south, avoiding the trees. And, that is how Bill and I learned about "density altitude".

#37	Delphi, Indiana	Delphi Municipal Airport
Type:	Paved Identifier: 1I9	September 1, 1990

#38	Sheridan, Indiana	Sheridan Municipal Airport
Type:	Paved Identifier: 5I4	September 1, 1990

| #39 | Muncie, Indiana | Delaware County Airport |
| Type: | Class D Identifier: MIE | September 1, 1990 |

| #40 | Bluffton, Indiana | Miller Airport |
| Type: | Grass Identifier: C40 | September 1, 1990 |

| #41 | South Bend, Indiana | Michiana Regional Airport |
| Type: | Class C Identifier: SBN | September 1, 1990 |

FLYING WITH NANCY

THE FLYING OF September 1, 1990, a total of five airports, was a special trip for me. There was nothing extraordinary to see or do, nowhere exceptional to go and there was nothing peculiar about the weather. Rather, this was the first trip that I made with my wife.

When we first bought the airplane, there hadn't been but two or three hours on the engine in several years. While it had acceptable compression readings at the annual inspection, engines must be run routinely to be reliable. A decision was made that I would fly the airplane alone for the first 50 hours. An engine likes to fix itself in many regards. Compression ratios are amongst those items that respond favorably to a steady accumulation of flying hours.

The time had come for a passenger. Nancy, my loving and adoring wife, would be my first passenger now that the plane had proved itself. How appropriate!

We took off in the early morning hours while the air was cool and slightly misty. It was a smooth ride, so it was good for Nancy. Nancy is not crazy about flying. Actually, she does not like to fly at all. She does, however, put up with her husband's hobby of sport aviation.

Our landing at Delphi was uneventful. We were there quite early, so no one was around. Delphi is a typical Indiana airport just inside the Hilltop MOA (Military Operations Area). Because it caters to only a few flyers in the area, the activity at the field is minimal.

Our next stop was Sheridan, Indiana. There were two fields in Sheridan and I would visit Sheridan - Blackhawk at a later date. Here at Sheridan Muni, we became acquainted with a kindly gentleman whose name we have forgotten. He was retired and managed the Fixed Base Operation (FBO) to keep busy. He had recently become enamored with personal computers. Don't forget, this was 1990, when the programs available depended upon BASIC language and memory was measured in double digit kilobytes and not triple digit megabytes. He had a program that could determine Biorhythms and wanted us to see it. It was fun to play around with the program, but it was more fun to see how excited this old man was to show it to us.

Some care had been put into the airport to make it more attractive. While our plane was being refueled, we could sit in the shade on a wooden swing in a white gazebo. The mid-morning sun began to bring up the temperatures, so gently swaying in the swing with a canopy over our head to provide some shade was welcome. We have good memories from there.

Delaware County Airport is the home of Vince's Restaurant. Vince's and Muncie Aviation cater to flyers and their guests. Each airplane is met by two linemen and accompanied to a parking space. Fuel and oil service orders are taken immediately while people deplane. The restaurant is only 25 feet from the parking ramp. The restaurant is fully glazed for a solarium effect. There are flowers and ivy plants located everywhere. Flyers from miles around come to Vince's for lunch on weekends. The lunch that Nancy and I had at Vince's will always be a memorable one.

Miller Airport in Bluffton is a two-runway airport with the north-south strip forming an "L" shape with the east-west strip. Both were 2,600 feet long. A Cherokee 180 by its nature is a nose-heavy airplane. This is especially true of the shorter, pre-1967, models. Putting in full fuel and two adults in the front seat made rotation at takeoff a little more difficult. Bluffton added a few more complications to that equation. The field was rough, the grass was almost to the leading edges of the wings, and the air temperature (by now in the middle 90s) was driving up the density altitude. Being fully fueled, the runway's 2,600 feet would be enough for take-off, but it would be a little dicey. Using the Midwest farmer's trick for such fields, we accelerated to rotation speed and then pulled in one notch of flaps. Regardless, the take-off roll was noticeably longer than Nancy was used to seeing. There was some talk about that on the way to South Bend.

At Michiana Regional Airport in South Bend we met up with my parents. They had come out to see us to say "Hello." As with all the other airports we visited, a number of snapshots were taken. As I came closer to my goal of landing at all the airports in Indiana, one of these snapshots appeared on the front page of the South Bend Tribune when the newspaper decided to write a human-interest story on my endeavor.

The trip was thoroughly enjoyable. In a single day, Nancy got to fly to (1) an airport in a Military Operations Area at Delphi, (2) a non-controlled airport with a paved strip at Sheridan, (3) a tower-controlled airport at Muncie, (4) a grass strip at Bluffton and, (5) a radar surveillance airport in South Bend. She had seen a representative cross section of Indiana airports. She still doesn't like flying, but she tolerates it.

| #42 | Attica, Indiana | Riley Field |
| Type: | Paved Identifier: 1I2 | September 3, 1990 |

| #43 | Frankfort, Indiana | Frankfort Municipal Airport |
| Type: | Paved Identifier: FKR | September 3, 1990 |

| #44 | Flora, Indiana | Flora Municipal Airport |
| Type: | Grass Identifier: 5I2 | September 3, 1990 |

| #45 | Lafayette, Indiana | Aretz Field |
| Type: | Paved Identifier: 3AR | September 3, 1990 |

"OH, MAN!"

SEPTEMBER 3ʳᴰ, 1990 was a special day for me and a young man by the name of Malcolm Maxwell. Malcolm and I were matched together in the initial year of a mentor program during his last semester of high school. We developed a close friendship through his graduation and entrance into Ball State University, where he studied law enforcement. I was always impressed by Malcolm and his intense desire to make something of himself. We became friends for life. Naturally, Malcolm was one of the first people that I wanted to take flying.

He had never been in an airplane, so everything was new. We weren't going to go on any long distance flights, but he had to be part of the adventure of flying to all the airports in Indiana. The furthest we went was less than 100 miles.

The trip to Attica was under perfectly clear skies. There we saw some men flying radio controlled model airplanes. Malcolm had never seen that before, either. As always, we took a few pictures to document the fact that we had visited the field, including several of Malcolm with the model flyers.

We also visited Frankfort Municipal, Flora Municipal (a grass strip) and Aretz Field, which is just east of Lafayette. None of these fields is more than 50 miles apart, but it was a good day's flying for someone who had never been in an airplane.

Taking off from Aretz, we had a 70-mile trip home. There was some "fair weather cumulus" with bases at 3,000 feet M.S.L. I explained to Malcolm that we could ride beneath these clouds and get bumped around for about 45 minutes but it would be better if we got above them to have a smoother ride. We spotted a hole big enough to climb through to about 4,500 feet, if I put the airplane in a maximum climb attitude. This would get us above the clouds. Normally, my airplane has unusually good visibility over the nose. But a Cherokee 180 at a maximum climb angle causes the nose to block out most of the horizon and destroys forward visibility. At, 4,500 feet, I rolled the airplane into level flight and looked over at Malcolm. He had the biggest smile on his face and his eyes were wide open. He had never seen clouds from this vantage point before. Just at rolling out, he looked at the big, white, fluffy cloud tops and simply said "Oh, man!" I had a camera ready and was fortunate enough to get a picture of him at that exact moment.

Once home, that photograph became the focal point of a montage of the shots we took during the trip. It was a terrific present for Malcolm and a wonderful memory for me.

#46   Huntington, Indiana   Huntington Municipal Airport
Type: Paved Identifier: HHG   September 15, 1990

#47   Winchester, Indiana   Randolph County Airport
Type: Grass Identifier: I22   September 15, 1990

#48   New Castle, Indiana   New Castle Municipal
Type: Grass Identifier: Private   September 15, 1990

#49   Sheridan, Indiana   Blackhawk Field
Type: Grass Identifier: Private   September 15, 1990

LLOYD AND FLOYD

BLACKHAWK FIELD IS a grass strip that runs 10 degrees and 190 degrees. As such, it is tricky to spot from the air. It must have been an active field at one time, because the remains of several airplanes are scattered about the area. The property owner pointed out the various types of frames and skeletons as we walked about the premises. The old maintenance hangar was stuffed to the rafters with wings, tail sections and engines from old Cubs, Stinsons and Taylorcrafts. I could not tell one from another, but Floyd could.

I am not quite sure of the name of the man who owns the

property - either Lloyd or Floyd. He owned a dog when I was there in 1990; a golden retriever. I doubt that the dog is still alive, as it was in deplorable condition when I visited. Whatever the owner's name was, the dog's name was the other. If Lloyd was the owner, then the dog was Floyd. I believe the owner was Floyd and the dog was Lloyd.

The dog was blind, but he tracked after his master by sound. As Floyd walked around with me, Lloyd was right behind him. Each time Floyd stopped, Lloyd ran into the back of Floyd's legs. I believe that the dog's hearing was bad also, as he sometimes lagged behind. Floyd had to yell for the dog so he would catch up to us. Walking and talking with Floyd and joining him in his love for old general aviation gave me a warm and soothing feeling. It was hard to leave those two.

Blackhawk Field did not exist long afterward. The specifics of its closing are lost to obscurity. I often wonder what happened to all those old parts and components.

#50   Waveland, Indiana   Shades State Park
Type: Grass Identifier: 812   September 22, 1990

THE MOST BEAUTIFUL STATE PARK

SHADES STATE PARK is one of the more beautiful places in which we landed. The runway is 3,000 feet long and about 300 feet wide. During our visit, it was as smooth and as level as a pool table. Naturally, the airplane was photographed from all angles. Every shot turned out perfectly. With the well-manicured grass and mature trees in all the backgrounds, the little Cherokee never looked better. The sun was shining brightly, which really highlighted the little red and white plane against the lush green grass and deep, dark trees. I have dropped in there several times.

This field was also the only place that ever charged me a landing fee. (Meigs and Midway in Chicago also do so years later.) Actually, it was an admittance fee for the park. During one of my visits, a park ranger, a young woman of about 20, approached me and asked to see my annual park sticker. I didn't have one so she told me that I would have to pay a daily entry fee. She hastened to add that it would be good all weekend. I told her that I would be on the ground less than an hour, but she was not going to be talked out of what she thought was the right thing to do. With her right arm outstretched, she pointed to the little rustic toll booth about 300 yards away and said "It's only three dollars. You can pay there." A couple of little worry lines creased her forehead as she started to walk away. Clearly, she anticipated additional reluctance or resistance from me. There was no need; like she said, it was only $3.

Paying the fee was funny. Cutting through a clump of trees, I went directly to the ranger's booth. The toll taker, about 18 years old and experiencing his first taste of authority, admonished me about jumping ahead in line. So I stepped aside and gave him working room with the cars that were lined up to enter. This wasn't good enough for him - the fare gatherer was quickly turning into a dictatorial tyrant. I had to take my place in line waiting to pay the entrance fee. There were three or four cars in line. I couldn't be sure whether the drivers were staring or glaring at me. It wouldn't be right to cut in front of anyone so I got in line. As each car pulled up forward, I moved up a space. It felt more and more awkward just standing there and then moving with the line. Really, I should have cut in and been ready for verbal abuse. But I didn't. I wonder what the other folks in line thought about me.

| #51 | Indianapolis, Indiana | Terry Airport |
| Type: | Paved Identifier: I52 | September 22, 1990 |

| #52 | Elwood, Indiana | Elwood Airport |
| Type: | Grass Identifier: 3I1 | September 2 2, 1990 |

MY FAVORITE LUNCH STOP

ELWOOD QUICKLY BECAME one of my favorite fields to visit. No matter where I was flying on any given weekend, Elwood was usually less than 45 minutes away. It was easy to stop for lunch.

It is two grass strips in an "L" configuration. The runways are in an East - West (2,243 feet long) and North - South (2,076 feet long) orientation with the intersection at the southern-most and eastern-most points. For some reason, the field captured my heart, and I found myself returning there, time and time again.

Elwood is the home of a small café that fronts on the street that runs alongside the airport. Cars park in a gravel lot in front of the building, and there is room enough for about four or five airplanes on a small grass yard in the back. There is a faded old Coca Cola sign in back - the type that is white with green lettering. Once, these signs were all over America. This sign read:

"Welcome To Elwood.
The Home Of The World's First Fly-In Drive-In."

The food was average, greasy and loaded with salt. Most of the taste came from heavy doses of salt. The people working there were extraordinarily friendly and accommodating. The other patrons, while not always pilots, were also friendly and interesting to talk to. I enjoyed coming to Elwood for a bite to eat and good conversation.

#53   Alexandria, Indiana   Alexandria Airport
Type: Paved Identifier: I99   September 22, 1990

#54   Marion, Indiana   Marion Municipal Airport
Type: Paved Identifier: MZZ   September 22, 1990

#55   Peru, Indiana   Peru Municipal Airport
Type: Paved Identifier: I76   September 22, 1990

| #56 | Terre Haute, Indiana | Hulman Regional Airport |
| Type: | Class C Identifier: HUF | September 30, 1990 |

| #57 | Clinton, Indiana | Clinton Airport |
| Type: | Paved Identifier: 1I7 | September 30, 1990 |

| #58 | Terre Haute, Indiana | Sky King Airport |
| Type: | Paved Identifier: 3I3 | September 30, 1990 |

| #59 | Brazil, Indiana | Clay County Airport |
| Type: | Paved Identifier: 0I2 | September 30, 1990 |

| #60 | Franklin, Indiana | Franklin Flying Field |
| Type: | Paved Identifier: 3FK | September 30, 1990 |

| #61 | Lebanon, Indiana | Boone County Airport |
| Type: | Paved Identifier: 6I4 | October 13, 1990 |

| #62 | Anderson, Indiana | Ace Airport |
| Type: | Grass Identifier: 3AE | October 13, 1990 |

| #63 | Kokomo, Indiana | Glendale Airport |
| Type: | Grass Identifier: 8I3 | October 13, 1990 |

| #64 | Converse, Indiana | Converse Municipal Airport |
| Type: | Grass Identifier: 1I8 | October 13, 1990 |

"WHAT IS THAT? A STOP SIGN?"

HAD NO UNDERSTANDING of the sight that awaited me at
Converse. According to the sectional chart, this was a paved

runway 2,000 feet in length. The Flight Guide warned of gravel and stones on the runway. This is the type of warning that goes with a seldom used strip with a concrete surface that has been neglected. A pilot has to come in at the slowest possible safe speed with the nose high and avoid taxiing at a high RPM setting. Often this field is shown as being for "Emergency Use Only." But there was more to Converse airport than that.

Approaching from the west and a little south of the field, I would be set-up well for a left downwind pattern for Runway 24. The octagonal shaped field could be seen for miles away. The field looked like a giant, concrete stop sign. It was so remarkable that I took a picture of it just prior to the downwind leg.

Converse airport was a gigantic circular pad of concrete measuring 2,000 feet in every direction. The runway was painted on the surface. It didn't mean much though. A pilot could land 20 or 30 degrees off the wind or even at a right angle to the wind direction and still be on concrete. Or, to really simulate carrier landings, all landings could be made straight into the wind regardless of the day's wind direction. Actually, the 2,000 foot dimension is at the four opposing corners of the field. The real size of the octagon is 1,800 feet. This convenient shape made pilots and saved airplanes.

There are three metal hangars on the field, all painted in bright reddish-orange and white. They appear to be in good condition. While there were no other pilots or aircraft to be seen, there were about 50 to 75 people there with radio controlled model airplanes. This was a great affair with barbeques going in several places and lots of coolers. This was truly a family affair with many wives and children present. When the 35 mm picture came back from processing, it was almost impossible to pick up the people and cars in the left downwind photo. Such is the insignificance of a 72" inch person relative to a 1,800 foot airfield!

The story behind this field goes back to World War II. We know that Bunker Hill Naval Air Station - now Grissom Air Force Base - originally had 26 satellite airfields established for off-site training purposes. These were called OLF's (Outlying Landing Fields). The military set up this type of field to accommodate cross-wind landings. By merely giving the student a heading on which to land, the instructor could present the student with as much or as little cross wind as he thought necessary. The solution was quick and cheap. The home-field traffic was greatly diminished for a very low cost.

Major General Doolittle set-up one of these fields for his 1942 mission over Japan. The 26 aircraft originally selected to form the 17th Bomb Group practiced short-field take-offs on a number of these 'auxiliary fields' in the Florida panhandle. From take-off, they would fly out to the Gulf for navigational training. I had the opportunity many, many years ago to land at one of those Florida bases on a runway that had a small portion of its length painted black. It was extended somewhat to simulate a carrier deck assuming a 35 knot head wind. I could have taken off in that length with the little Cessna I was flying at the time but I sure as heck wouldn't try the same take-off in a loaded B-25 off of a carrier!

The original name of our Indiana field is lost to history. No one knows if it even had a name. The common practice was to use the name of the nearest town and add an OLF on the end. In this case, it would have been Converse OLF. The local townspeople and the historical records at Grissom AFB have no information regarding the date it was built or commissioned, what it was called, or when it was turned over to civilian use. This situation is the same with similar fields which were mostly grass with one or two concrete strips. The OLF's seemed to rise from the ground without much to-do. They were needed and they were built. It was as simple as that. In digging into this story, it was also revealed that the Galveston, Indiana airport is the same "stop sign" design. Converse and Galveston airports are about 100 to 120 acres of land area.

Contrast this to the modern day effort by our Navy to establish an OLF within Washington County, North Carolina. Yes, they still use the term OLF for these fields. In this case, the Navy needs 2,000 acres for a runway, and additional 30,000 acres surrounding the field to prevent encroachment, a one year construction budget of $49,000,000 with 433 workers which will be followed by a full and part time operating staff of 50 people and an annual budget of $1,200,000! Things have changed since the early 1940s. For one, the Navy learned how to spend money.

The best sources of information for these sorts of fields are Abandoned & Little-Known Airfields by Paul Freeman and Forgotten Fields of America, by Lou Thole. These two fellows deserve a lot of credit for the research and documentation they have done to prevent the story of these fields from being totally lost. Please accept my gratitude for the background on these and other stories in this endeavor. Congratulations, my friends!

#65   Fort Wayne, Indiana   Fort Wayne International
Type: Class C Identifier: FWA   October 13, 1990

THE HISTORY OF BAER FIELD

THE PRESENT FORT Wayne International Airport was another of the air training bases built at the onset of World War II. In early January of 1942, Fort Wayne was given a caveat proposed by the government in that they would build a training base southwest of Fort Wayne if the townspeople would hand over the deed to the 700 acres of land that the Federal Government specified. Furthermore, the deed must be tendered within 30 days. This was an almost impossible task, - even in the early days of 1941 when war fever was at a high pitch. It would be difficult, but not impossible.

With the efforts of some 30 businesses coordinated with 4 major local banks and the cooperation of the land owners who would be ready to move out in 15 days, the land was secured for military use by February 1st, 1942. The land was tendered to the consortium and the Federal Government signed a $1 per year lease for the land. Construction started immediately.

The field, with three paved runways of 6,000 feet, 6,230 feet and 6,297 feet was turned over to the active branch of the Army Air Corps on October 31st, 1942.

The new field was named after Paul Baer, a Fort Wayne native who was born in 1894. Paul Baer serviced in the Lafayette Escadrille and the 103rd Aero Squadron in the AEF Air Force. Pilot Baer was an ace with 16 victories. He was awarded the Distinguished Flying Cross, the Legion of Honor, and the Croix de Guerre. After returning home from the war, Paul Baer participated in aviation experiments. Later, he pioneered many new air-mail routes around the world. He died on December 9th, 1930 while flying mail and passengers when his Loening C-2-H amphibian crashed on takeoff from Shanghai, China. He is buried in Fort Wayne.

Assigned to Baer Field during the war was the 31st Pursuit Group flying P-39 Airacobras, the 78th Fighter Group flying P-38 Lightning's and, most importantly, the I Troop Carrier Command.

The I Troop Carrier Command was responsible for combat equipping and modifying all C-47's to the latest configuration as soon as they flew out of the factories. This included removal of all unnecessary equipment and installation of new equipment suitable for the airplane's final destination and theater of operation. Post modification flight testing was then conducted on the aircraft. Lou Thole, in writing <u>Forgotten Fields of America</u> concluded that well over half the cargo aircraft over Normandy on D-Day, 1944 received their check flight out of Baer Field.[2]

And I was there in my Piper Cherokee some fifty years later.

#66   Sullivan, Indiana   Sullivan County Airport
Type: Paved Identifier: SIV   October 20, 1990

#67   Bloomfield, Indiana   Shawnee Field
Type: Grass Identifier: 1I3   October 20, 1990

#68   Indianapolis, Indiana   Greenwood Municipal Airport
Type: Paved Identifier: HFY   October 20, 1990

#69   Greenfield, Indiana   Pope Field
Type: Grass Identifier: GFD   October 20, 1990

---

2 "Preparing C-47's For War"; Forgotten Fields of America. Lou Thole, 1996

#70	Anderson, Indiana	Anderson-Darlington Airport
Type: Paved Identifier: AID		October 20, 1990

#71	Indianapolis, Indiana	Mt. Comfort Airport
Type: Paved Identifier: MQJ		October 20, 1990

#72	Westfield, Indiana	Wheeler's Field
Type: Grass Identifier: I72		October 20, 1990

#73	Marshall, Michigan	Brooks Field
Type: Paved Identifier: 5D8		October 27, 1990

#74	Logansport, Indiana	Logansport Municipal Airport
Type: Paved Identifier: GGP		October 28, 1990

#75	Galveston, Indiana	Galveston Municipal Airport
Type: Grass Identifier: 5I6		October 28, 1990

The Galveston airport is another of the OLF's (Out Lying Fields) left over from the government in WW II. This field is a round field similar to Converse which I visited on October 13th, 1991. But the Galveston airport is grass whereas Converse was concrete. Actually, the strip is paved as is Converse. The surface has since been covered over by dirt and sand to the point where grass grows on it. This sod is almost a foot thick. At a small corner of the octagon, the local model airplane club has stripped back enough for its hobby activities. There was some talk about breaking out the concrete and returning the field to tillable condition. This idea came to an end when the concrete borings revealed that it was four feet deep!

Furthermore, where Converse had a deteriorating surface, the grass at Galveston was typically well maintained. When I was there, the grass had been cut and was in excellent health. This field is maintained by a nearby farmer for the U.S. Government on an annual contract basis.

The field is not used much anymore. No aircraft are stored on the field. There are no buildings of any sort. It is estimated that only 25 aircraft visit the field each year. This is probably due to the fact that it is inconveniently located about 4 statute miles from the end of Grissom Air Force Base's Runway 23. Runway 23 is 12,000 feet in length and most of it is used during take-offs from Grissom. Grissom is home to the 931st Air Refueling Group. I suspect that the Air Force doesn't like light airplanes operating in front of the heavily fuel laden KC-135 and KC-10 aircraft which routinely take-off from Grissom.

Like Converse, not much is known about the origin of this airport, its name, or when it was opened to general aviation. But Converse and Galveston are unique. In all my other trips, I never saw these fields duplicated, although I was to learn later that the municipal airport at Kokomo had its beginning as an Out Lying Field, and it was probably round as well.

| #76 Union Mills, Indiana | Flying U Ranch |
| Type: Grass Identifier: 4C1 | October 28, 1990 |

HOW TO FIND A LOST (GRASS) FIELD

U NION MILLS is quite close to our home field. In fact, we would pass over it routinely en route east or upon returning. I never thought much about it since long distance, all-day flights were the norm. When it came time to visit the field, it wasn't to be found.

Anyone who has flown over northern Indiana terrain understands that it is one farm after another interspersed only with little towns and a couple of larger cities. Almost all farms look like they could be a landing strip of some sort. This was the case with Union Mills. The field could not be distinguished from adjacent farm land.

I tried on several occasions to find it with the LORAN and VOR coordinates, but to no avail. On one flight, a friend came along to help locate the field. Again, there was no success. Then an idea came to mind.

We had to wait out the season. We had been trying to find a rich, green landing strip in Indiana during the summer means trying to find it in the midst of equally rich, green crops. Merely waiting for the season to change would be the answer, sure enough. Come the middle of October, all of the crops were fully grown and most of them were harvested. All the crop land had acquired its golden hue of maturity. Union Mills landing strip was still that bright Kelley green. Contrasted with the surrounding farms, it stood out brightly. It was visited on October 28th, 1991 and that was that!

#77	Mishawaka, Indiana	Mishawaka Pilot's Club
Type:	Paved Identifier: 3C1	November 3, 1990

#78	Fort Wayne, Indiana	Smith Field
Type:	Paved Identifier: SMD	November 3, 1990

It was out of Smith Field that 1st Lieutenant Horace E. Diamond took off on a practice flight in his PT-17. While flying over the under-construction Paul Baer Field southwest of Fort Wayne, he decided that he would be the first to land at the airdrome. And, in fact, he was the first pilot to land at Baer Field. In the early 1940's it was considered to be great sport to be the first pilot to land at whatever new airfield was nearing completion, and there were hundreds of them around the Midwest. Typically, the pilots would use the pathetic excuses of "rough engine" or "low fuel" or "lost."

Everyone would look askance at the pilot but that was about all the superior officers could do in these cases. Horace made no such claim and simply admitted that he wanted to be the first to land on the field like every other student pilot was doing. Horace was subsequently reprimanded. He lost privileges and rank for his action.

Horace did wrong and was punished severely. It is good sportsmanship to applaud his candor and honesty!

ANOTHER STORY ABOUT SMITH FIELD

THIS TALE STARTS with an article written by Brenda Burn Kellow in July of 1998.It is titled "TRACING OUR ROOTS". It is subtitled "Couple Helps Family's Search for Relatives". Eventually, after many twists and turns, this story will end up at Smith Field! It goes like this:

Collin County has many heroes, and this story is about four such people in the North Texas genealogical community. Through a series of amazing coincidences, they find and bestow upon an unsuspecting researcher a treasure from the past.

Twenty years ago, a family moved out of a rented house in Dallas that was owned by Diane and Frank Andor of Princeton, Texas. The tenants left behind some items. One of them was an oval wedding picture with marriage information printed on the bottom of the picture. Diane, a budding genealogist at that time, did not know how to contact the people who left it behind. Hoping the family would miss the picture and call to inquire of its whereabouts, Diane kept it. No one ever inquired. She has been keeping the picture all this time.

On February 1, 1998, twentieth century researchers Marie and Mike Biggs, Jr., Diane's sister and nephew, decided to try to locate someone who deserved the picture. After a little research on the then-exploding internet and one phone call, they located Bob and Nancy Hechlinski, a relative of the couple in the picture.

Bob and Nancy of Dyer, Indiana are two of four active Hechlinski researchers. They were home alone watching the CBS presentation called "THE LOVE LETTER." The major element of this screenplay involves an exchange of photographs. Enter one of those serendipitous moments! Little did Bob and Nancy know that the phone call from Mike and Marie would be an ominous forbearance of what was to transpire!

Marie told them about the abandoned photograph that Diane and Frank had saved all those years. Indeed, it belonged to the Hechlinski's early American family. It was a 1924 wedding photograph of Kazimer Hechlinski and Carrie Kucharska. The picture of the couple is simply wonderful and it is still in good condition. While the photograph was not Bob's direct lineage, he promised that he would give the photo to Patty Ritter of nearby Ft. Wayne, a direct bloodline descendant of Kazimer and Carrie Hechlinski.

Diane mailed the picture replete with curved, convex glass and oval walnut frame within the week, at no charge to the Hechlinski's. Before presenting the picture to Patty, Bob made a camera copy for himself and the two other Hechlinski researchers. He also arranged for snapshots of the presentation and sent copies to Diane and Frank. Bob is also a hero. They are all heroes!

From this unassuming family, only Marie had this to say, "You meet such neat people in genealogy." She's right, too.

(Brenda Burns Kellow is a Certified Genealogist and a Certified Genealogical Instructor with a bachelor's degree in history, and a genealogy instructor at Collin County Community College.)

It was with familial pride that my cousin Bill and I could pack ourselves into the Cherokee for a second trip to Smith Field. It would be to deliver the precious photograph to Cousin Patty Ritter! It would be my second trip to Smith Field. (See comments about this grip at Airport 488)

#79   Garrett, Indiana   Shenk Field
Type: Grass Identifier: 3C2   November 3, 1990

#80   Butler, Indiana   Harrold Airport
Type: Grass Identifier: 2IN6   November 3, 1990

#81   Portland, Indiana   Portland Municipal Airport
Type: Paved Identifier: PLD   December 8, 1990

#82   New Castle, Indiana   Henry County Airport
Type: Paved Identifier: UWL   December 8, 1990

THE WRIGHT CONNECTION

NEW CASTLE IS located in northeast Henry County and there are two airports. One, Henry County Airport, is paved and New Castle's field, #48 visited in September 15, 1990, is grass. Of these two fields, Henry County is nearer to Millville, Indiana. Millville is a mere two or three miles from Henry County Airport.

It was in Millville, Indiana that Wilbur Wright was born on April 16, 1867. The Wright family lived there for almost another two years. Orville Wright would be born in Dayton, Ohio, some 50 nautical miles east on August 19, 1871. According to his father Milton's diary, Wilbur took his first steps while living in Millville. There is a small stone with a bronze plaque commemorating this event.

Concurrently, we must consider Octave Alexander Chanute, who was working in Chicago to pioneer aviation. He was born in France in 1832, and immigrated to the United States with his parents when he was seven. Chanute spent his life in the rail industry. He was chief engineer for the Chicago and Alton Railroad. During his professional career, he designed and built several railroad bridges in the Midwest. He designed the first bridge across the Missouri River and designed and built the Chicago and Kansas City stockyards. Later in his career, Chanute helped to design the early elevated train system of New York City.

After a brilliant career in civil engineering, his interest was drawn to the dream of man in flight, and he spent his retirement years pursuing powered flight in Chicago. He did some remarkable research concurrent with the Wright brothers. The three of them exchanged thoughts, ideas, and results of research with each other. Chanute knew that the far better opportunity for the discovery of powered flight lay with the Wrights. Chanute's greater contribution to powered and controlled flight was to serve as a clearinghouse of developmental information. He put an end to his trials and gave most of his instrumentation, many of his books and all of his data to the Wright brothers. Octave Chanute died in 1910.

Also consider that Chanute, living in Chicago, needed a good breezy location to test his full scale models. His conclusion was to select the dunes area of Indiana which is located where the little community of Miller now stands. Miller, then known as "Miller Beach, " is a suburb of Gary which is the site of US Steel's largest steel mill. Chanute conducted glider tests for several years starting in 1896.

The Wrights, also in need of a test area that is ripe with strong and consistent winds, selected Kitty Hawk. Hoosiers have always felt that we have a claim to the birthright of aviation because of Chanute's work. It was here in Indiana that he coined the word, "aviation". In fact, a model of Octave Chanute's Wing glider (48 pounds and built by John Lichenburg of Chanute, Kansas circa 1989-1990) proudly hangs from the ceiling of the Gary Regional Airport.

This forces a hypothetical question. What if the positions were reversed and Chanute had become enamored with the North Carolina seacoast and the Wrights opted for Gary, Indiana? Hmm. Northwest Indiana; the birthplace of aviation?

Nota bene. I submit my apologies to Allen Wright, my friend and colleague of many years. Allen and I were employees of the now extinct Pullman-Standard Company in the late 1970's and early 80's. Allen was in the Marketing Department and I was in Field Service Engineering. Pullman-Standard employed some 12,500 people in a variety of plants and sites. Allen and I were with the Passenger Rail Car division. This division was located in northwest Indiana and in Pullman, Illinois a south Chicago suburb. Since the collapse of Pullman, Allen has formed his own consulting company, rendering his services to a myriad of rail car manufacturers and transit properties in the United States, Europe and Canada. His company is appropriately called "The Wright Connection." Sorry, Allen. I couldn't pass up the title!

#83   Hagerstown, Indiana   Hagerstown Airport
Type: Grass Identifier: I61   December 8, 1990

#84   Shelbyville, Indiana   Shelbyville Municipal Airport
Type: Paved Identifier: 3SM   December 8, 1990

TIED FOR THE "MOST UN-FRIENDLIEST"

SHELBYVILLE PILOTS KEEP very much to themselves. The first time I visited there was December 8th, 1990. I tried to get into a conversation with the people, but they really didn't like the idea of talking with strangers. Some folks are like that, I suppose.

Unfortunately, I did not get a photograph while I was there the first time. That necessitated a second trip, just to get a picture of the airplane on site. Certainly, this would be an opportunity to see a different side of the Shelbyville flyers. I landed there with a friend about six months later.

We encountered strange behavior again from these folks. Both of us felt as though we were deliberately being excluded from their close, little group. Try as we might to be friendly, no one would talk to us. We concluded that there was nothing of interest at the Shelbyville airport, so there wasn't any need for either of us to go back again.

| #85 | Indianapolis, Indiana | Brookside Airport |
| Type: | Paved Identifier: I21 | December 8, 1990 |

| #86 | Indianapolis, Indiana | Eagle Creek Airpark |
| Type: | Paved Identifier: I14 | December 24, 1990 |

MY LAST FLIGHT WITH GEORGE

THE MIDWEST HAD just been hit with a double weather whammy. Technically, the snowfall couldn't be called a blizzard, but it certainly was a close cousin. We took 13 inches of snow in 24 hours. As usual, sharp Midwest winds drifted snow everywhere.

The temperature dropped to 15 degrees below zero and the wind chill factor was out of sight. To say we had a bite of old man winter was an understatement.

This was the week that Nancy's folks were our house guests. Californians to the core, they were not prepared for weather to which Midwesterners have become accustomed. Their outer clothing was inadequate, as was their footwear. Nonetheless, Dad was game to go flying with me.

Once aloft we found even more hostile conditions. The temperature fell another 20 degrees. The winds were in the 40 to 45 mph range, mostly from the west. We landed at Eagle Creek and hurried as best we could to the warmth of the FBO. Dad usually loves flying in light airplanes and he was keenly interested in our airplane. But this cold winter day, with the raw wind screaming across the Midwestern openness of an airport it was more than this Californian could tolerate. His thoughts were not here in the northern suburb of Indianapolis. No, he favored the idea of being in a warm house, in front of a roaring fire. A snifter of good brandy would be nice, too. No, he wasn't as keen as I on getting to know Eagle Creek airport. The sooner we got back into the plane and headed northward, the better he would like it.

I managed to get Dad to pose for a photograph by the plane. It is the shot that represents Eagle Creek in my book of airport photographs. Within an hour of our landing, we were aloft again. It was too late. Dad had gotten chilled to the bone and would remain cold for the rest of his visit. Adding to the chill that he picked up at Eagle Creek, the airplane never got warm, either. The wind had shifted to a dead head wind out of the north. I couldn't find an altitude that had less than 45 knot winds and all flight levels were head winds. I recall being in sight of Grissom Air Force Base for more than 30 minutes.

Dad spoke highly of our trip and continued to do so until his death a few years later. But I knew it was sheer misery for this man used to the warmer climes of Auburn, California. Nonetheless, he did make one airport in my quest, and that was important to me. I miss you, my friend.

#87	Evansville, Indiana	Evansville Regional Airport
Type:	Class C Identifier: EVV	December 31, 1990

#88	Jeffersonville, Indiana	Clark County Airport
Type:	Paved Identifier: JVY	December 31, 1990

#89	Indianapolis, Indiana	Speedway Airport
Type:	Paved Identifier: 3SY	February 9, 1991

#90	Indianapolis, Indiana	Metropolitan Airport
Type:	Paved Identifier: UMP	February 9, 1991

#91	Elkhart, Indiana	Elkhart Municipal Airport
Type:	Class D Identifier: EKM	February 10, 1991

#92	Connersville, Indiana	Mettel Field
Type:	Paved Identifier: CEV	February 10, 1991

#93	Greensburg, Indiana	Decatur County Airport
Type:	Paved Identifier: I34	February 10, 1991

#94	Columbus, Indiana	Columbus Municipal Airport
Type:	Class D Identifier: BAK	February 10, 1991

ATTERBURY ARMY AIRFIELD

THE ORIGIN OF Columbus Municipal had its roots in the massive construction process immediately after Pearl Harbor in 1942 and 1943. The pace of military construction projects was frantic. We were fighting a war on two fronts and the plan was to train 70,000 pilots a year. This was a major undertaking in terms of facilities and manpower. The airfield was to be separate from the Army Post called Camp Atterbury, which was some 25 miles away.

The airfield was to be one of the more substantial fields with permanent runways but less than permanent buildings. The notice to begin construction was July 29th, 1942. Although the budget was set at $1,000,000 per day, occasionally the limit could be raised, with a simple phone call to a superior, to $10,000,000 per day. Five months was allotted to the building of the base, which translated into a total cost of $130,000,000, a sizable sum of money even with today's purchasing power.

Twelve farms were bought to accommodate Atterbury Air Field. Roads were paved into the site, as well as a Pennsylvania Railroad spur. The field was handed over to the Army Air Corps on December 31st, 1942. It consisted of over 2,000 acres and 140 buildings.

Atterbury Airfield became the home of the 618th and 619th Bomb Squadrons of the 477th Bombardment Group. The training force alone consisted of 1,400 officers and men. The training was varied but concentrated on C-47 flight and crew training and CG-4A Glider training. For a while, some B-25 and B-26 flight and crew training took place.

The hospital at Atterbury, Wakeman General Hospital, was one of the largest military hospitals in the United States. Atterbury Air Base became the receiving site for the wounded flown-in for treatment and care from the European and Asian fronts.

While the general, massive training program stopped with the cessation of fighting, deactivation came slow for Atterbury. This was mostly due to selection of Camp Atterbury for a more permanent status as a training base. Later, in 1954, the base was renamed Bakalar Air Force Base in honor of Lt. John Bakalar of Hammond, Indiana who was killed in aerial combat over France in September of 1944 while flying a P-51. The base was finally evacuated by the Department of Defense in January of 1970. In 1972, the city of Columbus received the title and changed the name to Columbus Municipal Airport.

While most of the original buildings are gone, the airport has a fine museum - the Atterbury-Bakalar Air Museum. It was built in memory of all the military and civilian personnel who served there during the war years.

#95	Hobart, Indiana	Hobart Sky Ranch
Type:	Paved Identifier: 3HO	February 12, 1991

#96	Vincennes, Indiana	O'Neal Airport
Type:	Grass Identifier: OEA	April 6, 1991

#97	Evansville, Indiana	Skylane Airport
Type:	Grass Identifier: 3EV	April 6, 1991

THE TREE OF KNOWLEDGE

THE VISIT TO Evansville's Skylane Airport was followed by a pleasant surprise at Patoka's Hull Field. Skylane is a short north and south grass strip only 2,000 feet long with questionable over-runs at both ends. That early April day when I flew in was unseasonably hot and the grass was long. While it was pleasant for landing, the take-off was substantially more labored than I like.

I met some great pilots at Skylane. They invited me to sit with them below the "tree of knowledge". After listening to a number of their tales, I began to suspect that many of their flying stories had been stretched more than a little. When I questioned them about some of the details, they all remarked that I had already benefited from the tree of wisdom! Knowing that I had been set-up by these wiseacres, I bid them farewell.

#98	Patoka, Indiana	Hull Airport
Type:	Grass Identifier: IN30	April 6, 1991

TWO CHEROKEES AT PATOKA

I MET BOB GERARD at Skylane. He has a Cherokee the same color and paint scheme as mine, but it has a 235 horsepower engine. He took off before me.

When I landed at Hull Airport, Bob Gerard was already there. He wanted to be part of my adventure. This made him the only person to accompany me to a new airport in another airplane!

We had lunch and talked a lot about flying. We also noted a peculiarity about our names: his name is Robert Gerard and my first and middle names are Robert Gerald, a coincidental oddity. We flew on to Boonville together as well.

#99   Boonville, Indiana   Boonville Airport
Type: Grass Identifier: I91   April 6, 1991

#100   North Vernon, Indiana   North Vernon Airport
Type: Paved Identifier: OVO   April 6, 1991

#101   Decatur, Indiana   Decatur Highway Airport
Type: Grass Identifier: DCR   May 10, 1991

JOSEPHINE, THE FLYING MACHINE

I T WAS A late afternoon flight going into the Fort Wayne area, and an evening flight returning. By this time, I had started my IFR training with CFII Brian Conrad, so the trip across the Fort Wayne ARSA (then) or Class C airspace (now) was going to be intensive training. Handling the airplane and increased radio work was good experience.

The runway at Decatur Highway is exactly north and south, grass, 180 feet wide and 2,000 feet long. It was in excellent condition. Brian and I spotted the airplane and looked around. We started a conversation with a family that was sitting out on their porch enjoying the coolness. After a while, I noticed a woman looking over the Cherokee, and I went to see her. That is when I met the owner of Decatur Highway Airport, Josephine Richardson.

Josephine is an outgoing woman who has been in aviation all her life. She and her husband started Decatur Highway and have run it ever since. It seems that he passed away some time back, and Josephine has taken on all the duties of the airport maintenance and operations. She cuts the grass, trims the trees, maintains the hangars, monitors the Unicom, and generally sees to the needs of the resident pilots and aircraft owners. She has done very well! The field was immaculate, in excellent condition, and appealing.

Josephine doesn't know how many flying hours she has, but concedes that "it's considerable." She has two airplanes but doesn't fly them anymore. She lost her medical. Nonetheless, Josephine, in her words, "still flies in her dreams."

Josephine is an inveterate inventor also. While we visited, she showed me an insect trap made from a plastic soft drink bottle filled with some vegetable and fruit scraps. She explained how the traps worked for particular bugs. She changes the fruit and vegetable content to attract different species. As I recall, banana scraps worked best for Japanese beetles.

Josephine was not too pleased with the city fathers of Fort Wayne either. On a regular basis, she scolded them unmercifully with scathing letters to the editors of the local newspaper. Typically, she was upset with the development that was going on without due regard to water drainage. Given a good rainstorm with flooding, she would write again to the paper reminding everyone that the flood damage could have been avoided if they had heeded her past warnings. Looking back, she was often right!

All things considered, Josephine is a remarkable person. A pilot, airport manager, inventor and public conscience, she made her presence known, and her charm is persuasive. For several years afterward we would exchange letters and, occasionally talk on the phone. Certainly, she impressed me, but more than that, I liked her a lot. She was a real sweetheart. The most impressive thing about Josephine was that she had retained all this capability at 75 years of age! It is a flight I will remember forever because I will remember Josephine forever.

#102	Westville, Indiana	Orthodontic Field
Type:	Grass Identifier: Private	May 11, 1991

#103	Kokomo, Indiana	Kokomo Municipal Airport
Type:	Paved Identifier: OKK	May 12, 1991

#104	Greentown, Indiana	Howard County Airport
Type:	Grass Identifier: 5I8	May 12, 1991

#105	Vevay, Indiana	Robinson Field
Type:	Grass Identifier: 8I1	June 2, 1991

SWEATING OUT A TAKE-OFF IN VEVAY

JUNE 2ND OF 1991 was one hot and humid day. It was also the day picked for an IFR cross-country training flight. All the way south from Gary, my flight instructor, Brian Conrad, pumped and pushed instrument flight information into my head. Brian demands the highest skill and professionalism in IFR flight. He almost crucified me when he saw me holding a steady altitude of 40 feet above my 'assigned' flight level. "If you can hold that error so well, why not spend the same energy and maintain the correct altitude?" He was relentless in searching for excellence.

A little south of Indianapolis, we began to question our landing at Vevay. The length of the runway (1,670 feet) was a little small for the temperature and humidity conditions. The grass told us that it would be harder to get off the ground. With the Airplane Operating Manual in hand, Brian did the math and thought it would be an achievable landing. The obstruction at the end of the runway bothered him though. He dismissed the issue and returned to the intense instruction. A small part of my mind remained with the question of runway length and trees.

Once on the ground, we met a charming youngster whose name is lost to my memory. He had just started flying and had purchased an ultra-light airplane to accumulate flight time. He was full of stories. Brian was fascinated by his enthusiasm. My eyes kept darting over to the trees. There was only the tiniest of zephyrs for a breeze, and it was favoring the tree-ward end of the runway. The grass was a player in this problem too. It had been a long time since it was cut and it was fully 10 to 12 inches tall. I also thought about the extra weight that I was carrying and how I had put off going on a diet.

We broke away from the youngster and sauntered over to the Cherokee. Brian suggested that we get as far back up against the windward end of the runway (there was a crossing road there), apply full power, and bring in a notch of flaps right at V1 air speed. It should be all right.

I did as he said and, glancing over, I saw his eyes glued on the up end of the runway and the trees. His hands were at the ready an inch away from the throttle and control column. The grass and weeds seemed a lot longer than I thought. True to her design intent, the little Cherokee nosed up at 57 mph and sniffed for altitude. The trees came upon us fast, but the gain in altitude outpaced them. We were free and clear, albeit wobbly in our climb. I looked over to Brian and he was already setting up the next IFR problem. He didn't even break a sweat. Once airborne, it became clear to me; that you only do it wrong once!

| #106 | Scottsburg, Indiana | Scottsburg Airport |
| Type: | Grass Identifier: IN46 | June 2, 1991 |

| #107 | Seymour, Indiana | Freeman Municipal Airport |
| Type: | Paved Identifier: SER | June 2, 1991 |

JACK NORTHROP'S FLYING WING

THROUGH AVIATION'S SHORT history, it is remarkable how often the State of Indiana has been touched during its development. Freeman Field is an example.

Born of necessity with the rapid start of World War II, ground was broken on May 2, 1942, and the base was operational as of December 1 that same year. It was a remarkable achievement, as were all of these hastily constructed air fields. It was built on 2,560 acres of theretofore farmland and sported four runways of 5,500 feet each, and 413 buildings. The base was utilized as an Advanced Twin Engine Aircraft training field.

In March, 1943, the field was officially named the Freeman Army Air Field. Richard S. Freeman was born on June 22, 1907 in Winamac, Pulaski County. He graduated from West Point and was assigned to the Army Air Corps. He earned the Distinguished Flying Cross. He died on February 6, 1941 when his plane crashed in Nevada.

Less known about Freeman is the fact that it was the site of some of Jack Northrop's last test flights in his radical, controversial Flying Wing, the N-1M. Jack Northrop was convinced that the future of high performance aircraft was limited not only by the amount of power available but also the high amount of aerodynamic drag with which every airplane was cursed.

His concept of an aircraft without a tail and without a distinguishable fuselage was promising. The design was proved by Northrop's succession of flying wings, from the N-1M with the original Lycoming 0-145's of only 60 horsepower, up through the series to the more powerful N-9M, which was powered by two Franklin engines of 117 horsepower. With development, the flying wing progressed into the extremely promising YB-35 powered by four R-4360 engines, and then the YB-49 with no less than eight non-after burning Allison J-35 jet engines of 5,600 pounds of thrust each. These Allison engines were manufactured in Indianapolis, Indiana.

The N-1M was presented to the Army Air Force at Freeman Field in 1945. With the war over and demobilization in high gear, the urgency for aircraft development was ebbing. It appeared that the Air Corps did not know what to do with the N-1M aircraft. So, it went into storage and out of mind. Time passed and while the plane was not actually lost, it was apparently thoroughly forgotten. The story goes that during random postwar housecleaning at Freeman Field, the N-1M was "found."

There are other cases of "lost and found" priceless airplanes at Freeman Field. For example, they found one of three prototypes of Curtiss-Wright's XP-55 Ascender built in the later years of World War II. Two of these were lost in flight testing. The third, S\N 42-78846, was flown and extensively tested at Wright Field in Dayton prior to being flown to Freeman Field where it was tested further and eventually stored. The airplane's presence at Freeman was over-looked for many years. As in the case of the N1M, no one knew it was there for decades. Since its "discovery" it was taken to the Kalamazoo Aviation History Museum in Michigan.

It seems that Inventory Control at Freeman was a matter of "put it over there for now and we will figure out what to do with it tomorrow."

The Smithsonian wanted the Jack Northrop brain child for display but it was far from being in museum quality condition. In 1946, the flying wing was shipped from Freeman Field to the Museum Storage Depot at Park Ridge, Illinois for restoration.

The N-1M has been completely restored to its original configuration. It is now on display in the Smithsonian Institution. I have not seen the plane in its new home but I do believe that it is there, and it probably still has a little Indiana farm dust on it!

THE DARKER, DESPICABLE SIDE
OF FREEMAN FIELD

WHEN I FIRST bought N8369W in early '91, it was hangared at the Gary Regional Airport. Conveniently enough, the lease of the hangar could be transferred directly to me whereby I could avoid being placed on a 'waiting list' of potential renters. It wasn't much of a hangar, as it dated back to World War II, and maintenance had been a thing of the past for many years. In fact, the airport authority planned to tear down these old relics in a short time. Nonetheless, it provided decent cover for the airplane, and it was cheap.

Being at the Gary airport enabled me to become better acquainted with Quentin P. Smith, the president of the Gary Regional Airport Authority. His work at the airport was a second career for Quentin. Previously, he had spent almost 50 years in the Gary School system. We would have a chance now and again to talk about the airport's future. Local economic development was amongst the mutual activities we shared. The Northwest Indiana region had suffered greatly with the deterioration of the steel industry which was vital to our local economic well-being. The nation was trying to recover from the back to back recessions suffered in the early 80's. Northwest Indiana only had one recession but it lasted 5 years. During that dark time, we lost over 50,000 jobs. Most of these jobs came from the steel mills and surrounding and supporting industries. It was a monumental struggle to get those high hourly rate manufacturing jobs replaced. It was during this time that all of us worked hard toward developing the Gary (Indiana) Regional Airport into the third Chicago airport.

Our acquaintance goes back to 1988 when both Quentin and I were involved in the Career Beginnings program. This effort was the brain child of the Center for Corporate and Education Initiatives of the Heller School at Brandeis University. The program offered youngsters help with their career goals. The children selected were from lower income families and questionable neighborhoods. In other words, it was directed toward "at risk" kids.

The program used a three-pronged attack. First, there were lectures and workshops on career initiation and development that required the children to attend classes at the local sponsoring university. In this case, it was Indiana University Northwest in Gary, Indiana. The classes went on for several months and they were conducted on Saturday mornings. It was a true commitment on everyone's part.

Secondly, there were jobs for the teenagers in the local area for the summer. Where possible, the candidates were placed in those jobs in which their career objectives were present so that they could see first-hand the inner workings of their career. That is, if a student or intern expressed a desire to follow a career in bookkeeping or accounting then the system would try and place them in a CPA firm. These jobs paid the minimum wage which was covered by the Federal Government through their JTPA funds or the successor to that agency. No, it wasn't a lot of money but it was more than the kids ever had in their pockets.

The third aspect of the program is where Quentin and I became more deeply acquainted. During the senior year of school, each student was assigned to an adult mentor; a one on one relationship for the whole of their senior year. The first class of Career Beginnings interns (as they were called) numbered 115 and we were fortunate enough to get 115 mentors from business and industry. As I recall, Quentin Smith was quite a presence in the program at the onset. After the initial gathering, there was only an occasional opportunity for all the interns and mentors to gather as one group again. I no longer had a chance to see Quentin but I began to pick up some scattered information about him in his early years.

Mr. Smith's background was both intriguing and fascinating. It had to do with his time in the Army Air Corps and his tenure at Freeman Field in Seymour, Indiana. Quentin, as I found out, was one of the Tuskegee Airmen; the all-black squadrons that were trained at the Tuskegee Institute in Tuskegee, Alabama. Quentin was in one of the first graduating classes out of Tuskegee. Most of the graduates were intended for fighter duty. First Lieutenant Quentin P. Smith, a relatively tall man, was not allowed to continue his training in fighters, and was transferred to medium bombers - specifically, the

B-25 Mitchell built by North American. This training was to take place at Freeman Field in Indiana.

Quentin moved to Freeman Army Air Corps Base in late 1944. As with most training bases, activity was beginning to wind down at Freeman Field by the time 1945 arrived. During the three years in which it functioned as an advanced aerial training base for medium bomber training, some four thousand pilots had earned their wings. Let there be no doubt, Freeman performed as expected and Quentin was still to be part of the field's history.

There is a lot of Deep South influence in southern Indiana. Chances are good a visitor would soon recognize distinctive southern drawl and word pronunciation among the residents. There were southern feelings, too. Sundown Laws, for example; while not written, it was enforced. Simply put, black people better not be on the street come sundown. There were drinking fountains and toilets for men, women and colored. Here in Jackson County segregation was rampant, and civil rights applied only to white people. "It was nearly impossible to find in Indiana a public place, institution, or group where whites accorded blacks an equal and open reception," noted Indiana University Professor of History James Madison in his history of the state from 1920 to 1945. While this was especially true in Seymour, it was the case throughout Indiana.

The feeling was deeply imbedded in the military as well. Soldiers of color were not assigned to white outfits; it was white with white and black with black. The white supremacy element was there as well. All black outfits had white commanders. No white people were assigned to a black superior. Frankly, no one knew what to do with black fighting units. No commander wanted to commit them to combat overseas and no stateside commander wanted them on his base or post. The tendency was to keep moving black units from base to base. This is what happened to Quentin and his fellow airmen of the 477th Bombardment Group when it arrived at Freeman.

In that age, accepted race relations meant "separate but equal" when it came to facilities. For example, black pilots and air crew stationed at the airfield could not use the white USO club in Seymour. Rather, the USO Council established a separate facility for them on West Tipton Street. "Separate", but far from equal. More demeaning was the Officer's Club on base. It was here that the ugly racial confrontation which initially erupted at Selfridge Field located near Detroit was to re-affirm itself. Here, the 477th Bombardment Group initially attempted to use the club, as was their right as officers. They were refused admittance by the commanding officer and the 477th was quickly moved to Godman Field in Kentucky.

At Godman, black officers were able to enjoy full use of the officers' club. But race relations were not as appealing as they appeared on the surface. White officers relinquished the club at Godman to the black officers. The white officers repaired to the officers facilities at the segregated Fort Knox post. Segregation prevailed, and it was insult after injury to the black flyers.

Here at Freeman Field, the black pilots wanted to end the racism and resolve the conflict without compromising their rights of fair and equal treatment as officers in the Army Air Force. A statement would be made at the Freeman Field Officers Club.

Freeman's Officers Club was open to blacks until 5:00 P.M., then it would become a "whites only" establishment. They would attempt to change that soon.

The leader of the plot was Lt. Coleman Young, who would go on to become Detroit's only mayor to serve five consecutive terms. Their intentions were straightforward and would serve as a model for Equal Rights activists in the 1960s.They would participate in a non-violent protest that would be totally legal but rebellious. Black officers would enter the officer's club before five o'clock in small groups of no more than five men at a time in close enough intervals to be supportive, yet not appear to be a mass coordinated direct confrontation group. They would remain in the club past the 5:00 deadline. The last thing they wanted was to show a mob effort. They would wait for the white faction to make the first move.

On the evening of April 5th, 1945 the entrance of its segregated Officers Club was physically blocked by the Officer of the Day, Lt. J. D. Rogers, who represented the commander of the 477th, Colonel William L Boyd. Lieutenants Roger C. Terry, Marsden A. Thompson and Shirley R. Clinton took the point. It was 9:00 PM when the three men attempted to enter the club by simply pushing aside Lt. Rogers. They demonstrated that they were through tolerating crass racial discrimination and expected unimpeded entrance into the club. The three pushed Rogers aside. Boyd immediately ordered the three to be arrested and remanded into the custody of the provost marshal.

But the plan was still in effect. For the next day or so, more groups of black airmen showed up at the Officers Club until 101 of them were arrested. There was no violence, but the tolerance of racism within the officer's corps was coming to an end. After the incident, each arrested officer was presented with a new directive from Colonel Selway. This directive instructed the black officers to admit they were trainees and, according to club regulations, had no right to use the officers' club. One by one they were brought into Colonel Selway's office and presented with a document that required their signature. Smith recalled that when asked to sign the new directive, he replied loudly, "No, sir." He continued to refuse signing. But he felt his voice crack slightly. He refused even when he was threatened by the colonel with Article 64. (Article 64, 'failure to obey a superior officer's direct order' is a serious offense.) The article provides for punishment up to and including the death penalty. In the face of this threat, Smith stayed his ground. With the country at war, it would not be hard to press a case of insubordination and to garner at least a 20-year sentence in Leavenworth.

In an oral history interview with Indiana Historical Society, Editor Doug Clanin, Smith remembered: "The immediate major said, 'I order you to sign.' I didn't have any breath; I didn't have any saliva left to say anything. I shook my head because I couldn't even talk. So I said, 'no' [in a high voice]. He rapped a gavel and said, 'you go out that door.' When I went out that door a soldier said, 'Go back to your barracks, don't put your head out, don't come out, when suppertime comes, we'll bring you your food.' So I'm sitting there by myself thinking; 'now this just can't be true. I'm just about 190 miles from home and this just can't be happening.' But it was."

About that time, the commander of the 477th was replaced by none other than Colonel Benjamin O. Davis, former commander of the famed 332nd Fighter Group, the original all-black unit that distinguished itself in combat over Europe. With the hue and cry becoming louder, aid rushed to the embattled 101 blacks.

From the federal ranks came New York Congressman Adam Clayton Powell, then a freshman Representative in the 79th Congress. From Indiana came Congressman Louis Ludlow who would serve with distinction in nine straight Congresses. They were incensed by the goings on and campaigned against this court martial. The NAACP stepped up and encouraged a young black attorney named Thurgood Marshall to defend the 101. Thurgood Marshall would become the first black man to serve on the Supreme Court of the United States. These powerful additions to their ranks strengthened the position of the 101 and brought wholesale disaster to the ill-conceived *de facto* segregation brought about by Selway and Hunter.

There was a court martial, but only against the original three 'offenders.' Thompson and Clinton were cleared of all charges. Terry was found guilty of "offering violence against a superior officer" (whatever that means). The claim is that Terry intended harm through battery when he physically touched Rogers to push him aside. He was fined a paltry $150. Quentin Smith was not brought up on charges and was released from custody.

Segregation died a welcome death in the Air Corp and bigotry was dealt a severe blow. Three years later, President Harry Truman would sign into effect Executive Order 9981 which brought an end to racial segregation in the United States military forces.

With the events of Freeman Field behind him and the war over, Quentin Smith went back to school and earned another degree from Indiana University. He went on to teach for 50 years at Gary schools and served as president of the Gary Regional Airport Authority from 1986 to 1996. Today, in his eighties, Quentin looks fit and healthy. He should feel good, too, because he is owed a debt and is entitled to the prayers of a grateful black America for what Quentin and his 100 flyboys did for the black situation that had sunk so low in the United States.

He tells me that the '101 Club' has "made its peace with the Freeman Field participants." Further, he has continued to fly and maintains a close relationship with other pilots and the Gary Airport board. There are semi-regular reunions at Seymour which he tries to attend as often as possible. He treats the incident with a smile. I think it should be a grin.

| #108 | Indianapolis, Indiana | Post Air Airport |
| Type: | Paved Identifier: 7LB | June 2, 1991 |

| #109 | Richmond, Indiana | Richmond Municipal Airport |
| Type: | Paved Identifier: RID | June 7, 1991 |

| #110 | Muncie, Indiana | Reese Airport |
| Type: | Paved Identifier: 7I2 | June 7, 1991 |

| #111 | Erie, Pennsylvania | Erie International Airport |
| Type: | Class C Identifier: ERI | June 7, 1991 |

A VISIT WITH RON AND CATHY PRINDLE

ON THE FEBRUARY 1990 cover of the Piper Owner's Magazine, a very pretty Cherokee 180 was featured. The airplane was white with blue trim in exactly the same factory paint scheme as our airplane. Moreover, the tail number was N8379W! The tail numbers were exactly 10 digits off. This plane was almost a twin sister to ours. I had to give the owner a call. His name was listed as Ron Prindle in Erie, Pennsylvania, and he had a publicly listed number. We struck up an immediate friendship over the phone. Over the years, we exchanged letters, photographs and stories. While I had never met Ron or Kathy Prindle, I felt as if they were old friends.

One day, Ron sent some advertising posters for a Fly-In his EAA chapter was sponsoring at Erie Airport. He asked that we put them up at our airport and, if possible, perhaps I could join in. It was thought provoking. It was only a few days off. It would be a trip of about 400 miles, but the week-end weather looked good.

I intended to fly to Richmond and Muncie, Indiana on Saturday anyway. What the heck? Why not simply continue on to Erie for the weekend? I really wanted to visit Ron and Kathy! Bob Smith was to join me on the visits to Richmond and Muncie. He agreed that the trip to Erie would be a great adjunct to the trip already planned. It was set, then. First, it would be visits to Indiana airports #109 and #110 and then on to Pennsylvania!

It was late afternoon when we arrived. We secured the Cherokee and got a cab to the hotel. The next morning, we got a lift from the hotel courtesy car to the field. The crowd was sizeable, even at 8:00 AM. The first people to greet us were Ron and Kathy. Ron was effusive. He told us that putting together the Fly-In had taken a lot more strength than he thought. He was almost physically and mentally spent. When he went to the airport the night before, he said that he was encouraged and re-invigorated when he saw N8369W sitting on the ramp. If his friends came 600 miles to his Fly-In, then he had to make it the best Fly-In and show that he could manage.

The first thing Ron did was reposition his airplane and ours next to each other. Both airplanes were prominently spotted in the center of the day's activities where they could be seen by all attendees. From that point on, he told everyone and anyone about the owner/pilots of N8379W and N8369W, how we met and how our subsequent friendship developed. Ron had a good time that day.

Despite having in excess of 1,000 people at the Fly-In, Ron and Kathy Prindle made it their business to treat Bob Smith and me as if we were the only folks that mattered. Not that any other aspect of the show went unattended or anyone else was neglected; they simply did all they could to make us feel at home. Ron convinced the local television station that the adventure of flying to all of the airports in Indiana (plus our long cross country trip to attend the Fly-In) was newsworthy and an interview was taped for the evening news. Ron sent a copy of that tape for our enjoyment.

We saw a lot of airplanes, talked with a lot of people and investigated many interesting displays. But the day had to come to an end. We took off from Erie (after being 17th in line for departure) and set a nearly direct VFR course for Elkhart, Indiana. Both Bob and I had very little to say. The visit was great. The work that they put into the Fly-In was enormous and the results were testimony to their great effort. We were overwhelmed by the gentle, caring ways of both Ron and Kathy. We were treated like long lost relatives or, better, like lifelong dear friends. Ron and Kathy Prindle have been special to us. They will remain in our hearts forever.

#112	Indianapolis, Indiana	Indianapolis International
Type:	Class C Identifier: IND	July 6, 1991

MAINTAIN BEST POSSIBLE AIR SPEED

PART OF MY agreement with Colonel Larry Wheeler is that Grissom Air Force Base would not be the second-to-last airport visited in Indiana but the very last airport. It was going to be a special landing at Grissom. It was made special because my Mom and Dad would be there with several other friends.

Regrettably, in making this decision, I was going to pre-empt Jack McCarthy in Indianapolis. Jack had been the publisher of the Hammond Times, a Howard publication. He was a feisty Irishman of the first order. He was a newspaper man inside and out. Jack would be very much at home at the Billy Goat Tavern in Chicago. I can almost see him elbow-to-elbow with the likes of Mike Royko, the late and great columnist of the Chicago Tribune.

Jack had spurred growth in the Hammond Times and made it a true regional paper. Prior to Jack coming on the scene, the Times served, well, Hammond. Jack broadened the paper's venue to encompass the dozens of small communities that northwest Indiana had become. A Merrillville resident would be comfortable reading the Times because it covered Merrillville news very well. The Times did the same for Highland, Griffith, Whiting and all the other towns of Lake and Porter County.

Then one day it happened. There was a change in top management at the paper and Jack was out of a job.

Jack McCarthy drew upon his inner strength and began to look, not for a job, but for a paper to buy. On the strength of his character, he lined up financing and saw his opportunity. Not with just one paper but two; the largest circulation was the Plainview Dealer. With Jack as the owner and publisher his only complaint was that he worked for a real son of a bitch!

The deal was that we were going to make a day of the landing at Indianapolis International. I wanted to have lunch with Jack and have a photo opportunity if he thought it was worthwhile. He told me to bring my golf clubs and money.

But all that was trashed now. I wouldn't be there as the noteworthy last airport but second to the last. It wouldn't matter to his readers as much now. I would have a chance to meet with Jack at a later date. Now the trip to Indy was a lot less sensational.

The day was perfect for flying at all altitudes; "severe clear" as pilots put it. No adverse winds at any flight levels, and visibility was limited only by one's imagination. Smooth and perfect flying was the order of the day.

About 40 miles north of Indy, I tuned into Approach Control. Some jet with the call sign of "Blue Streak" reported in and was advised to expect a straight-in approach for Runway 23 Right and that he was the seventeenth in line for landing.

"SEVENTEENTH FOR LANDING! What was going on?", the pilot of Blue Streak asked. The controller couldn't give him a reason for all the traffic in front of him, only that it had been like that all day long. There was no Indianapolis Colts game, no college graduations, no civic events. There was no reason for all the air traffic. Just get in line and watch your interval.

What was I going to do? Fly into Ohio and get in line. Oh my! This perfect flying day took a turn for the worse. I continued to monitor Approach Control. Not much changed. Soon, I was 25 miles out and it was time to call in. The exact words that were used in our exchange are not clear in my memory, but the message is burned into my brain. It went something like this:

8369W: 'Indianapolis Approach, Cherokee 8369 Whiskey is 25 north inbound with "ATIS" '

Indy: 'Roger 8369 Whiskey, Turn right to a heading

of 200 degrees. Keep up best possible air speed for traffic.'

Some time passes and it is apparent from the radio traffic that there are DC-9's and 727's all around me, converging on the same runway to which Indy Approach is directing me. Cockpit temperature is climbing. Indy calls again:

'Cherokee 69 Whiskey, Turn left to one eight zero, descend to 2,000 feet. Maintain best possible air speed.'

Their broadcast is acknowledged. Engine RPM is a touch above 2700 rpm; the maximum allowable power setting. Within seconds, Indy calls again.

'69 Whiskey turn right now to 190, maintain 2000 feet and keep up best possible air speed.'

The throttle has never been pushed in this far for so long. It is still at 100% power. Indy's last instruction is repeated, and I thank heaven there is a newly rebuilt engine under the cowling. Indy Approach is busy with non-stop transmissions. There is a lot of traffic, and they are handling it well. My air speed is nearly in the 'yellow' band of the air speed indicator. The time spent in the yellow is very limited. With each passing minute, the engine degrades as if it had spent a hundred hours at a normal cruising RPM. Indy calls again:

'69 Whiskey, turn now to a heading of 230 for final approach to Runway 23 R. You are second to land behind American 727. Please maintain best possible air speed for traffic.'

Now the little Cherokee is in a slight angle of descent. Coupled with the high power setting, the air speed is firmly in the yellow. No sharp control movements, Bob. Take it easy. Good grief! I am on a long final that is usually done at 80 knots and screaming in at over 140 mph. Cylinder head temp is higher than I have ever seen it. Oil temp is nearly in the red. This is a dicey situation. Then there was another call from Approach.

> '69 Whiskey, continue on course. Contact tower on 120.9. Maintain best possible forward air speed.'

Now the oil temp is in the red zone. I am less than 2000 feet off the threshold of Runway 23 R at maximum "flap down" speed. I can feel the jets lined up behind me with their JT-8 engines guzzling jet fuel at an astronomical rate. The cockpit temperature is elevated as well. It was getting hotter and hotter with each request to "maintain best possible forward air speed." Keeping mindful of the runway turbulence ahead and the absolute need to get the airplane down quickly and solidly, the throttle and mixture are held tight against the panel so as to prevent them from creeping back. I can see the expansion cracks in the runway pavement. Indy approach's latest order was answered:

> 8369W to 120.9 … and sir, I am beating the thunder of this poor Lycoming.'

With more than a small amount of laughter in the background, Indy Approach, with a lighter tone in his voice calls back.

> 'Indy appreciates your cooperation. Contact tower at this time.'

The little Cherokee came over the threshold at over 100 knots. In order to clear the runway as soon as possible, I stomped on the brakes and swung onto the Beech dealership ramp without even bothering Ground Control. I spotted the airplane in a parking slot and pulled back the mixture control. The engine became quiet and still. I was sweating like hell.

#113   Peru, Indiana   Grissom Air Force Base
Type: Military Identifier: GUS   July 20, 1991

THE AIRPORT!

THIS WAS THE one. This was the field that I had been waiting for; number 111 in the state of Indiana. With Grissom Air Force Base, I will have visited all the airports in Indiana.

I had Grissom's permission to land there. By their rules, my insurance had to be changed to accept all responsibility while there. The insurance company was reluctant. They finally asked how many times I was going to do this. When they discovered it was only a once in a lifetime occurrence, they finally agreed.

The date of my visit was picked by Grissom command. Saturday, July 20th was their Open House and Air Show. The landing was going to put a little "Hoosier flavor" into the show. They asked for my presence on July 19th, the day before the show. It was going to be their media day. The Air Force would not let me land at Grissom that Friday but rather nearby Peru. An officer and a car would be there to take me onto the base.

My landing at Grissom at 12:10 PM, was to be the opening event of the show. During that Friday, we went over the timing and post landing procedure. We were to land, pull off the runway at Taxiway Bravo, and then proceed to the front of the VIP reviewing stand.

Grissom's officer in charge would be Colonel Larry Wheeler. Larry Wheeler is a most impressive man. Experienced, intelligent, confident and astute, we would become friends immediately. This friendship lasts until this day.

Nancy and I had a press conference at Gary airport on the 20[th,] just before take-off. The trip to Grissom would take 54 minutes. Naturally, Grissom operates by the book. They don't like VFR straight-in flights. We flew to the nearest navigational aid, Knox VOR. Once we were established on a heading to Grissom, I called approach control with a simple announcement.

69W:	"Grissom approach, this is Cherokee 8369 Whiskey."

GAFB: "Go ahead 69 Whiskey."

69W: "8369 Whiskey is 30 miles north on the 175 radial
               out of Knox VOR, inbound."

The fact that I was inbound stopped the controller cold. Certainly, he thought he was going to have an easy day. Grissom was closed to all traffic. No traffic to worry about and an Air Show to watch from a great vantage point. But here we were, inbound and the show was just about to begin. He needed time to think. He replied,

GAFB: "Stand by, 8369 Whiskey."

We augured on. We called in plenty early, there was no rush. He came back on the air.

GAFB: "8369 Whiskey, say again your destination."

69W: "69 Whiskey is inbound Grissom for landing."

After this transmission, it became apparent that things were not improving for this controller. None of this had any meaning for him. He needed help but he didn't want to ask us. When he came back, I would have to fill him in with a lot of the details. But it wasn't he who contacted us next. Now, a different voice came on the air. This voice was not casual and unassuming but deeply serious and blunt.

GAFB: "8369 Whiskey this is Grissom. What are your
               intentions?"

N8369W: "8369 Whiskey intends to land at Grissom. To help
               you, we are scheduled to land at 12:08, just after the
               parachute team lands but before the A-10 Warthogs
               take-off for their demonstration flight."

The light came on. Now it all made sense to him. Everyone at Grissom must have been nodding in agreement with each other by now. In a relieved and acknowledging tone, he simply came back with,

GAFB: "Oh, it's you, Bob."

THE INSTRUMENT RATING

NOW THAT THE objective of flying to all the airports in Indiana was accomplished, it seemed as if there were nothing left to do except to fly out for the fabled $100 hamburgers every Saturday and Sunday. This is a favorite pastime of most pilots. But another objective came to the fore. The thought of studying for an instrument rating started to become intriguing. The scare that we had flying out of Bloomington was a serious factor in my decision. All the IFR pilots with whom I talked about a rating were very encouraging. Each had a tale to tell how the rating saved their bacon at one time or another. We had several excellent instructors on the field, and they were all supportive as well. Clearly, the time had arrived when I could no longer avoid an instrument rating. There are several reasons why pilots seek an IFR rating, and I experienced all of them.

Economically, flying insurance is reduced by some 25% to 30% with an IFR ticket, and that was appealing to me. Owning an airplane, I kept reminding myself, provided a means of flying whenever I wanted, and that convenience was very valuable. It seemed to offset the monthly cost of a hangar, the annual inspection and insurance Of these, only insurance could be decreased somewhat. A little extra money at the end of the month would be nice.

Most of the time, pilots get the hell scared out of them at one time or another and they rediscover religion and the benefit of an instrument rating. When I learned to fly in the 60's and 70's, instrument conditions were simulated for the shortest of periods. Mostly, I was taught to seek an immediate place to land or execute a 180-degree turn out of danger. The log book only shows about two hours of IFR training.

#114	Kalamazoo, Michigan	Battle Creek International
Type:	Class C Identifier: AZO	August 10, 1991

#115	Decatur, Illinois	Decatur Airport
Type:	Class C Identifier: DEC	January 20, 1992

#116	Culver, Indiana	Fleet Field
Type:	Paved Identifier: Private	June 27, 1992

THE AIRPORT THAT RUBEN FLEET BUILT

CULVER MILITARY ACADEMY is an outstanding college preparatory school for boys. It can be argued that, being located in the rural heart-land, it is an ideal setting leading to extensive academic and character building. The school also includes some of the finest athletic programs in the country.

Over 99% of Culver graduates continue their educations at the world's leading institutions such as Dartmouth, Princeton, Colorado-Boulder, Vanderbilt, Purdue, Yale, Northwestern, and Indiana University. Once there, they compete successfully for placement in advanced professional programs, athletics, and other constructive activities. Here students, or cadets, can learn to fly, participate in crewing, theater, fencing, or ride in the renowned Black Horse Troop.

While a youngster, I knew several students at Culver Military. Since then, I have met a number of graduates. They are a breed of men that are well focused and distinctly set apart from others. Truly, Culver helps youngsters develop discipline, skills, and the confidence to achieve almost any goal a student may desire.

On the sprawling academy property, Stifel Field is a two-runway flying field in an "L" configuration, with the longest being 2,400 feet. The strips are hard surfaced and easily seen from the air. The nearest visual cue is that it is on the southeast side of Indiana's second largest lake, Lake Maxinkuckee. The airport is named after Ruben Fleet, who was a graduate of Culver Military.

Most Americans will remember Ruben if they are told that he is the pilot standing next to President Hoover in a 1920's photograph. He was the pilot who accepted the first bag of air mail to be transported across the country. Ruben Fleet became a successful industrialist in aviation. Among his early design and manufacturing successes is the PBY series of float and amphibious aircraft prior to and during World War II. It was Ruben Fleet who founded Consolidated Aircraft Company.

Being that Fleet Field is private, permission has to be granted to land there. Passing near Culver on the way home from a business trip one day, I took advantage of the opportunity and stopped at the field. The personnel staffing the field are young and friendly. There are a few airplanes on the field with four of them belonging to the Academy. The Academy planes are all Piper Warriors.

The procedure there is to bring in four students from school every two hours. The students are taken-up, each with their own instructor, for an hour long lesson. Upon their return, the instructor-student pairs go through a debriefing and some ground instruction. All of this takes about two hours. Then the next students arrive and start the pre-flight inspection the airplanes. The station wagon takes the previous students back to school. Ground school is held at the Academy.

It is a process geared to getting a lot of students through a flight regimen leading to a private pilot's license. Sometimes five sets of students will get their hour of flying in during the day. That means that some 100 students will get an hour's worth of flying and instruction during the week, leaving the weekend free for solo flight. It would be very hard for a youngster to matriculate at Culver Military Academy and not be able to get his private pilot's license. As a sport aviator, I would like to see this arrangement replicated at more airports.

A more thorough understanding of Reuben Fleet can be garnered from the following article as written by the San Diego Aerospace Museum:

'Reuben Hollis Fleet graduated from the Culver Military Academy in 1906. It appears that he tended to re-invent himself every so often. From his first footsteps as an adult,

1. Formed a successful real estate business, and amassed a fortune while very young.
2. Became a state legislator.
3. Became the 74th Army pilot.
4. Trained nearly 11,000 pilots in the Army.
5. Established the first mail delivery from Washington D.C. to New York.

'In 1919, Major Fleet was reassigned to the U.S. Army Flight Test Center at McCook Field, Dayton, Ohio as business manager. It was here he acquired the experience that inspired him to enter the aviation industry, leaving the military service in late 1922 to begin his distinguished career as an aviation industrialist. Acquiring the assets and engineering talents of Gallaudet Aircraft Corporation and the Dayton-Wright Airplane Company, he combined the two into a new firm in 1923 known as Consolidated Aircraft. In a leased factory, the new company developed a successful series of training planes in which literally every military pilot learned to fly during the next decade. It was, however, the great flying boats developed by Fleet and the Consolidated team in 1929, that made his company an industrial giant. Large contracts from the Navy for Seaplane Patrol Bombers required a larger factory and year round test flight capability. With typical Fleet determination and courage, he elected to move his entire company to San Diego, California. In the spring of 1935, in a move unprecedented in industry, he transferred his entire Consolidated operation in 157 freight cars of machinery and materials as well as moving employees and their families to the newly constructed factory in San Diego.

The famed *Catalina* PBY Patrol Bombers production required several expansions of the factory to keep pace with the flood of orders from the Navy. The introduction of the four- engine B-24 "Liberator" Bomber for the Army Air Forces added further growth.

Fleet personally managed this entire operation along with actively flying and testing of his products.

In late 1941 this captain of industry, one of the last of the industrial tycoons who built and led their own large corporations, retired from active management of Consolidated as it was acquired by other interests. When war came to the United States a few weeks later, Fleet immersed himself completely as advisor and consultant to industry and government. In the postwar years he devoted his time and fortune to works of philanthropy: Culver Military Academy, hundreds of scholarship programs, a variety of charities, the Fleet Space Theatre and Planetarium, and the International Aerospace Hall of Fame.

From: *These We Honor, the International Hall of Fame*; the San Diego Aerospace Museum, San Diego, CA.1984

#117   Champaign, Illinois   Willard Airport
Type: Paved Identifier: STQ   September 17, 1992

ON TO 500 AIRPORTS!

IMMEDIATELY AFTER OBTAINING an instrument rating, my flying life took a hard left turn toward boredom. I still showed up at the airport every weekend but there was no longer any sense of duty or obligation. There was a lot more 'hangar flying' and coffee drinking and a lot less long distance flying. The strong desire that once burned within had been dramatically subdued to a small, flickering flame. I had become so accustomed to flying with a goal that I was rudderless without one. Saturday morning breakfasts and Sunday late morning brunches were becoming more commonplace, but the word "routine" started to grate on me. If I were truthful, I would admit that I was forcing myself to go to the airport and to the airplane. Another goal was needed and needed in a hurry.

"All the airports in Indiana" are not really all of them. There were well over a hundred farm fields that had not been visited. Maybe that was the answer: Re-fly the state and catch them all. Indiana's Aeronautical Department provided a floppy disk which listed all the private fields. The spread sheet included the name of the owner, field description, address and telephone number. It seemed more and more plausible.

The Cherokee was good on unimproved fields. One person aboard with full fuel did not even come close to the gross weight of the aircraft; it would still be 300 pounds under gross. The 180 horsepower engine was very strong and would not be a limiting factor, either. It had 6.00 x 6" tires all around. If the field was rutted or chuck holed, the nose wheel could be held back during takeoffs and landings. The idea might work.

There were several flies in the ointment, however. Some of these fields tend to disappear if the prices for cash crops create a demand for more growing space. Those fields may not be here today and reappear next year. A trip may be wasted in this case. Or worse, a landing may be made on a field of crops that appears intended for aircraft use.

Other fields are extremely short and intended as landing strips for ultra-lights. I love the way the little Cherokee handles a grass strip, but a 600-foot runway is too short and there is no getting around that fact. It became apparent that some farmers "alter" the length (read "drastically reduce") which could pose problems on our hot and humid summer days.

What's more, some fields don't exist, except on the Sectional maps. In making some phone calls to owners, they were hesitant to talk with me about their field until I convinced them that I was not with the FAA. All they were doing was setting aside some land where a strip once existed or, they anticipated building a strip in the future. One of these men was constructing a home on his intended flying field. Not bad, having a runway in the back yard. He didn't want to maintain it until he was ready for it. In the case of a grass strip, there is a lot of lawn to be mowed each week; so the field remained fallow. For whatever reason, just because a field shows up as a named entity on the sectional, there is no guarantee that it is really there!

It was obvious that I could never count on visiting all the airports in Indiana, or any other state for that matter. No one could, unless they start letting ultra-lights fly into Chicago O'Hare. There were a few private fields I wanted to visit, however, and I filed them in the back of my head. What would be the goal? That was still the key question to be answered.

It was only a short step to look beyond Indiana state lines. The number "one thousand" came to mind, but it didn't last long. That was a little too ambitious. I would be going to 10 or 12 mid-western states to complete that objective. The new goal had to fit into my life without a total displacement of my other activities, duties and responsibilities. After all, somebody had to cut the grass and shovel the snow!

How about 500 fields? Indeed! Why not? That would be the new target. It was attainable. Surrounding states should provide enough opportunities. There could be a few overnight trips, but an occasional Remain-Over-Night would be acceptable.

In fact, there could be flying weekends. I could catch up with all the chores at home during the week, then take advantage of the big high pressure areas that frequent the Midwest during the summers. I would take-off on Saturday mornings and return on Sunday afternoons. Overnight trips did not have to be too frequent; only occasional swings around the region, such as a trip around Lake Michigan or something like that. The interesting farm fields that surfaced in the Indiana records would be part of the goal. Five hundred airports was a good fit.

| #118 | Streator, Illinois | Streator Airport |
| Type: | Paved Identifier: DTG | March 5, 1994 |

| #119 | Dwight, Illinois | Dwight Airport |
| Type: | Paved Identifier: I88 | March 5, 1994 |

THE SKINNIEST RUNWAYS

THE WEATHER HAD finally broken in the Midwest. We had been besieged with several days of heavy rain. The week looked good with a complete lack of clouds. The only detriment to flying was a brisk south wind of about 15 knots. The airplane hadn't stretched its legs in a while, so it was time to go airport hopping again. The easiest airports to reach were in central Illinois; Streator and Dwight, for example.

Streator has an east-west runway, so that meant a very healthy cross wind landing. I over flew the airport to get a good look at the wind sock and conditions on the ground. All the terrain in the Midwest had standing water and mud from the torrential downpours we had experienced during the past several days. From the perceived narrowness of the runway, I felt that I was much too high to enter the landing pattern. But the altimeter showed that the altitude wasn't too high, the runway was extraordinarily narrow! I pulled out the flight guide and looked up Streator. The paved runway was only 19 feet across. The Cherokee has a 10-foot wheel base so that meant I was going to land in a considerable cross wind, with standing water and mud on both sides of the runway and just 4 - ½ feet of clearance on each side of the airplane.

I made the landing. I made it with one hand on the control column and the other on the throttle so that, in case of an anomaly, or any odd eventuality, I could push the throttle forward to full power and abort the landing. There is a wide runway listed for the field but it includes a wide grass portion which is sometimes used for grass landings.

Flying on to Dwight, I found the same thing: a narrow runway in a dead cross wind. According to the flight Guide, the runway was 21 feet wide. Now I had a clearance of 5 -1/2 feet outside of each wheel.

Dwight's strip also ran east and west, and it was also rimmed with standing water and mud. But there was other activity on the field so the surface winds must have eased a bit. I landed with the same extraordinary caution as with Streator.

I have never come across narrower runways among all subsequent airports after these two. The vision of those two runways with borders of standing water and mud are still clear in my mind.

#120   Pontiac, Illinois   Pontiac Municipal Airport
Type: Paved Identifier: 0C1   March 6, 1994

#121   Lacon, Illinois   Marshall County Airport
Type: Paved Identifier: C75   March 6, 1994

#122   Peru, Illinois   Illinois Valley Regional
Type: Paved Identifier: VYS   March 6, 1994

#123   Ottawa, Illinois   Ottawa Airport
Type: Paved Identifier: C13   March 6, 1994

#124   Morris, Illinois   Morris-Washburn Airport
Type: Paved Identifier: C09   March 6, 1994

A TRIP WITH ROCKY

BILL RAKSANI HAD been a friend for over 20 years. We met when we were both employed at the Pullman-Standard Manufacturing Plant in Hammond, Indiana.

Pullman-Standard was a 115 year old company that built passenger railroad cars. The history of the company was rife with familiar names. George Mortimer Pullman was founder and first president of the original Pullman Silver Palace Car Company. Its second president, none other than Robert Todd Lincoln, the first born of President Abraham and Mary Lincoln. In 1930, because of a buy-out of Standard Car Company, we gained a Standard executive known nationwide for his flamboyant life style, James Buchanan Brady. He was better known as "Diamond Jim" Brady. This gathering of famous personalities continued to the end when I was there. In fact, my last boss at Pullman was Colonel Jim McDivitt. You will remember that Jim McDivitt who, with Ed White, manned the Gemini IV space mission in 1965.

Pullman was building three different fleets of rail cars at the time I met Bill (everyone called him "Rocky").He was a specialty machinist who had a very large and well equipped shop all to himself. Mostly, he had no assigned tasks relative to the production line. Rather, he was given hot jobs that had to be done to keep the line moving. He had to be ready for scores of special requests; mostly from the Engineering department on a "'cut and try" basis.

Rocky was a true machinist, not just a machine operator. He could handle a mill or an engine lathe or any of the dozen other major pieces of equipment in the shop with equal proficiency. Especially at his diminutive size, he was worth his weight in gold. He handled every task that came into his shop single-handedly and he did it well.

Rocky trained as a B-17 pilot in World War II, but washed out. He continued training as flight gunner. Accordingly, he accumulated a considerable amount of time in B-17's. Sometime in July or August of 1943, Rocky signed on as a temporary crew member under Captain Charlie Morgan on the famous Memphis Belle (S\N 41-24485) during their bond selling tour and public relations visits throughout the United States. His interest in flying continued to grow. He was a lifelong private pilot but never owned an airplane. The horrible costs of keeping a plane conflicted severely with the financial demands of a family with growing children.

In his basement were parts and pieces of a Pazmany two-place, low wing airplane. Rocky had been building it for over 15 years. His work pace may not have satisfied a hard-nosed and man-hour sensitive production superintendent but the quality of his work was superb. No matter what part was scrutinized, there could be no comparison as far as workmanship was concerned. Particularly interesting was the layout of the building process. All sub-assemblies were built with removal from the basement in mind. When finished, all the components were brought out of the basement with only Rocky and a friend.

After Pullman-Standard was destroyed by corporate take-overs, buy-outs and consolidations, Rocky and I separated for several years. It was by chance that we met again in a doctor's waiting room. We were both scheduled for flight physicals on the same day and the same time. His airplane was finished and it was hangared at Griffith Airport. I didn't own one yet, so I started renting at Griffith. Our friendship was as strong as ever. We began to see each other more frequently.

Rocky took an avid interest in my quest of flying to all the airports in Indiana. He often asked me about the different airports and compared his recollections with mine. When the decision was made to fly to 500 airports, I asked him to accompany me on one of the Saturday adventures. This was the weekend.

We made it more memorable with him as a safety pilot on our first leg, the trip to Pontiac, Illinois. I needed some hood time and a non-precision approach so we made an IFR currency flight. It was the first time Rocky ever saw an entire flight done under the hood. When I pushed up the hood on final approach, locked on final and at approach altitude, all Rocky could say was "I'll be damned!"

#125	Kankakee, Illinois	Greater Kankakee Airport
Type:	Paved Identifier: IKK	April 9, 1994

#126	Paxton, Illinois	Paxton Municipal Airport
Type:	Paved Identifier: 1C1	April 9, 1994

#127	Lewis, Missouri	Lewis County Airport
Type:	Paved Identifier: 6M6	May 28, 1994

#128	Kirksville, Missouri	Kirksville Regional Airport
Type:	Paved Identifier: IRK	May 28, 1994

#129	Queen City, Missouri	Applegate Airport
Type:	Grass Identifier: Private	May 28, 1994

| #130 | Memphis, Missouri | Memphis Memorial Airport |
| Type: | Paved Identifier: MO16 | May 28, 1994 |

| #131 | Kahoka, Missouri | Kahoka Municipal Airport |
| Type: | Grass Identifier: MO05 | May 28, 1994 |

| #132 | Keokuk, Iowa | Keokuk Municipal Airport |
| Type: | Paved Identifier: EOK | May 28, 1994 |

| #133 | Monmouth, Illinois | Monmouth Municipal Airport |
| Type: | Paved   Identifier: C66 | May 28, 1994 |

| #134 | Lostant, Illinois | Hartenbowers Hectares |
| Type: | Grass Identifier: IS56 | May 29, 1994 |

THE PAINS OF VIETNAM

HARTENBOWERS HECTARES FIELD is a 2,000 foot long, north-south grass strip very close to the Illinois River near Lostant. It is owned by a retired Air Force officer; Milton Hartenbower. He told me that he named the field at a time when he was convinced that the United States was going to switch to the metric system. He named his field in the metric vernacular, but the U.S. did not go metric.

Milt Hartenbower was there this particular Sunday morning, as were two other guests. The pilot's lounge had a lot of Vietnam era photographs on the wall. The war soon became the major topic of conversation. Milt soon invited the three of us to the 2nd floor of the building.

It was here in this private room that Milt had kept his most personal memorabilia of his tours of duty in Vietnam. There were mementos and souvenirs everywhere. Milt was obviously there in the later years of the war, during the heavy air bombardment action. He pulled down several photo albums and leafed through them deliberately. He began to tell the story about his many tours of duty in Nam. He stopped at each picture and told us the names of each of the men as well as some poignant aside of each individual. All too often, he would add a finalized thought such as "...he didn't come back from his 24th mission." Or, "We lost him over Hanoi." There were tears welling up in his eyes but he didn't cry. He continued until finally he felt he had gone on enough. Mostly he complained bitterly about how the "Whiz Kids" in Washington micro managed the war. Milt said it seemed as if we were there to be the chess pieces for their daily board games.

I thought back. He was right, it was a crummy war. We didn't dare to lose it and we couldn't win it. It was frustrating and confusing even with our strength, technology and esprit de core. He was forced to follow direction as it came straight from Washington. It wasn't good, it wasn't right and it wasn't effective. But, it did come from above and orders, unfortunately, are orders.

He put the photo books away and tried to change the subject. He told us that the local flyers have a pancake breakfast every Saturday morning. They are a good bunch of guys and we should try to attend next week. We all said that we would see him the following week. I was the first to leave.

The rest of the day, my mind kept returning to Milt and his demons at Lostant, Illinois. I saw the heavy emotional load that Milt Hartenbower was carrying. The names and memories of his men returned to mind. Moreover, I saw his reaction to the mention of the names Lyndon Baines Johnson, Robert McNamara and Jane Fonda. Clearly, Milton was disappointed with the behavior of his government and disgusted with the seditious conduct of those high school dropouts we revere as movie stars; but he drew strength from the heroism of his fighting staff, Each day in Vietnam he suffered another loss of a well-trained and superbly disciplined pilot. Compounding his pain was the fact that each one of these fine young men was a personal friend of his. Probably, each was more like a son than a subordinate which made the anguish harsher.

A lot of veterans share his memories to this day. It was a crummy war; one we shouldn't have been in. Certainly it was not fought the way it should have been. There are strong arguments that Rolling Thunder, for example, could have ended the war if we let it go forward. But, McNamara wanted to show the North Vietnamese how we could turn the pressure on and off at will. Then there was "Hanoi Jane" Fonda. I wonder how many North Vietnamese she inspired to kill more and more America fighting men? Like Milt, we all have bad memories of that terrible time.

Hectares and Milton Hartenbower held my mind captive all through the day. He was carrying the hurt of his personal Viet Nam each day and he will have this burden for the rest of his life. It is right to pray for the souls of his lost pilots. It is also right for Milton Hartenbower to gain peace in his memories. If it is any consolation Milt, prayers are offered for our Vietnam vets in my church every day.

#135   Gibson City, Illinois   Shertz Airport
Type: Paved Identifier: C34   May 29, 1994

#136   Kankakee, Illinois   Koerner Field
Type: Grass Identifier: 3KK   May 29, 1994

I MEET DELBERT KOERNER

KOERNER FIELD, THE "other" Kankakee airport, was much more interesting than Greater Kankakee Airport. This airport was started and was being run by one of the old-time greats of aviation, Delbert Koerner. When I met Delbert he was 90 years old and a slightly built man. Regardless, he was still active in management of the Fixed Base Operation.

Delbert Koerner was mechanically minded all his life. He was equally fascinated by aviation. He traveled to nearby Peoria, Illinois in 1926 to learn how to fly. He not only soloed in a Curtiss OX-5 powered Standard biplane, he bought the plane and flew it back home. Delbert and his brother started an airport in 1927 but soon moved to Kankakee. They added a Waco 10 to their holdings to start Koerner Aviation Inc. Delbert's license was signed by Orville Wright.

During WW II, Delbert was a B-24 test pilot for Ford at Willow Run, Michigan. He also worked for Curtiss-Wright in Buffalo, New York. After the war, he returned to Kankakee, his brother and Koerner Aviation. Delbert is an Honored Member of the Illinois Aviation Hall of Fame (1984).

On November 20, 1999 Delbert Koerner was presented with the Master Mechanic Award by the FAA. To be nominated for the Master Mechanic Award a mechanic nominee must have spent 50 years in aviation maintenance, be a U.S. citizen, and be recommended in writing by at least three A&P mechanics.

Delbert was interested in my project of flying to many airports. He took me around the shops and hangar for a personal tour. I felt favored by this gesture. There were four antique airplanes in various stages of restoration, including a Piper Cub and a stripped biplane that I didn't recognize.

Delbert had an extraordinary number of Wright 2600 radial engines around the shop. Some, still with cowlings on them, came from North American B-25's. The two shops in the operation were well equipped and fully stocked with very old parts. The shops, with a well-worn look and a soft industrial patina on the wooden work benches, had the appearance of having been very active in the past, but not used in several years.

Delbert Koerner got around very slowly. I enjoyed the time that he allowed me that day. All over the walls of the shop and office were yellowed newspaper clippings about this well-known Kankakee pilot. It was a pleasure to meet and talk with him. Although we spent little together, I felt comfortable with Delbert.

Delbert passed away shortly after my visit. I felt honored to have met him. Sport Aviation will miss him. He was quite a man.

#137	Burlington, Iowa	Burlington Regional Airport
Type:	Paved Identifier: BRL	June 4, 1994

#138	Mt. Pleasant, Iowa	Mt. Pleasant Municipal Airport
Type:	Paved Identifier: MPZ	June 4, 1994

#139	Albia, Iowa	Albia Municipal Airport
Type:	Paved Identifier: 4C8	June 4, 1994

#140	Centerville, Iowa	Centerville Municipal Airport
Type:	Paved Identifier: TVK	June 4, 1994

DID SOMEONE MOVE ANTIQUER?

THERE IS A little grass strip at Blakesville, Iowa. It is a private field that caters to old aircraft. On the chart it is called Antique Airport, but the club members call it "Antiquers Airdrome." This field is a frustration to me because I never landed there. I really wanted to, you understand, I just couldn't find it. And it's not because I didn't try.

After I left Mount Pleasant, Iowa, bound for Antiquers, I couldn't spot it so I circled lower and slower... no luck. I skipped over to Albia, which is about 5 miles west. Some folks there were well aware of Antiquers and they gave me specific headings and mileage info. I thought I could find it but, after circling for about a half hour, still no luck.

I went on to Centerville, Iowa, now completely frustrated. How in the dickens am I qualified to fly to various airports if I can't find one after two tries? While at Centerville, I met a guy who understood my problem and advised me of yet one more way to find Antiquer's. It sounded good, so back I went. He told me there were no straight lines so don't look for a straight runway. Rather, he confided, I have to check out landing marks (stripes of landing gear) on the field. I wasn't sure about that but, what the hell, I was right there so I might as well try again.

This time I came down to an altitude of 200 feet above ground and I still couldn't find the runway. I could have thrown a rock at Antiquer's given, of course, I could recognize it!

#141	Bloomfield, Iowa	Bloomfield Municipal Airport
Type:	Paved Identifier: 4K6	June 4, 1994

#142	Keosougwa, Iowa	Keosaugwa Municipal Airport
Type:	Grass Identifier: 6K9	June 4, 1994

#143	Fort Madison, Iowa	Fort Madison Municipal Airport
Type:	Paved Identifier: FSW	June 4, 1994

#144	Monee, Illinois	Sanger Airport
Type:	Paved Identifier: C56	June 27, 1994

#145	New Lenox, Illinois	Howell Airport
Type:	Paved Identifier: 1C2	June 27, 1994

#146	Frankfort, Illinois	Frankfort Airport
Type:	Paved Identifier: C18	June 27, 1994

#147	Danville, Illinois	Vermillion County Airport
Type:	Paved Identifier: DNV	July 10, 1994

THE COOLEST BACHELOR PAD IN AMERICA

THIS TRIP TO Danville was made during the evening of July 10th. The excursion was an easy one at about 3,000 feet altitude heading directly south down the Indiana - Illinois line. According to the sectional, Danville is a non-controlled airport. Accordingly, I made my radio announcements at 10 north and then at 5 miles north. As Danville came into view, I saw the distinct profile of a control tower. I quickly re-checked the chart and was reassured that the field was not under the control of a tower. I radioed my intention to enter the appropriate runway and kept an eye on the tower for possible signal light indications. There were none.

Once on the ground, I taxied over to the FBO. On the way, I saw movement in the tower. What was going on?

While I sipped on a soft drink, I asked the FBO attendant what the story was on the tower. The guy behind the desk rolled his eyes back and smiled. He told me that the tower is not in operation. He assured me that the field is indeed, pilot-controlled. It seems that the Federal government removed the tower operator in a cost cutting measure. The city was saddled with the responsibility of staffing the tower. The city could not come up with the funds to replace the controller so the tower sits empty.

Still smiling through his explanation, the FBO attendant continued. He said that the city was approached by a young man who wanted to rent the tower. The city saw an opportunity for a little revenue and gave him a year's lease. The young man promptly moved in and made the tower, in the breathy words of the FBO guy ..."The coolest bachelor pad in America!"

#148   Paris, Illinois   Edgar County Airport
Type: Paved Identifier: PRG   July 10, 1994

#149   Kewanee, Illinois   Kewanee Municipal Airport
Type: Paved Identifier: EXI   July 10, 1994

#150	Sterling, Illinois	Whiteside County Airport
Type:	Paved Identifier: SQI	July 10, 1994

#151	Dixon, Illinois	Charles R. Walgreen Memorial
Type:	Paved Identifier: C73	July 10, 1994

#152	Polo, Illinois	Radio Ranch
Type:	Grass Identifier: 1C6	July 10, 1994

WARNING: FIELD MAY BE ABANDONED

RADIO RANCH IS one of those airports that time has passed by. It is called Radio Ranch because it used to be an aviation radio repair center. Radio Ranch Repair Service moved its operation to Whiteside County Airport in Rock Falls, Illinois. The name remained with the old airport.

The field at Radio Ranch is of north - south orientation and is grass. Flying over it, the surface appeared rough and lacking in maintenance. Judging from 1,000 feet over head, however, is difficult. Flight Guide is a private organization that gathers and publishes data on all the airports in America. The book is updated a couple of times per year to reflect the best information they have. They rely upon various sources such as material provided by their subscribers as well as official government documents. The listing for Radio Ranch airport included a warning: "Caution. The field may be abandoned."

While the field may appear rough, it was certainly clear of debris and obstacles. Prepared for a surprise, I continued my approach. The weeds and grass had grown without cutting for several weeks. The taller weeds were big enough to grab at the leading edge of my wing. The prop was having a good time, too: it was acting as a horizontal lawn mower. The sky in front of the cockpit was green and filled with chlorophyll. It became apparent that my plans to take-off from this field started with action now. I kept up power and continued the landing roll almost to the end of the runway. At the turn coming back, I tried to "cut grass" adjacent to the strip that was cleared by the landing. There was more chlorophyll, more green skies.

There was a concrete ramp near the approach end of the runway to park. I got out of the airplane and walked over to look down my landing track and taxi back lanes. The two semi-circular lanes were plainly visible. The good news is I was down safely; the bad news is that I had to take-off again from this field. This was a low density day. The temperature was in the high 90s and the humidity was too. While the Cherokee was lightly loaded and had above-average power, the take-off could be interesting. This would have been a good time for a cigarette, if I were a smoker.

There was no one to talk to and very little to see. Take-off time was upon me. I taxied the airplane alongside the fence and lined up with my freshly mowed prop trails. I held the brakes until the engine went to full power. At about 50 to 60 miles per hour, I pulled in 10 degrees of flaps and eased back on the control column. The Cherokee jumped into ground effect and mushed through the air for a few seconds at about 10 feet of altitude. Free of the drag from the tall and thick weeds, the Cherokee mercifully gained air speed. Within a few seconds, I eased pressure off the elevators and the airplane settled into a 100 mile-per-hour rate of climb. There was no more need for flaps.

Radio Ranch Airport was a nice field to visit ...once!

#153   Rochelle, Illinois   Koritz Field
Type: Paved Identifier: 12C   July 10, 1994

#154   DeKalb, Illinois   Taylor Municipal Airport
Type: Paved Identifier: DKB   July 10, 1994

#155   Bresson, Illinois   Bresson Airport
Type: Grass Identifier: C82   July 10, 1994

#156   Newark, Illinois   Cushing Field
Type: Grass Identifier: 0C8   July 10, 1994

#157   Joliet, Illinois   Park District Airport
Type: Paved Identifier: JOT   July 10, 1994

THE GIFT

AFTER VISITING A hundred or more airports, I felt an obligation to return the kindness of the various owners and operators. Friends and acquaintances were made at many airports. Additionally, I brought back some photographs of interesting things that I had seen at many fields. I left nothing behind and that bothered me. The people I met were generous with their friendship and hospitality. Emptiness existed that was ungentlemanly. Somehow, these kind people had to have their kindness repaid. I thought carefully about what that return gift should be for a long time.

A few restrictions had to be imposed. For example, the gift would have to be inexpensive; after all, I would be passing out hundreds of them. It would have to be distinctive also. The theme of the gift must include a feeling of sport aviation. It must have a personal essence that reminded them of me and the little Cherokee. My first thought was to send each field a picture of my plane. However, the last thing an airport needs is yet another picture of yet another airplane. For a photograph to be an appropriate gift, it would have to be unique.

Other options came to mind, but the thought of a photograph kept coming back. If I did my work correctly, the photo could be of my airplane. The shot would characterize the airplane as one that visited a lot of airports. The picture would have to be eye-catching and memorable. The resulting photo accomplished all of these goals.

It has nothing to do with computer aided graphics. The original picture is from the space program and is called "Earth Rise." The picture was purchased in 11" x 17" size from NASA. It was photographed by the astronauts of Apollo 14 (Alan Shepard, Stuart Roosa and Edgar D. Mitchell, the lunar module pilot) as they circled the backside of the moon. Each of the three astronauts claimed that he took the picture. Consequently, each of the astronauts claims that the other two are lying about the picture's authorship. The photo eventually became the subject of a first class postal stamp. It is important to include a quotation that is naturally linked (and beautifully so,) with this photo. From (now Dr.) Edgar Mitchell,

> "Suddenly, from behind the rim of the moon, in long, slow-motion moments of immense majesty, there emerges a sparkling blue and white jewel, a light, delicate sky-blue sphere laced with slowly swirling veils of white, rising gradually like a small pearl in a thick sea of black mystery.It takes more than a moment to fully realize this is Earth ...home."

And then, at a later date:

> "My view of our planet was a glimpse of divinity."

Superimposed on the picture of "Earth Rise" was our Cherokee. The airplane was photographed from several angles at its home base. I stood on a tall ladder to get the proper perspective. The shadows of the airplane matched the shadows on the moon quite closely. It was simply a matter of cutting out the airplane with scissors and pasting it on the large picture. It looked great. Never mind that the adjacent craters are actually several hundred miles across; the airplane looks at home! It was distinctive and memorable. Moreover, it brought to mind an airplane which visited a lot of places.

I took the time to copyright the composite image. It now has an official copyright and is called "Lunar Visit 1995". Literally hundreds of these have been sent to airports around the Midwest. Several phone calls and a couple of letters have resulted from these mailings.

My intention is to re-visit some of the folks who took the time to write or telephone.

#158   Findlay, Ohio   Findlay Airport
Type: Paved Identifier: FDY   August 6, 1994

#159   Fostoria, Ohio   Fostoria Metro Airport
Type: Paved Identifier: FZI   August 6, 1994

#160   Tiffin, Ohio   Seneca County Airport
Type: Paved Identifier: 16G   August 6, 1994

#161   Fremont, Ohio   Fremont Airport
Type: Paved Identifier: 14G   August 6, 1994

GOVERNOR RHODES DOES HIS OHIO PROUD!

AS I BEGAN to travel to the first few airports of Ohio, I enjoyed talking with my new pilot friends and told them what I was doing. I had just finished visiting all of the airports in Indiana. Because I enjoyed it so much and because it gave me an excuse to get into the air more often, I thought it would be an inspiration to others. Perhaps it would break the normal pilot's routine of Fly-In breakfasts and the $100 hamburger trips.

Very often, the comment would be made that 'you should have good flying here; there is an airport in every county in Ohio.' I thought it odd that they should have that little tidbit so readily available, and I had no idea what the situation was in my home state of Indiana. Furthermore, it was repeated frequently as I traveled from field to field. Once aware of this, I questioned the next flyer to mention that little fact and found out about the massive airfield construction across the state in the late 1960's. Supposedly, a great number of airports were built in a short time frame. With this effort, highways became runways, civic pride was rejuvenated and the birthplace of aviation regained it birthright under the determination of a concerned governor of 30 or 40 years ago. Once it was understood, the story begged to be told. This is the tale of how all the counties of Ohio got their own airports.

It was late 1964. The world had suffered through the Bay of Pig fiasco, the US-supported war in the Belgian Congo, the Cuban missile crisis, and the murder of President Kennedy. Armed mainly with our innate American resiliency, a federal tax cut and a rugged determination to build a better future, America's economy saw better days ahead. This optimism was obvious wherever one went. Well, almost everywhere.

Ohioans were considerably more pessimistic about their future. Ohio was not growing as fast as the rest of the country. This was especially true in the southeast hinder regions, where chronically depressed Appalachia sprawled over into several Ohio counties. Governor James A. Rhodes was painfully aware of his state's economic vulnerability. He knew the weak areas of Ohio's infrastructure and he was intent about doing something about it. In order to generate the high paying industrial jobs, he had to present a state that was willing to make the improvements necessary to attract such business. He was gunning for industry and high paying factory jobs. Minimum wage work, casual labor or tips based waiter and waitress positions were not on his radar screen.

Governor Rhodes was about to challenge his aviation team. He was also a good manager; he knew the answers before he asked the questions. To their credit, his Aviation Division was ready. Pertinent to his challenge that more industry is needed in Ohio, he asked, "what influence and status does the airport have in the business world?" Adding another thrust, Governor Rhodes continued with "what can we offer to persuade businesses to relocate to Ohio?"

His Aviation Division, under the leadership of Norman Crabtree as Chief of Ohio Division of Transportation responded with less than complimentary data. Of the 88 counties in Ohio, only 30 had runways capable of handling small business aircraft - a runway that is at least 3,500 feet in length. This may seem short by today's expectations, but remember, this is before the massive growth of the business jet market. Furthermore, most of these were north on the periphery of Lake Erie. The Appalachia section in the south and east counties of Ohio was especially lacking in adequate air facilities. Aviation-wise, Ohio was in a fix.

Detailed analysis of the state's airports revealed that only 23 counties had airports with paved runways that were 3,500 feet or longer. This was considered to be the minimum length needed for business aircraft and their higher landing speeds. Not only that, there was some question as to the structural soundness of some strips. Among the slightly smaller airports of the 88 Ohio counties, only nine had runways with length between 3,000 and 3,499 feet. And, of these nine, two had inadequate runway strength.

Ohio's Aviation Division told their Governor what he suspected: industry relied upon nearby, serviceable airports to conduct business. The locale of business had been slowing changing over the years; big cities no longer held a tight grip. The lower cost of land, ample opportunity to expand, more productive and cheaper labor in smaller communities, and the speed and ease of transportation brought on by the nations new and developing interstate highway system lured businesses to small town America. The Aviation Division staff acknowledged that prospective companies look at Ohio in their search for a competitive and profitable atmosphere. But when they were flown into cow pasture airstrips or had to be driven 30 to 50 miles to prospective sites, interest dwindled noticeably. A key element remained unchallenged in the business world: "Time is money." Wasting time to travel to and from local flying fields was counterproductive to business's objective.

Governor Rhodes and his small cadre of aviation experts went into action. With their guidance, Ohio enacted and the voters passed the Capital Improvements Bond Issue. The attack was logical. They went immediately to the 58 counties that had no airports whatsoever and designated $100,000 for each of them as an outright grant if they met the state's 10 requirements which were:

1. Title to land for an airport.
2. A complete plan to build an airport.

3. Tracing titles complete with signatures of the county and city officials.
4. A letter verifying the correct zoning for the site.
5. Complete set of specifications for the project.
6. A set of bidding sheets to be sent to contractors.
7. An estimate of the engineering costs
8. Proposed timetable or schedule for construction.
9. A letter from the governing body which guaranteed monies were available.
10. Four signed copies of the grant agreement.

This is a logical, straightforward and well-focused approach. Nothing in the above list should hinder a well-intentioned local government. Rhodes and his company sped forward.

In the first year of the program, state operatives met with local governing bodies to explain the need and to promote the demand for desirable aviation facilities in each county. In 1965 alone, there were in excess of 400 meetings and conferences for this purpose with recently appointed officials of the new county airport authorities. Even with this work, the benefit of air travel proved valuable. The Aviation Division team consisted mostly of Norman Crabtree's Assistant Chief, John Cornett, Mark Carr, Gerry Chambers and Ed Arn. They used light, single engine planes to move quickly to-and-from grass strips of the various counties.

Governor Rhodes had a budding success on his hands. Success of the Airport Program brought about a subsequent passage of House Bill 886 which allotted another $1,200,000 in July of 1967 so that 12 new counties could participate in the growth. By 1970, 62 of Ohio's 88 counties were establishing airports with grant money. Keep in mind, "grant money" is a gift and does not need to be repaid.

There was a growing optimism in the state because of this extraordinary effort. The Federal Aviation Administration was anxious to get its name associated with the success of Rhodes and company. There was a danger here and Ohio knew it. Once the FAA got involved, they would bring along their influence and demands. The airport program was going well and it didn't need adverse interference even if it came from the "well-meaning" FAA.

For example, the FAA wanted to dictate that only federally approved construction materials and methods be used to construct the actual runways. Rhodes knew that Ohio contractors were not familiar with runways construction, but they were expert in highway building. Part of the economic development advantage of the airport program was the immediate creation of jobs for the Ohio labor force. Exercising his state's rights, Governor Rhodes rejected the FAA's insistence on runway standards, and set down Ohio's own civil engineering standards. In essence, the construction companies were to build the runways as if they were laying down a new highway. The result would be a high quality runway, built by experienced and knowledgeable contractors and work crews in the least amount of time. No learning curves here, no misinterpretation of specifications and certainly, no rookie mistakes to slow progress.

By 1970, there was no mistaking the positive impact that the airport program had upon the state, the counties and the residents. The movement was massive, well directed and well managed. The pending and apparent success was contagious and community pride blossomed. Civic groups such as Kiwanis, Rotary, the Lions and the Knights of Columbus supplied excellent help and performed much needed groundwork in many communities. Contractors and vendors became caught up in the benefits of the movement. As the state personnel so eloquently put it, "pencils were sharpened" at every turn. No one wanted to be in the way of this feat of progress. Everyone wanted to be a part of it. Land for new airports was provided via various means. In some cases, land was exchanged instead of money changing hands. Removal of overburden was sometimes donated and in most cases done for a fraction of the normal cost of landfill.

The Perry County Airport, just outside of New Lexington, is an excellent example of creative land acquisition. While the minimum size runway that could be built under the Airport Plan was to be 3,500 feet, there were still clearance problems in the area surrounding the field. The best location and the cheapest land available in hilly Perry County ended at a section of railroad track. The FAA would require strict minimum altitudes over the tallest obstacle. Most of the approach end of runway near the track would have to be painted with yellow chevrons to indicate runway length that cannot be used.

The authorities made a couple of astute decisions. They would preserve the runway length, location and the favorable prevailing wind orientation. They would opt to move the runway more to the west and build a bridge across the railroad track. The bridge would become part of the runway! Now they did not need the air space clearance between the landing airplanes and the trains. They had a runway between them for the protection of each. And the two have lived happily together ever since.

Between the inception of the program in late 1964 and the end of 1970, there were no less than 50 new airports dedicated in Ohio and 16 more were in progress. In fact, in October of 1967, a total of 13 airports were brought into commission. Six of these were dedicated on one Sunday afternoon, with four dedicated on another Sunday, and the last three on yet a third Sunday. Clearly, this phenomenal aviation growth and development is unprecedented and, I am sure, has not since been duplicated, let alone eclipsed.

Governor Rhodes was rewarded for his foresight and determination. There has been significant and measurable economic development throughout the counties which opted for new airports. In a survey of 150 manufacturing concerns located in the counties with new fields, most responded that they use the airport frequently for business purposes. Nearly half of all traffic in and out of the new airports was by corporate planes or commercial cargo aircraft.

Regarding employment and income, the new airport counties experienced an average rate of a payroll increase that was 3% higher than comparable counties which had not yet added airports. In the same comparison, the rate of employment increased by 5%. Because of the program, Ohio netted over $250,000,000 in additional personal income, and enjoyed the creation of over 60,000 new jobs. Not always counted in such successes are the retail trades. The participating counties enjoyed an increase of retail revenue sufficient to support an additional 200 stores.

Industrial development and capital investment benefited as well. Nearly 1,500 new or expanded industries and an estimated $1,000,000,000 in industrial capital investment have been credited to the program. Additionally, 20 new industrial parks have been constructed adjacent to the new airports, and more are being planned.

As anticipated, land value within these counties has escalated to everyone's benefit. Fully 90% of the participating counties experienced land price increases of more than 100%. In some instances, this figure was nearer 500%. The highest increase reported was in Delaware County, near Columbus, which was selling land next to the airport for $7,000 per acre whereas prior to the airport's existence, it had a value of $400 an acre.

Landing at the county airports is a thrill for a businessman such as me. I know the value of up-to-date infrastructure to a business. It is impossible to hear the main wheels squeak onto the asphalt runways of these fields and not feel a smile come across my face. But for the acute vision of one man and the overwhelming support of his staff and popular constituency, these airports would never have been. Not only do business people acknowledge the benefit of these airports and what it has done for Ohio's economic health, but sport aviators also appreciate the convenience. Well done, Jim Rhodes. You are a man among men. When Sir Isaac Newton commented that we have the vision of the ages because we stand on the shoulders of those who went before us, he was talking about you, James A. Rhodes!

My appreciation is extended to David Dennis, Aviation Planner at the Ohio Department of Transportation, who graciously provided so much help and cooperation in order that this story could be told.

#162   Bowling Green, Ohio   Wood County Airport
Type: Paved Identifier: 1G0   August 6, 1994

#163   Ottawa, Ohio   Putnam County Airport
Type: Paved Identifier: OWX   August 6, 1994

#164   Ruhe, Ohio   Ruhe Airport
Type: Paved Identifier: 39OI   August 6, 1994

#165   Napoleon, Ohio   Henry County Airport
Type: Paved Identifier: OH17   August 6, 1994

#166   Defiance, Ohio   Defiance Memorial Airport
Type: Paved Identifier: DFI   August 6, 1994

FRIENDS DON'T LET FRIENDS FLY CESSNAS

THIS VISIT TOOK place on the weekend immediately following the EAA Convention at Oshkosh, Wisconsin. My wife and I spent 4 days at the Fly-In and, like everyone else, we managed to pick up our share of flying memorabilia. A dear friend, Keith Grill, has a Cessna 172 Skyhawk. For some childish reason or another, we have developed a rivalry based upon his high wing versus our low wing airplane. It is nothing serious, just enough to kid each other. While at Oshkosh, I bought a T shirt that read "Friends don't let friends fly Cessnas." This was perfect for my relationship with Keith.

On the morning of August 6th, 1994, I put on the T-shirt and went to his hardware store. Much to my disillusionment, he wasn't there. It seems that he was on Chicago's north side picking up some material and wouldn't be back until later in the day. It was a small disappointment, but not enough to keep me from flying. He would see the shirt another day.

I visited 10 airports that day; a lot of flying in anyone's book. The trip started in the Findlay area and stretched east-ward, then back west for the trip home. Toward the end of the day, I thought that one or two more airports would be as many as I could fit into a day. From where I was, Defiance Memorial was on line with my route home. Defiance, Ohio! What a great name. A good, strong Republican name! I had to stop in.

There wasn't much radio traffic from 10 miles out, so I expected no congestion over the field. I over flew the airport to get a feel for the wind. While overhead, I saw that there were dozens of aircraft on the ground. This was terrific. A field with a lot of general aviation activity; this is my kind of place.

Upon landing and roll out, it was apparent that it would be difficult finding a place to park. The asphalt ramp was full of airplanes. In fact, there were airplanes parked three rows deep on the grass. I found a suitable opening and shut down the Cherokee. Something was wrong. Wait a minute. This was not just a gaggle of airplanes. These were all Cessna 310's. All model years, all colors, and all versions of Cessna 310's. Virtually every one was in pristine condition; show quality. Defiance, as it turns out, is the center of all Cessna 310 activity in the United States. Defiance is the gathering point and an information clearing house for all 310 owners and pilots. But I didn't know that at the time.

I started to walk toward the FBO and saw that there was a real picnic going on. Charcoal broilers were smoking everywhere and about a hundred people were having a good time. All this Cessna activity and now comes this Cherokee pilot. Holy smoke! I became extremely conscious of the T-shirt I was wearing. I was in trouble, for sure.

These were, however, flyers. This is the brotherhood of flight. Maybe the shirt was in poor taste but they made the best of it. It started all sorts of discussions and conversations. There were Cessna flyers with shirts like mine only they read something like "I would rather fly a Cessna than push a Piper." Folks were putting their arms around me to have their picture taken. This visit turned out to be a lot of fun! It was mutually enjoyable. I'm sure that the pilots there don't remember me but I am also certain that they haven't forgotten the guy who showed up one day with a funny T-shirt.

#167   Bryan, Ohio   Williams County Airport
Type: Paved Identifier: 0G6   August 6, 1994

AN AIRPORT OF HISTORIC NOTE

THIS STORY IS not of the present Bryan Airport, but the original airport north of town. Because of its location, midway between Cleveland and Chicago, Bryan was a stop on the early air U.S .mail route. The town cleared a field, where the first mail plane landed on September 9th, 1918. By December 11th of the same year, a modest hangar had been built. Fortunately, it remains on North Main Street. After the airport moved south of town, the building was used by a succession of businesses, most recently a glass company. Sliding hangar doors big enough to accommodate a de Havilland DH-4 were removed long ago and replaced with bricks and smaller doors.

Today the building is vacant. The owner is willing to sell for a goodly amount; however, no one has come up with the cash. Local pilots and others proud of Bryan's place in aviation history would like to see the building donated or somehow preserved. Surely, this must be one of the oldest remaining hangars in the country and, the only tangible link to Bryan's historic place on the transcontinental air mail route. After surviving this long, it surely deserves to be saved forever, and a way must be found. The surrounding area, however, is being developed.[3]

#168 Muscatine, Iowa Type: Paved Identifier: MUT	Muscatine Municipal Airport August 14, 1995
#169 Washington, Iowa Type: Paved Identifier: AWG	Washington Municipal Airport August 14, 1995
#170 Fairfield, Iowa Type: Paved Identifier: FFL	Fairfield Municipal Airport August 14, 1995
#171 Ottumwa, Iowa Type: Paved Identifier: OTM	Ottumwa Industrial Airport August 14, 1995

---

3 Remnants of Glory. A Light Plane Tour of Aviation's Past by Russell Munson. Air & Space, September 1999.

DEJA VU ALL OVER AGAIN

AUGUST 14TH WAS a day filled with beautiful VFR flying. All of it was in Iowa at non-controlled fields. After a while, I began to recognize a repetition in radio announcements. With the northwest breeze of 10 to 15 knots, I kept saying something like:

> "Cherokee 8369 Whiskey is crosswind over the field for left traffic on 31."

Downwind, base and final announcements were equally repetitious. I felt that I had repeated this for all the airports visited this day. Finally, I looked back at the airport diagrams in the flight guide and, sure enough, all the airports had a runway 31 and 13. The airports were all alike. There were a lot more airports like these. Clones!

At Ottumwa I mentioned this to the line man. He told me that this was, indeed, a fact. Most airports in Iowa were identical or nearly so. The Navy had come through during World War II and built 65 or 70 airports and each was exactly like the one before.

I had two difficult facts to accept. The first is that the United States Navy had decided to have a massive presence in Iowa. This means they concluded that Iowa, 1,000 miles from the nearest salt water, had to be the site of not one, but 65 naval air bases.

Secondly, the U.S. Navy determined that the prevailing weather conditions all over Iowa are identical; therefore the runway orientation for 65 airports all over Iowa should be identical.

Strange things happen in this world. The most peculiar events seem to have their roots in our U.S. government.

#172 Oskaloosa, Iowa
Type: Paved Identifier: OOA

Oskaloosa Municipal Airport
August 14, 1995

#173 Iowa City, Iowa
Iowa City Municipal Airport

Type: Paved Identifier: IOW
August 14, 1995

THE FIRST U.S. AIRPORT WITH ELECTRIC LIGHTS

IOWA CITY, IOWA, was once the only mail stop between Omaha and Chicago. Boeing Air Transport, later United Air Lines, built a hangar there in 1930. The airline pulled out in 1959, but the hangar is still in use.

In the mid-30s, Boeing Air Transport built a nearly identical hangar in North Platte, Nebraska, which now houses Trego Dugan Aviation. The most noteworthy aviation artifact in North Platte, however, is a man named Louie Drost.

Louis C .Drost Jr. was born on December 14, 1901, almost two years to the day before the Wright brothers first flew a powered airplane. Louie's family moved from Iowa to North Platte in 1904. Once airplanes and airports were invented, Drost was drawn to them, never as a pilot, but as a starry eyed teenager hanging around the North Platte flying field. The airmail pilots were heroes. When they went to the Place Café for coffee, everyone wanted to sit next to them.

As Drost recalls, he went to work for the postal service around 1920 or 1921 as a field and mail clerk for $100 per month. He stayed until 1927 when the Federal Government signed over the San Francisco-to-Chicago route to Boeing Air Transport. During that span he drove mail between the airport and the train station, set bonfires on the airstrip for the air mail pilots to land between at night, got weather reports by telephone from towns along the route, and helped recover aircraft that had made emergency landings. "Those Liberty engines stripped gears a lot," he said and that would force aircraft into the nearest field or, in the case of Jack Knight, into the North Platte River. Drost rode in the mail bins of DH-4s and helped install the cables when North Platte became the Nation's first airport with electrical lighting.[4]

---

4 Remnants of Glory A Light Plane Tour of Aviation's Past by Russell Munson. Air & Space, September 1999.

#174 Rantoul, Illinois National Aviation Center
Type: Paved Identifier: 2I5 August 21, 1994

#175 Lincoln, Illinois Logan County Airport
Type: Paved Identifier: 3LC August 21, 1994

#176 Mattoon, Illinois Coles County Airport
Type: Paved Identifier: MTO August 21, 1994

#177 Casey, Illinois Casey Municipal Airport
Type: Paved Identifier: 1H8 August 21, 1994

#178 Tuscola, Illinois Tuscola Airport
Type: Paved Identifier: K96 August 21, 1994

#179 Urbana, Illinois Frasca Field
Type: Paved Identifier: C16 August 21, 1994

FRASCA INTERNATIONAL

U RBANA WAS A refueling stop and a change to enjoy a soft drink. While roaming around the field, I learned of Frasca International and, more specifically, about Rudy Frasca. He is some kind of flyer!

Frasca International was founded in 1958 by Rudy Frasca. Rudy began taking flying lessons at the age of 14 and soloed shortly thereafter. In 1949, Rudy joined the Navy and was stationed at the Glenview Naval Station, where he worked as a flight instructor teaching pilots on the early Link trainers. After the Korean War, Rudy left the Navy to attend the University of Illinois, where he did research in Aviation Psychology and honed his interest in the field of flight simulation. The more Rudy worked with that early generation of pilot training devices, the more he realized that there had to be a better way. In 1958, putting together everything he had learned in the Navy and the University, Rudy built his first flight simulator at home in his garage and Frasca Aviation was founded.

Walking around the field and looking into several hangars, one can see Rudy's avocation. In addition to his time in naval aviation and having flown hundreds of aircraft over the years, Rudy Frasca collected several planes - including some "War Birds," all in flying condition. He has a P-40, a recently restored Spitfire Mk XVIII, a Wildcat, an SNJ, a T-34, a Fiat, and a Zero replica.

Rudy is active in many areas of aviation and has held every office in the War Birds of America organization. He has been a member of the Experimental Aircraft Association (EAA) since 1956 and has loaned several of his aircraft to the EAA Museum for enjoyment of the general public. He has received numerous awards for both his personal efforts and for Frasca International's success in the simulation industry.

Courtesy of Frasca.com, September 3, 2002

#180 Toledo, Ohio
Type: Class C Identifier: TOL

Express Airport
September 11, 1994

#181 Toledo, Ohio
Type: Class D 1994

Metcalf Airport
September 11, 1994

#182 Port Clinton, Ohio
Type: Paved Identifier: PCW

Keller Airport
September 11, 1994

THE PORT CLINTON PATRIOTS

AWARTIME PRACTICE THAT was initiated 200 years ago and continued through World War II was the grouping of fighting units according to the state or other geographic origin. Consequently the five Sullivan brothers, who together enlisted in the Navy, were assigned to serve on the light cruiser, the USS Juneau. The ship was struck by a torpedo attack and was lost with almost all hands including the Sullivan brothers. After 1945, the armed forces discontinued this practice.

Similarly was the devastation to the population of Port Clinton in early 1942. A number of young Port Clinton men formed the backbone of Company "C" in General MacArthur's 192nd Tank Battalion on duty in the Philippines. This unit was wiped out on the Bataan Peninsula. It was at the Standard Products Plant in Port Clinton that recompense for this loss was made.

The Standard Products Company of Detroit, Michigan, made window channels, door locks and other stamped parts for the automotive industry. One of its divisions was in Port Clinton. This division was to manufacture the .30 caliber carbine.

In August of 1943, Iron Age magazine published the following article addressing this terrible loss and the reaction of Port Clinton's residents:

> With the burning recollection that 25 fellow workers and 140 brothers, husbands and sons of the people of Port Clinton, Ohio were among those lost on the Bataan Peninsula when the Japanese overcame those troops that held out to the last to give other American Forces in the Pacific more time, workers at Standard Products Company are personally aiming to see that American forces at any battlefront will never run short again - at least of caliber .30 M1 carbines. From a population of 4,350 in 1940, this town has grown in size until today there are some 7,300 people living there. The fall of Bataan will long remain a

memory to those folks, since about three percent of the entire population was lost or annihilated in one single stroke.

The relatives and friends of those soldiers killed or taken prisoner by the Japanese were more than eager to help produce a weapon as personal as the carbine. Grandmothers learned to operate milling machines and drill presses; many young people received their first paychecks from Standard Products, and farmers, after a day at the plant, hurried home to do their chores. It seemed that everyone in the area, from orchardists to commercial fishermen, stood up to be employed. Except for the Ordnance inspectors and the production specialists, who were mainly New Englanders, there were few "in-migrants" among the general plant personnel. The plant cafeteria, which fed the numerous employees daily, boasted real home cooking, most of the women who cooked and served there had never before worked outside their own home kitchens. Some employees lived as far as fifteen miles from the plant, a considerable distance in those car-and-gasoline scarce days, and a 'share the ride'" plan was instigated to provide transportation.'

Standard Products still exists. It is now known as Cooper-Standard, a division of Cooper Tire & Rubber Company. With their sacrifice and patriotism, its employees have earned their place in America's heart. Their proud heritage is a gift to America.

Such is the America spirit.

#183 Clyde, Ohio   Bandit Field
Type: Grass Identifier: 5D9   September 11, 1994

A VISIT IN TIME

BANDIT FIELD WAS a visit to World War II. While no one was there with whom to talk, the array of equipment was like museum pieces: Personnel carriers and amphibious vehicles. Light armored equipment and scout planes. There were even some antique aircraft that I had never seen before.

The field itself was interesting because it was a grass field with a road going across it. Landing on a field with such an addition proved to be no problem whatsoever. The only thing is, I hadn't done it before.

#184 Upper Sandusky, Ohio
Type: Paved Identifier: 56D

Wynadot County Airport
September 11, 1994

#185 Kenton, Ohio
Type: Paved Identifier: I95

Hardin County Airport
September 11, 1994

#186 Bluffton, Ohio
Type: Paved Identifier: 5G7

Bluffton Airport
September 11, 1994

#187 Van Wert, Ohio
Type: Paved Identifier: VNW

Van Wert County Airport
September 11, 1994

#188 Galesburg, Illinois
Type: Paved Identifier: GBG

Galesburg Municipal Airport
September 18, 1994

#189 Sigourney, Iowa
Type: Grass Identifier: Private

Nell Ruby's Field
September 18, 1994

THE STORY OF NELL RUBY & SYLVAN VAVERKA

THIS BEAUTIFUL SEPTEMBER day was made for flying. The air was cool and still and the sky was free of clouds. Flying at any altitude was smooth and effortless. Typically, these kinds of days make me turn to grass strips. An airfield like Sigourney is a good example.

Sigourney is a two-runway airport with the strips in an "L" shape with the north-south runway being much more suitable for a Cherokee. The strip is 2,250 feet long and 165 feet wide. I landed from the north.

I met Nell Ruby and Sylvan VeVerka that day. Nell, the owner, manager, operator and chief mechanic of the field, was helping Sylvan VeVerka with his early model Cessna 172. Nell was a widow and easily in her early sixties. Sylvan was somewhat older, possibly in his late 70s.

The Cessna was a tricycle-geared airplane, but with a straight tail left over from the conventional geared 170 series. The airplane was built in 1956 and it certainly showed its age. The tail number was N6910A.

There was a distinct sadness between these two folks. In conversation, Sylvan revealed that he was taking his grandchildren for their last airplane ride this day. He was about to hand over the airplane to its new owner.

Sylvan said that he had owned the airplane since it was nearly new. He learned to fly in it. Sylvan had put a lot of hours on the airplane but those days had come to an end. His wife was ailing badly. She was suffering from some sort of dementia, it seems. Whenever Sylvan left for the airfield, she presumed that he was not coming back. He had to leave her in the care of a nurse while he was gone. Even then, she thought the worst. Obviously, Sylvan had to spend all of his time with his wife to avoid these complicated circumstances that caused his wife so much anxiety and discomfort. He was forced to say good-bye to 10 Alpha. The airplane had to go.

He had a buyer, but Sylvan did not share his name with me. It mattered not. This was a day for Sylvan, his grandkids and the Cessna that he had loved for so many years.

I stayed around that morning to see Sylvan fly N6910A for the last time. As usual, I had my 35-mm camera with me and took a few shots of his last flight. Once Sylvan was gone, I said my good-byes to Nell and set off for Pella. My mind stayed at Sigourney for a long time, however. Both Sylvan and Nell remained in my thoughts.

Naturally, I had two copies made of the pictures and sent a set to Sylvan in care of Nell Ruby. Sylvan replied with a touching note. On occasion, I look at the note and it brings back fond memories. It was a great trip.

I thought the Sigourney story was done at this point, but I was wrong. Just over a year later, the Experimental Aviation Association (EAA) magazine for January 1997 arrived at our house. On the cover of that issue was Sylvan's Cessna 172. It now belongs to Joel Miller of Sollen, Iowa. He was the gentleman who bought the airplane from Sylvan VeVerka. He brought insight to the VeVerka Cessna 172 story. This is, in part, what he wrote in the January 1997 article for "Sport Aviation":

> I started learning to fly in 1977 and almost immediately got to know Sylvan VeVerka, from Kazoo, Iowa. Sylvan was in his late 60s at the time and was also learning to fly, but he was learning in his own 1956 Cessna 172.
>
> After Sylvan got his license, he liked to have others fly with him, so he and I spent a lot of time in his airplane together. I guess I fell in love with specific 172.
>
> I think the first time I asked Sylvan if he would sell me his airplane was in 1978. But, he was too much in love with it to let me have it. We'd fly it together, but no matter how many times I asked, he wouldn't sell.
>
> Finally, in 1994, Sylvan agreed to sell me the airplane. I was excited and, with some help from my Dad and the support of my wife, we wound up with our very own 1956 Cessna 172. It was special to me for a

couple of reasons, including the fact that I felt as if
Sylvan was passing his treasure on to me.'

I suppose this story is not done. Eventually, it is easy to expect
to see N6910A as the subject of yet someone else's affections. In the
meantime, enjoy your Cessna 172, Joel!

#190 Pella, Iowa   Pella Municipal Airport
Type: Paved Identifier: PEA   September 18, 1994

#191 Grinnell, Iowa   Grinnell Regional Airport
Type: Paved Identifier: GGI   September 18, 1994

#192 Marshalltown, Iowa   Marshalltown Municipal
Type: Paved Identifier: MIW   September 18, 1994

#193 Belle Plaine, Iowa   Belle Plaine Municipal Airport
Type: Paved Identifier: 0I4   September 18, 1994

#194 Vinton, Iowa   Veteran's Memorial Airport
Type: Paved Identifier: VTI   September 18, 1994

#195 Monticello, Iowa   Monticello Municipal Airport
Type: Paved Identifier: MXO   September 18, 1994

#196 Tipton, Iowa   Mathews Memorial Airport
Type: Paved Identifier: 8C4   September 18, 1994

#197 Davenport, Iowa   Davenport Municipal Airport
Type: Paved Identifier: DVN   September 18, 1994

#198 Clinton, Iowa   Clinton Municipal Airport
Type: Paved Identifier: CWI   September 18, 1994

#199 Allegan, Michigan   Padgham Field
Type: Paved Identifier: 35D   December 26, 1994

8369W GETS A NEW ENGINE

THE TRIP TO Allegan, Michigan was a proving flight for our new engine. For the previous several weeks, the airplane had been laid up while G & N Aviation re-built our Lycoming engine.

This was to be an almost-new engine. Prior to work, we made a number of decisions regarding the configuration of our power plant. During the teardown, mechanics found that the crankshaft and cam shaft suffered from light to moderate corrosion. Because these parts couldn't be reconditioned, they had to be replaced with new. We had opted for all new cylinders and pistons. All pumps were replaced with new. The old factory supplied-magnetos were a constant money drain. It seemed that some, ultra-expensive part had to be replaced at each annual inspection because of a factory issued Service Bulletin. So we replaced the old Bendix magnetos with a new pair of lighter, more economical to operate Slick magnetos.

The Cherokee 180 is a heavy nosed aircraft. Piper designed the airplane to accommodate a variety of engines in the airframe, most of them based on the much lighter O-320 power plant . The 180 horsepower O-360 engine is clearly the heaviest offering. As a consequence, the airplane suffers an air speed loss due to control surface aerodynamics needed to carry the extra nose weight. Whatever weight can be removed from the nose would help cruise speed. The new magnetos reduced the nose weight by three or four pounds. The starter motor, hung way out in front next to the propeller, was a 1940s design. It was not light. Technology now provides us with a much lighter starter motor with much more cranking speed. Midwest pilots always need more cranking power, especially in the winter. The 10-pound weight savings so far forward was Heaven sent.

We rounded out our overhaul with new engine mounts, a new firewall treatment, copper electrical cables to replace the original aluminum wire, and a propeller balancing. It is easy to see why the trip to Padgham Airport was more of a flight test than a visit. For this purpose, the cruise speed was kept at a high RPM level with occasional increases to 100% power for several minutes at a time. It was good flight.

Naturally, the folks at Padgham were interested in the new engine. Pulling the cowling off and letting the shiny new power plant sparkle (I thought it sparkled) in the sunlight. They seemed to approve of the overhaul. I would have loved to chat for a while, but it had been several months since last flying and I had to get back in the cold, January air.

#200 Peoria, Illinois
Type: Paved Identifier: 3MY
Mt. Hawley Auxiliary Airport
February 5, 1995

#201 Canton, Illinois
Type: Paved Identifier: CTK
Canton-Ingersoll Airport
February 5, 1995

#202 Pekin, Illinois
Type: Paved Identifier: C15
Pekin Municipal Airport
February 5. 1995

#203 Bloomington, Illinois
Type: Class D Identifier: BMI
Bloomington-Normal Airport
February 5, 1995

#204 Benton Harbor, Michigan
Type: Paved Identifier: BEH
Southwest Michigan Regional
February 18, 1995

#205 Holland, Michigan
Type: Paved Identifier: HLM
Park Township Airport
February 18, 1995

#206 Sparta, Michigan
Type: Paved Identifier: 8D4
Sparta Airport
February 18, 1995

#207 Big Rapids, Michigan
Type: Paved Identifier: 77D
Roben Hood Airport
February 18, 1995

#208 Ionia, Michigan
Type: Paved Identifier: Y70
Ionia County Airport
February 18, 1995

#209 Hastings, Michigan
Type: Paved Identifier: 9D9
Barry County Airport
February 18, 1995

FLIGHT TO GUN LAKE

OUR VISIT TO Hastings was a two airplane trip. Accompanying us was Bob and Dorothy Smith in their Piper Archer 52Y. Along with Bob and Dot was Dorothy's brother and wife. We joined 52Y about 100 miles from our field in Elkhart, Indiana. We agreed to fly in loose formation. That is, if one would call flying about a half a mile from each other 'formation flying.' Bob was cautious and I was afraid.

We were picked up at the airport by the owner of Water's Edge Restaurant. The restaurant is on Gun Lake, about 20 miles away. The owner is also a pilot having owned a Lake Buccaneer for several years. He sold the airplane to "make a down payment on the restaurant."

The timing of our trip demanded that we have the brunch offering. The food was outstanding, with several chefs contributing to the menu. My favorite was the pastry chef who knew she had an appreciative diner in me. Prudence (but not good taste) prohibited sampling more than two of her creations.

On the trip home, we flew in loose formation for only a few miles. Bob and his family went on to Elkhart, which is really quite close, and Nancy and I headed west to Gary Regional Airport, with yet another memory.

#210 Plainwell, Michigan
Type: Paved Identifier: 61D

Plainwell Municipal Airport
February 18, 1995

#211 Berrien Springs, Michigan
Type: Paved Identifier: C20

Andrews University
February 19, 1995

#212 Three Rivers, Michigan
Type: Grass Identifier: HAI

Dr. Haines Municipal Airport
February 19, 1995

#213 Coldwater, Michigan
Type: Paved Identifier: D96

Branch County Memorial
February 19, 1995

#214 Charlotte, Michigan   Fitch H. Beach Municipal Airport
Type: Paved Identifier: 07G   February 19, 1995

"SWEET CHARLOTTE"

LISTENING TO RADIO traffic prior to landing at Charlotte, the odd pronunciation of the name "Charlotte" became awkwardly noticeable. It was being pronounced not as "Char-let", but as "Char-lot" with the "Char" portion as char-coal and heavy emphasis on the first syllable. This seemed to be very peculiar. Upon landing and talking with some of the locals, I got the story.

The land on which the original village of Charlotte was laid out was purchased from the government by George W. Barnes in 1832. Because of its location at the geographical center of Eaton County, he named it Eaton Centre. Within a few years, Barnes sold his land to Mr. Edmund B. Bostwick. A letter from Bostwick to his business agent in 1835, however, indicated he preferred to name the settlement "Charlotteville" or "'Charlotte" after his newly married bride.

Bostwick's wife was very much loved by friends, neighbors and many of the citizens, but she was very shy. Even though she expressed to all of them that she was very uncomfortable with the town being named after her, no one wanted to change it. Finally, with pressure on her husband, he moved to change the town's name. However, the Village of Charlotte County Board of Supervisors liked the idea of honoring Mrs. Bostwick and wanted to keep the name and agreed that they would try and ease sweet Charlotte's anxiety by altering the way they pronounced it ever so slightly. Charlotte graciously accepted the change. So, to this day, all flight traffic announcements to 07G are Charlot.

#215 Holland, Michigan   Tulip City Airport
Type: Paved Identifier: BIV   February 19, 1995

#216 South Haven, Michigan   South Haven Area Airport
Type: Paved Identifier: 0D1   February 19, 1995

#217 Dowagiac, Michigan   Dowagiac Municipal Airport
Type: Paved Identifier: C91   March 25, 1995

#218 Jenison, Michigan   Riverview Airport
Type: Paved Identifier: 08C   March 25, 1995

#219 Fremont, Michigan   Fremont Municipal Airport
Type: Paved Identifier: 3FM   March 25, 1995

#220   White Cloud, Michigan   White Cloud Airport
Type: Paved Identifier: 42C   March 25, 1995

#221 Lakeview, Michigan   Griffith Field airport
Type: Paved Identifier: 13C   March 25, 1995

#222 Muskegon, Michigan   Muskegon County Airport
Type: Class D Identifier: MKG   March 25, 1995

JONATHON YOUNG GETS WINGS

JONATHON YOUNG WAS 12 years old when we went on this trip. It was his first time in an airplane. Jonathon would come with me to the hangar to help clean on many occasions. This was his exposure to pilots, airplanes and airport activity. His eyes were wide open during the first of these visits. Then we made short hops in the airplane. We didn't go far; probably 35- or 40-mile trips. He became accustomed to what was going on, so it was time to go on a long cross-country flight. Now he was going to be gone all day, which meant about six or seven hours of flying time. He looked forward to it.

We picked the west coast of Lower Michigan for our travels. Eventually, we called on five airports, which were all interesting. The important issue here is that Jonathon became totally aware of the sport of flying. He was comfortable in an airplane and showed no fear of flying. Jonathon was short, so looking out the windshield was difficult for him, even with cushions to prop him up. It wasn't long before he acquired a real feel for airplane control.

Jonathon was the highlight of each visit. Pilots seem to look upon youngsters like Jon as the heirs of sport aviation. Everyone made a profound fuss over him. All wished him the good fortune of becoming a good pilot.

All of his experiences were gathered on video tape. He showed this tape to his schoolmates at "show and tell," with no small degree of pride and accomplishment. He'll be a good pilot when he grows up.

#223 Sturgis, Michigan   Kirsch Municipal Airport
Type: Paved Identifier: IRS   May 6, 1995

#224 Niles, Michigan   Jerry Tyler Memorial Airport
Type: Paved Identifier: 3TR   May 26, 1995

N8369W BECOMES A COVER GIRL

THE LITTLE CHEROKEE achieved a little notoriety while we were together. Shortly after her 30th birthday in 1995, the Cherokee as depicted in "Lunar Visit" was selected as the Piper of the Month by the Cherokee Pilots' Association. The following is a reproduction of the article that accompanied the cover photo. The introduction was written by Terry Lee Rogers.

'Cherokees are much loved by their owners; some are even treated like family members. But the only real reason for the breed is transportation, and this month's first Piper of the Month is a good example of how useful they can be.

'N8369W is shown on this month's cover. No, she actually did not fly to the moon, but the 'doctored' photo is meant to convey the message that Cherokees are good for going to lots and lots of places. Bob Hechlinski of Dyer, Indiana, writes:

'When we found N8369W, she was in the last stages of a three-way partnership. The story is familiar: One member lost his physical, another had passed away and the last was very busy with his maturing family and career, which preempted his flying hobby. Nonetheless, the airplane was exceptional. Not only did it have reasonable airframe and engine time, but she spent all her life on the ground under cover of a hangar. The paint and outer skin condition, therefore, were in excellent condition.

'She is a 1965 180 C with tail number N8369W. She is a relatively low-time airplane with only 2,600 hours on the airframe and 700 hours on the engine.

'When I bought the plane in 1989, the old avionics presented the first action item. We installed some new (and one not so new) avionics. From the top down, it reads like this: an Arnav R-30 loran with data base, a Narco COM-810, a Narco 12D Nav-Com, a Narco AT-150 encoding transponder and a Narco NAV 122 navigation unit including marker beacons, localizer and glide slope.

We kept the old Bendix ADF unit, as it still works. The compass got a well-earned overhaul and we replaced some gyro instruments with more modern versions. In other words, we now have a fully instrument-capable airplane. That is, of course, if we use the Loran's distance measuring feature as a DME.

'The interior had lived a full life, however. With the help of folks at Airtex and my loving wife, N8369W now has a new interior. The seats were rebuilt and the entire interior was done over in a great looking light gray, wool fabric.

'It seems that every little item on the airplane could stand improvement. Everything we did to the plane made it look better. This includes the new stainless steel hardware, the bright and shiny wheels and brakes, all of the paint touch-ups that we have affected, and so on. Because my wife is an integral part of this pseudo-restoration, it has made the whole business of recreational flying much more acceptable to her.

'Because we had turned the aircraft into a viable IFR platform, I restarted my instrument training. I finally got my instrument rating in December of last year.

'As a Cessna trained and bred pilot, the change to a Piper was a skeptical move. The power, speed and stability of the aircraft were enough to convert me in an instant. It's a decision that I won't ever regret.

'Prior Cherokees of the Month have been very high quality aircraft. The ones that impress me more than others are the aircraft that have a part in extraordinary accomplishments.

'It is an easy thing to do. After all, the first thing I told you about is <u>what I did to our airplane</u>. The better story is what the airplane, a device of transportation, convenience and adventure, <u>does for us.</u>

'When we first considered buying our Cherokee, there was a question in my wife's mind about what we would do with it. Simply flying around did not seem to justify the purchase. There had to be some specific reason to buy the airplane.

'All wives ask these type questions; all husbands are obligated to come up with an answer. The answer is usually the first thing that comes into a husband's head. My response is that I would fly our Cherokee to every airport in the state of Indiana!

'I don't know why that came to mind. It had not occurred to me before, but now it was the reason to buy an airplane. Now, I had to see what I had let myself in for.

'In checking the Indiana sectionals, the AOPA Airport Directory and the Flight Guide, I came to the conclusion that there were one hundred and eleven airports in the state. Starting in March of 1990, I began to set out routes that would take me around the state on day-long sojourns.

'These routes would allow me to visit three or four airports on a given Saturday or Sunday. The routes covered as much of Indiana as was possible during the day. That meant over flying many airports, only to catch them later.

'At each airport, I would spend as much time as possible visiting with the folks there. I have at least one fascinating human interest or airplane story for every stop.

'The friendships that started during this escapade are unbelievable. I still write letters back and forth to many people I met. I continue to visit others periodically. One couple stopped by to say hello when they passed over Northwest Indiana.

'It was great adventure and I encourage everybody to do it in their home state. It was such a great adventure that I am going to do it again.

'In conducting this odyssey, over 200 flying hours were logged and over 25,000 miles were flown. Winter flying proved no obstacle, but the hot days of summer forced us higher and higher as the temperatures on deck began to approach the upper 90s.

'There is a complete photographic history of the project. I have at least one color photo in an album to represent each airport. As you might suspect, I go through this album from time to time.

'The greatest day of the whole journey was the final stop in Indiana and that took place on July 20, 1991. In applying for permission to land at Grissom Air Force Base, I ran into some paperwork issues, but most confounding was the problem of Desert Storm. Grissom's Air Refueling Wing was the principal player in aerial refueling during the pounding we gave the Iraqis.

'Patience proved to be the saver of the day, however. Finally, in early July, Grissom granted me permission but they were quite specific about when I should land. It had to be at 12:10 p.m. on the 20th of July. The reason they were so exact was that my landing would kick off their annual Open House and Air Show.

'The Air Show included a demonstration flight of the A-10 Warthogs, Air Force One, KC-135s, the F-117 Stealth fighter, and the Air Force Thunderbirds. I was ecstatic. Naturally, I cooperated with them in every regard.

'My wife and I flew into Grissom together and we were right on time and right on cue. Thankfully, the landing was a greaser. The Wing Commander, Colonel Russell Rinklin presented my wife and me with an engraved lithograph of the Thunderbirds to commemorate the event. We reciprocated with a gift for Colonel Rinklin.

'We gave him a rendering of the accomplishments of Octave Chanute. This print documented Chanute's work with gliders in Gary, Indiana during the turn of the century. (Terry, did you know that Octave Chanute coined the word 'aviation' while testing his gliders in Indiana? Save that for Trivial Pursuit.)

'Afterward, Nancy and I joined the Colonel and his guests in his reviewing box to watch the rest of the show.

'N8369W is a special airplane. Throughout the four years in which she took me around Indiana and surrounding states, she proved to be a totally predictable and reliable aircraft. At least a dozen people have flown safely with us in our Tour de Hoosier."

'Furthermore, we began receiving considerable radio and television coverage after we visited 80 or 85 airports. The Associated Press picked up the story for distribution. I understand that one report was even presented on CNN news. All in all, it was rather heady stuff

'In the midst of this escapade, I have picked up partial ownership of the title, 'The Hoosier Pilot.' Certainly, I have a love for flying and the State of Indiana. So if I am the Hoosier Pilot, then N8369W is the HOOSIER CHEROKEE.'"[5]

#225 Freeport, Illinois   Albertus Airport
Type: Paved Identifier: FEP   June 17, 1995

#226 Monroe, Wisconsin   Monroe Municipal Airport
Type: Paved Identifier: EFT   June 17, 1995

#227 Mineral Point, WI   Iowa County Airport
Type: Paved Identifier: MRJ   June 17, 1995

#228   Lone Rock, Wisconsin   Tri-Co Regional Airport
Type: Paved Identifier: LNR   June 17, 1995

---

5 Piper Owners' Magazine, Issue #172 October 1st, 1995. Terry Lee Rogers, Editor\Publisher

#229 Boscobel, Wisconsin   Boscobel Municipal Airport
Type: Paved Identifier: OVS   June 17, 1995

#230 Praire du Chien, WI   Praire Du Chien Municipal
Type: Paved Identifier: PDC   June 17, 199 5

#231 Cassville, Wisconsin   Cassville Municipal Airport
Type: Paved Identifier: C74   June 17, 1995

#232 Platteville, Wisconsin   Grant County Airport
Type: Paved Identifier: PVB   June 17, 1995

#233 Dubuque, Iowa   Dubuque Regional Airport
Type: Class D Identifier: DBQ   July 1, 1995

PRETTY AND SHY

GETTING THE AIRPLANE prepped for a trip includes a good washing of the windshields and leading edges of the wings and tail. This is easily performed at Griffith Aviation where they always have a garden hose ready. Prior to leaving for Iowa this day, I taxied over for the cleaning.

At the FBO there was also a young family of four getting ready to leave. One of them was a little girl was of about five. She was pretty and shy. I tried to get her to smile but she kept hiding her face behind her mother's dress. She never did smile back at me, but that wasn't for of the lack of effort on my part. Anyway, it was time to leave for Dubuque.

I flew VFR to Dubuque and we found out that the young family back in Griffith was also flying to Dubuque. We never talked to them but we recognized their airplane's tail number during several radio communications approaching Dubuque Regional Airport. We landed just behind their airplane. Not unexpectedly, we tied down next to them on the Dubuque ramp. As soon as they got out of their airplane, I tried to get the little girl to smile again. She had no idea how I got there. The look on her face was complete surprise and bewilderment. And, I finally got the smile I was after.

#234 Manchester, Iowa
Type: Paved Identifier: C27

Manchester Municipal
July 1, 1995

#235 Independence, Iowa
Type: Paved Identifier: IIB

Independence Municipal
July 1, 1995

#236 Oelwein, Iowa
Type: Paved Identifier: OLZ

Oelwein Municipal Airport
July 1, 1995

#237 West Union, Iowa
Type: Paved Identifier: 3Y2

George L. Scott Airport
July 1, 1995

#238 Decorah, Iowa
Type: Paved Identifier: DEH

Decorah Municipal Airport
July 1, 1995

#239 Caldonia, Minnesota
Type: Paved Identifier: CHU

Houston County Airport
July 1, 1995

#240 Reedsburg, Wisconsin
Type: Paved Identifier: C35

Reedsburg Municipal Airport
July 1, 1995

BOB & EMMY LASKOWSKI

THE SOIREE OF July 1ˢᵗ promised to be a good one. Midsummer days were long and I had an early start. The tanks were full, but the windshield needing to be 'de-bugged, so I taxied over to the FBO for service. As soon the airplane swung around in front of the office, a dear friend, Bob Laskowski, stepped out to say hello.

Bob explained how he had been putting in a lot of overtime, working 12 and 14 hour days and six days a week. This is a tough schedule for anyone. Bob was a good and honest man. It can be believed that he puts his all into his work. Nothing is held back. However, enough is enough. Saturday was coming and he needed to get airborne. A one-hour rental was not going to be enough.

He asked where I was off to and how long the trip would be. He wanted to know if this were going to be a solo affair or if I wanted company. Since company is always welcome and Bob is always a lot of fun, I asked him to join me. He accepted immediately.

I warned Bob that my trips are not short hops. That in a given day, seven to eight airports would be visited, and it would take about six to eight hours of flying and, by the time we returned home, we would peel ourselves out of the plane. He still agreed to go.

It was a great trip because Bob is great company. We ended up landing at six airports in Iowa, one in Minnesota and finishing at Reedsburg, Wisconsin. We had flown for almost seven hours. We both loved every minute of it.

Bob and his wife Emily (Emmy, for short) were favorites at Griffith Airport. Some would say they were "fixtures'" at the airport. They managed to endear themselves to all the pilots and airport bums. Each weekend, Emily would bake something or cook a pot of lunch for anyone who stopped by the field. On one occasion, they made cupcakes with white icing and then wrote the tail numbers of all the planes hangared at Griffith airport. Bob and Emmy touched the hearts of all the pilots at the field and they were much loved.

Bob is an electrician by trade and Emmy clerked at a local super market. They had a dream to go into business for themselves.

Specifically, they wanted to open a Subway sandwich shop in Hobbs, New Mexico and they followed that dream. We lost good friends when they left town. Before leaving, we had a party to honor them. At the close, they were given a plaque which read:

"Bob and Emmy,

We were always first in your thoughts. You will always be #1 in our hearts."

The Pilots and Flyers of 05C"

#241 Mansfield, Ohio   Lahm Regional Airport
Type: Class D Identifier: BJJ   July 8, 1995

THE DOUBLE CLICK

NO MATTER HOW long I live, I will always remember my flight into and out of Mansfield, Ohio. Mansfield was to be my first stop on an eight-airport journey to Ohio on July 8th, 1996.

The weather for the day was a scattered cloud layer at 3,000 feet with tops at 4,000. A big high pressure area was moving in, so the cloud cover would soon dominate the Midwest, especially Indiana and Ohio. The first leg of my trip would be IFR at 5,000 feet. The rest of the day would be VFR flying. The route would be all under radar contact with handoffs from South Bend then to Fort Wayne, with Toledo handling me all the way into Mansfield.

Nowadays, 30% or 40% of the controllers are female, so this isn't a surprise to any pilot. All the controllers that July day were male, except for the tower at Mansfield. About 15 miles out, I was told to contact Mansfield tower on 119.8 kHz. I was pleasantly surprised by an extraordinarily beautiful female voice. She was handling about six or eight aircraft at the time. During these conversations, I was impressed by how feminine and alluring her voice and demeanor were. Coupled with smoothness and professionalism, it was at the point of being sensuous. It was a pleasure to listen to her.

I really believed that the amount of inbound and outbound radio traffic was higher than the VFR conditions required. I believe that it was just so the pilots could talk with this woman or just to hear her talk. There were requests for wind and temperature checks. The conditions were light and variable. Not only that, she handled ground traffic also.

While getting refueled, I asked the line man about her and he just smiled and said that she was one of Mansfield's more pleasant assets. A lot of pilots are taken by her sweet voice.

About an hour later, I was back in the plane, ready for my trip to Wooster airport. She was still on duty. Through all the pre-flight duties, I smiled just listening to her. She had a soft and sexy voice. She cleared my taxi to the northwest end of runway 14.In that it is a 9,001 foot runway, I requested a run-up on Taxiway E and she approved the short cut. There was more chatter on the frequency. I don't know who those guys thought they were kidding. Being ready at "E", I got her clearance for takeoff.

After settling into climb to altitude on my departure heading, I called a few minutes later: "Mansfield tower, Cherokee 8369 Whiskey is five to the east. Ma'am, before changing frequencies, I must say that you have one of the finest radio voices I have ever heard."

Her response was telling. She gave me the pilot's shorthand for "Acknowledge." All I heard was the mike switch go "click-click"! That was the last I heard from her.

#242 Wooster, Ohio   Wayne County Airport
Type: Paved Identifier: BJJ   July 8, 1995

#243 Millersburg, Ohio   Holmes County Airport
Type: Paved Identifier: 10G   July 8, 1995

#244 Mt.Vernon, Ohio   Knox County Airport
Type: Paved Identifier: 4I3   July 8, 1995

#245 Mt.Vernon, Ohio   Wyncoop Airport
Type: Grass Identifier: 6G4   July 8, 1995

THE BANDITS OF WYNCOOP!

THE AIRPORT AT Mt. Vernon, Ohio has a hard surfaced, 5000-foot runway with headings 10 and 28. It is the Knox County Airport. It is non-towered with a great FBO on the field. I visited there on July 8th, 1996.

Like most pilots, I made all my radio calls: 10 miles out, five miles out and upon entering the downwind leg. All of a sudden, a blur of yellow passed below my right wing. It was a Cub less than 100 feet below me going somewhat the opposite direction. It gave me quite a start. The rest of the landing was uneventful.

I met some good people at Knox County. During our conversations, I mentioned that I was a little surprised by the closeness of the Cub while in the pattern. Immediately, the FBO people became upset. It seems that the flyers at a little grass strip a couple of miles north were notorious. The airport is Wyncoop Field. It seems that there was a long history of distrust and mutual disrespect between Knox County and Wyncoop. Knox County pilots complained that the Wyncoop fliers misused the common airspace, they were disreputable, they didn't use radios while in the landing air space and, overall, they were just in the way. Wyncoop sounded like my kind of place!

I jumped back into the Piper and maneuvered into position a downwind leg targeting the east runway at Wyncoop. Immediately, I realized that I was second in sequence with a yellow and red Aeronca ahead of me. As we both came onto a long final, it was apparent that there were two runways with an east heading and they formed a "V". The leg of the "V" that was southernmost was shorter and narrower. The other leg of the "V" slanted off a little to the north of east. It was wider and longer. Both were pretty, with lots of trees and rolling terrain around them. The Aeronca landed on the shorter runway and came to a quick stop. While he was turning on the runway, I continued on final to the longer strip. The grass was well cut and the runway smooth and flat.

Taxiing in, I saw there more than a dozen individual hangars around the property. I spotted some men standing around what could have been an old flight office. The old flight office, many of the hangars and some of the pilots there had some years on them. Only a couple of hangars still had doors, and all of the pilots were carrying a little extra weight. This was an old-time field.

I met four or five of the guys and really enjoyed the conversation and stories. Evidently, this group of men and the field in general catered to older airplanes; tail draggers, mostly. It was charming and cozy. The surroundings would have warmed the heart of any pilot.

Joining in the discourse, I mentioned that it was surprise to see the two runways in a "V" configuration. I told these men that while the Aeronca ahead of me was using the shorter strip, I felt more comfortable on the longer runway. I didn't expect a response. I was simply stating my preference. One of the fellows stepped toward me. He was a big guy, maybe 250 pounds and 5' 11". He moved a little closer, as if to share some deep secret or little known fact. He had this sly little grin on his face and he squinted at me while he talked. In a low, knowing voice he said: "That short field there is for us tail dragger guys. The longer one is for you boys with those new aluminum jobbies."

| #246 Mt. Gilead, Ohio | Morrow County Airport |
| Type: Paved   Identifier: 4I9 | July 8, 1995 |

| #247 Bellefontaine, Ohio | Bellefontaine Airport |
| Type: Paved   Identifier: 7I7 | July 8, 1995 |

| #248 Lima, Ohio | Allen County Airport |
| Type: Paved   Identifier: AOH | July 8, 1995 |

#249 Monon, Indiana   Gutwein International
Type: Grass   Identifier: Private   August 31, 1995

#250 Jackson, Michigan   Reynolds Airport
Type: Class D Identifier: JXN   September 2, 1995

#251 Gregory, Michigan   Richmond Field
Type: Grass   Identifier: 69G   September 2, 1995

#252 Howell, Michigan   Livingston County Airport
Type: Paved   Identifier: OZW   September 2, 1995

#253 Brighton, Michigan   Brighton Field
Type: Paved   Identifier: 45G   September 2, 1995

#254 New Hudson, Michigan   New Hudson Airport
Type: Paved   Identifier: Y47   September 2, 1995

#255 Fowlerville, Michigan   Maple Grove Airport
Type: Grass   Identifier: 65G   September 2, 1995

#256 Mason, Michigan   Mason - Jewett Field
Type: Paved   Identifier: TEW   September 2, 1995

#257 East Lansing, Michigan   Skyway Estates Airport
Type: Grass Identifier: 60G   September 2, 1995

ONE SWEET AIRPORT

SKYWAY IS LOCATED dead south of Lansing and is a grass field that is very easy to overlook. In fact, I had to remind myself to include it on the day's soiree. In my over flight of the field, nothing looked cramped or crowded, so it would be an easy landing.

The first thing that became apparent is this was no cheap or decrepit airport. The grass was like a putting green. Whoever designed and built this airport put in some expensive grass. Furthermore, it was plenty wide at 150 feet and very level; what pilots refer to as "pool table smooth.'" No surprises on this strip.

The air strip has public access but is surrounded by private homes. This is very unusual, in that these Fly-In strips are almost always private or limited access.

I met one of the owners at the field, but I have since misplaced his name. I am truly sorry for that. He was very kind and generous with his time and his hospitality. He showed me his beautiful Beech Bonanza in its hangar which was attached to his gorgeous home. Along the inside was the uncompleted fuselage of a Bede Jet; I believe it was a BD-9. Anyway, it was the model that was suspected to be a questionable design and was taken out of circulation. The man who owned this Bonanza and BD-9 bought his plans before the retraction of the BD-9.

I was shown the rest of the neighborhood - what a neighborhood it was. No homes here less than a million dollars. Everything was spacious and well planned. Every home, hangar, car and airplane was neat, clean and gleaming.

Behind the homes and between the run way was a generous amount of land. Each home included two acres of land adjacent to the runway. Why? A place to park the airplanes of visiting friends, of course!

#258 Yates City, Illinois   Tri County Airport
Type: Grass   Identifier: 2C6   September 4, 1995

#259 McComb, Illinois   Smith Field
Type: Grass   Identifier: C10   September 4, 1995

#260 McComb , Illinois   McComb Municipal Airport
Type: Paved Identifier: MQB   September 4, 1995

#261 Carthage, Illinois   Martin Airport
Type: Grass Identifier: I48   September 4, 1995

#262   Rushville, Illinois   Schuy-Rush Airport
Type: Grass Identifier: 5KY   September 4, 1995

#263   Mt. Sterling, Illinois   Brown County Flyers Club
Type: Paved Identifier: I63   September 4, 1995

#264   Pittsfield, Illinois   Pittsfield-Penstone Airport
Type: Paved Identifier: PPQ   September 4, 1995

#265 Jacksonville, Illinois   Jacksonville Municipal Airport
Type: Paved Identifier: IJX   September 4, 1995

The September 4th, 1995 trip took place with Bob Laskowski as a passenger and safety pilot. We managed to get a little hood time in during some the longer legs. It was a day for friendship and the pervasive enjoyment of flying. We went to eight fields, half grass and half paved. Most of them were bundled together geographically. In fact, the two McComb fields are across town from each other. There wasn't a lot of navigational skill required for this cross country flying.

#266 Schneider, Indiana   Huber's Farm
Type: Grass Identifier: Private   September 8, 1995

#267 DeMotte, Indiana   DeMotte Airport
Type: Grass Identifier: Private   September 8, 1995

#268 San Pierre, Indiana   Harrington's Farm
Type: Grass Identifier: Private   September 8, 1995

ONE SHORT RUNWAY

IT WAS DURING this trip that I discovered the pleasure of visiting farm fields. A fellow pilot, Ray Edling, accompanied me. Ray has been busy building an RV-6A. At some point in time, he thought the building was taking too long and he needed to fly in the interim so he bought a Piper Arrow. It was an earlier model with 180 horsepower. The RV-6A is still progressing, and Ray is also flying on a regular basis. We flew together often.

The three airports we visited started with a landing at Huber's Turf Farm. I met Wayne Huber when he was taking flying lessons on the grass strip at Lowell. He was an older man when he started to fly and he wasn't very far into his training when he decided that an airplane purchase was eminent. I suppose that he also knew which part of his turf farm he was going to set aside for his private strip. Regardless, he is obviously getting good use from his plane and his private airport.

Our second stop was DeMotte, Indiana. This is a field with a strange history. From one sectional issue to the next, we don't know if it is going to be listed as "public access" or "private". When we were there, it was public access. The north-south field is good sized at 2,200 feet, and has mature trees at the north end. These trees are well above the 50-foot FAA standard so a north departure has to be accurately calculated. A south departure has to contend with power lines along the south edge of the field.

The third and last field was the most memorable. I had called the Harrington's for permission to land during the week. They had an idea that I would be there on this Sunday afternoon. We spotted the field (a north-south 2,000-foot grass strip) and made a left hand pattern. The approach was a little warm, so it needed a side slip to lose some altitude. Altitude on approach was critical because of the tree line was right at the threshold of the runway. We got past the tree line and began a flare, but we were too long. I applied full power, raised the flaps and went around.

Paul had warned me about the tree line being a problem. He cut the trees several years ago to form a notch, but they had grown back considerably since then. The next approach was substantially slower and lower. We actually made our final approach between the trees tops which means the trees were about 20 feet off the wing tips. It's a wonder we didn't stub the wheels on the treetops beneath us. Once on the ground, there was no space for a rollout. Brakes came on immediately and we were able to turn back with only a few feet to spare.

Paul and Leona Harrington were waiting for us. They were a happy and content couple in their 70's. They had their arms around each other and were smiling as we taxied up to them. A great welcoming party!

They had seen us go around and, as a form of apology; I told them that I came in with too much speed and altitude for the warm day. I told them that the length of the field was surprising. The landing and the roll-out seemed to indicate a field much shorter than the 2,200 feet that the field is listed, but then, I merely attributed the sensation to the high temperature and humidity. The pilot's enemy, density altitude, had gotten to me. Or, so I thought.

No, that wasn't the case, explained Mr. Harrington. The field indeed used to be 2,200 feet, but he sold off some 600 or 700 feet of it several years back. The field really measures about 1,500 feet! With tall trees at both ends! Fifteen hundred feet is great for Cubs and Tri Pacers, but Cherokee 180s like 2,000 foot runways (or longer) much better.

This makes Harrington's Farm field, at 1,500 feet, the shortest runway on which I landed.

#269 Lowell, Indiana   Weitbrock's Farm
Type: Grass Identifier: Private   September 16, 1995

THE WEITBROCK'S OF LOWELL

LL THE TIME that I spent flying around different airports, I was told that Christine Weitbrock's's family had a private strip not more than 20 miles south of my home field. The Weitbrock's are nice people and it would be well worth my while to visit them.

Christine is a young Certified Flight Instructor at my home field of Griffith-Merrillville. She is a flight student in the great aviation program at Purdue University. This is the same program instituted by none other than Amelia Earhart. Christine is a pleasant and personable young lady. She is also very quiet.

It is easy to see where she got her poise and charm. Her parents are a sheer joy. Her father is a shift foreman at a nearby manufacturing plant and farms over 400 acres at the same time. Her mother is accommodating and energetic. "Charming" also describes her nicely.

Finding their field was difficult as it ran east and west like all the other land in the flatlands of Indiana. Furthermore, it is rough, narrow and short - which made it a perfect candidate for an actual short-field take-off. All of my landings on grass strips are done as if they were rough fields.

#270 Medaryville, Indiana   Sommer's Farm
Type: Grass Identifier: Private   September 23, 1995

LANDING TO GET DIRECTIONS

HE VISIT TO the private strip of Paul and Leona Sommers was great. A large family group saw me land. While I was immeasurably impressed by the Sommer family's hospitality and graciousness, there is a funny story how I got there.

First of all, Paul Sommers gave me directions to his farm. He told me the layout of the strip and what the prominent landmarks were including the fact that the hangar is silver and it is topped by an orange wind sock. After over flying the area for 20 minutes or more, I concluded that there were at least three likely spots that could be his strip; but I couldn't identify it conclusively. I went on to Winnimac for some help. That is where I ran into Kendrick.

Kendrick is a man in his sixties. He is a tall and imposing man who is obviously a farmer. I found out later that he, too, has a private farm strip north of the Summers' farm. When I asked him for directions, he pointed at the county road in front of the Winnimac airport and said:

> "Go on down the corner to the stop sign. At the stop
> sign, turn left until you get to a tee intersection and
> then turn right. Go about a mile and a half and Paul's
> farm is on the right."

I explained to Kendrick that I wasn't driving, but flying. I guess I successfully intimated that I needed different directions; something suitable for flying, not specifically for driving. Kendrick looked down at me and gave me a crooked little smile and a big, ole country wink and said....

> "Oh, in that case, go on down the corner to the stop
> sign. At the stop sign, turn left until you get to a tee
> intersection and then turn right. Go about a mile and
> a half and Paul's farm is on the right."

Kendrick skewered me right there on the spot. I had been "had." Then, with a twinkle, he continued to smile and told me to follow him. He promptly jumped into his blue and silver Stinson and flew to Sommer's farm. He made a low pass over the field with the little Cherokee in tow, indicating where I should land. I was right on his tail and followed his lead. Once, I taxied off the runway, I looked up and saw the blue Stinson coming over the field low and waving its wings!

#271 Knox, Indiana   Singleton's Farm
Type: Grass Identifier: Private   October 20, 1995

HAPPY ANNIVERSARY, WAYNE AND BERTHA!

THERE WAS ONLY one airport to visit on Sunday, October 20th, 1995. I had called ahead and received permission from Harry W. Singleton to drop in at his farm. They were only 30 or so miles from Griffith. Singleton's is an easy airport to spot. It is exactly north of the departure end of runway 18 in Knox, Indiana. I circled the field and ascertained that it was plenty wide and long enough and it seemed to be in excellent condition.

The landing must have been quiet. Mr. Singleton was immediately adjacent to the runway, but he was busy with his back to me and his head in his tractor. He never heard me roll past him. I taxied back to about where he was working.

He was a little surprised to see me there. We talked for a while and then we went to see my airplane. We wandered into a small shed alongside the runway. The place was full of farm equipment and paraphernalia. His 1947 Stinson 108-2 was also in this barn. Harry is one of the Flying Farmers and he told me that he often flew his dark red Stinson to their various Fly-Ins and breakfasts. I don't know much about Stinsons and even less about their Franklin engines, but from outside the cowling, it surely looked to be a heavy and bulky engine.

Before too long, Wayne's wife Bertha joined us. Wayne and Bertha are active in the local chapter of the Flying Farmers. They thought that I would be good candidate to join so they gave me some literature and a membership application. They held hands all the time that I was there.

Most importantly, however, was the fact that this was their 50th wedding anniversary. Wayne and Bertha were going to have dinner with some family later on in the afternoon. I was fortunate to be there. One of the pictures I got that day was Wayne giving Bertha a 50th wedding anniversary kiss. They are a cute couple! I wished them many more happy years.

#272 Kingsford Heights, IN   Shamrock Turf Farm
Type: Grass   Identifier: Private   November 22, 1995

#273 Momence, Illinois   Shamrock Turf Farm
Type: Grass   Identifier: Private   November 22, 1995

A GENTLE, SOOTHING DAY

THE VISIT TO the two Shamrock Turf Farms was a continuation of my visits to private fields. It was a wet and rainy day with low ceilings, but acceptable visibility - a good day to fly.

The coolness of the past few days and the gentle rains turned the grass and cropland a brilliant green. The blue-gray skies blended gently with my prevailing mood of quiet relaxation. Let's go flying.

The two fields were as beautiful to land upon as they were to look at. The Shamrock farms are famous for their Kentucky Blue Grass. From the air, they truly have a blue hue that is breath taking. The farms are terraced, to be easily harvested. That made for a pool table smooth landing strip. The quietness of the evening and the coolness of the air made for a pensive and reflective moment. Flying makes possible such retreats.

#274 Syracuse, Indiana   Wawasee Airport
Type: Grass   Identifier: Private   November 25, 1995

#275 Waterloo, Indiana   Walker-Rowe Field
Type: Grass Identifier: 4C2   November 25, 1995

#276 Millersburg, Indiana   Zollinger's Farm
Type: Grass Identifier: Private   November 25, 1995

THE NICEST GUY IN AVIATION

A PRIVATE AIRPORT ON the Chicago Sectional called "Zollinger's Farm" is just a little southeast of Goshen, Indiana. It is a grass strip 2,000 feet long and runs east and west. There is a house and some low structures at each end of the field. It was at Zollinger's that Lowell Ferron entered my life.

Lowell is a most likeable guy. He is an easy guy with whom to get along. He listens well and is understanding. He and his lovely wife are retired and live in the A-frame house at the west end of the runway. Next to his house is a combination shop and hangar. Walking into the building hangar is a pilot's reading room. Here are thousands of flying and airplane magazines and books. It appears that these books and periodicals go back to the time just after World War II. A pilot would have no problem spending hour upon hour there. Walk through the inner door and you enter the hangar itself.

Lowell's plane is a Luscombe 8A. It is kept in absolutely pristine condition. He obviously dotes on this airplane. The hangar is just a little bit bigger than the plane. In fact, Lowell used to have a problem with people walking out of the anteroom into his hangar and walking right into the wing tip of N077K. The metal wing tip caused more than one forehead injury. Lowell hung a scrap piece of white cloth at the tip as a warning flag but the head bashing continued without abatement. Then he replaced it with a red rag thinking that it would be more noticeable. Despite the color change, his guests were so taken back by pristine Luscombe that they looked beyond the caution flag and banged their heads into the wing tip as they always had.

I did not have that problem. In fact, it was just the opposite. My attention was instantly drawn to the wing tip area. You see, Lowell no longer had a white cloth or a red rag hanging from the wing tip. They had been replaced with ladies pink panties. Lowell claims that since he made the change, no man has missed the "warning pennant.'"

I know very little about Lowell Ferron and his finances except to say that he appears to be a man of modest means. His home is not ostentatious. He has no outward evidence of great wealth. He tends to substantiate this by claiming that he "...knows how poor a man can be and still fly."

Lowell is a nice man. I still drop in on him from time to time. Whenever I call, he always has visitors.

#277 Remington, Indiana
Type: Grass Identifier: Private

Culp's Farm
December 3, 1995

#278 Rensselaer, Indiana
Type: Grass Identifier: Private

Gilmore's Farm
December 3, 1995

#279 Mount Carmel, Illinois
Type: Paved Identifier: AJG

Mount Carmel Municipal Airport
February 4, 1996

#280 Fairfield, Illinois
Type: Paved Identifier: 2H3

Fairfield Municipal Airport
February 4, 1996

#281 Flora, Illinois
Type: Paved Identifier: FOA

Flora Airport
February 4, 1996

#282   Olney, Illinois
Type: Paved   Identifier: OLY

Olney-Noble Airport
February 4, 1996

#283 Lawrenceville, Illinois
Type: Paved Identifier: LWV

Lawrenceville-Vincennes
February 4, 1996

THE STORY BEHIND VINCENNES INTERNATIONAL

THE AIRPORT ALSO was a military installation. At the end of WW II, it was given over to the City of Lawrenceville, Illinois. It was a huge task to take on 3,000 acres; so the State of Illinois and the State of Indiana entered into a joint agreement and the airport is now under a joint board. Because of an inquiry I had made to the city, I received a message authored by Howard Hatcher, Mayor of Vincennes. It explains as follows:

"The board consists of eight members. The governors of Illinois and Indiana each appoint one member, the mayors of Lawrenceville and Vincennes each appoint three members. This is just a brief memo on the airport makeup. The language in the agreement became the template for O'Hare airport at Chicago, in which the State of Indiana is involved. I hope this explains the airport being in Illinois.

Regards, Hatch" [6]

#284 Oaktown, Indiana   Ed-Air Airport
Type: Paved Identifier: OTN   February 4, 1996

  This southern part of Indiana is rich with WW II military history; especially air history. Oakton was one of the four auxiliary fields for George Army Air Force Base in Lawrenceville, Illinois. In Lawrenceville, pilots were trained for duty in light and medium bombers - mostly A-10s and B-25s - but there was a smattering of P-47 training done here as well.

  (In World War II, Republic Aviation could not produce P-47 fighters fast enough at their Long Island plant so they constructed a plant near Evansville, Indiana. The Evansville plant built a total of 110 P-47Ds. Some of the P-47 flights landing at Oakton were fresh out of that factory.)

6 Howard William Hatcher, Mayor of Vincennes E-mail of September 27th, 1999.

This was a large airport when it was finished in 1943. It had two hard surfaced runways one of which was 4,500' and the other 5,800 feet. It was officially named "Emison Auxiliary #2 Oakton, Indiana, Auxiliary AAF." At the end of WWII, the field was deactivated. The Oaktown field was sold to Bob Green by the government. Bob Green is the construction contractor who built all five of the Lawrenceville fields on a Cost Plus basis. After the war the name "Emison" was dropped and it became Green Airport for a few years.

It was a little difficult getting permission to land at Ed-Air Field. While everyone in the vicinity knew the owner was Bob Green but no one knew the correct phone number. After several attempts, I finally got in touch with his son. His son was reluctant to allow me to land. I tried to assure him that my visit would be simple; a landing in VFR conditions and a short stay only to allow time for a look around and to get a picture or two. He thought that would be innocent enough and finally consented.

Most of the airport has been broken up and carted off over the years. The principal runway, 18/36, still remains the active runway with all traces of the other strip gone. The outline of the 5/23 runway can still be seen from the air, however.

The entire length of the field was lined with earth moving equipment and construction vehicles. This field was devoid of any human presence when visited and that'is too bad because I wanted to talk with someone about the background of the field.

Today, there is very little aviation activity at Ed-Air Field and, as with other low use fields, this saddens me. Please note that the field still carries the identifier of OTN for Oakton.

#285 Robinson, Illinois		Robinson Field
Type: Paved Identifier: RSV		February 4, 1996
#286 Peoria, Illinois		Greater Peoria Regional Airport
Type: Class C Identifier: PIA		February 24, 1996
#287 Manito, Illinois		Mitchell Field
Type: Paved Identifier: C45		February 24, 1996

#288 Springfield, Illinois
Type: Class C Identifier: SPI

Springfield Capital Airport
February 24, 1996

#289 Palmyra, Illinois
Type: Paved Identifier: 5K1

Zelmer Memorial Airport
February 24, 1996

#290 Shelby, Illinois
Type: Paved Identifier: 2H0

Shelby County Airport
March 3, 1996

#291 Taylorville, Illinois
Type: Paved Identifier: TAZ

Taylorville Municipal Airport
March 3, 1996

#292 Litchfield, Illinois
Type: Grass Identifier: 3LF

Litchfield Municipal Airport
March 3, 1996

#293 Greenville, Illinois
Type: Grass Identifier: GRE

Greenville Municipal Airport
March 3, 1996

#294 Centralia, Illinois
Type: Paved Identifier: ENL

Centralia Municipal Airport
March 3, 1996

#295 Salem, Illinois
Type: Paved Identifier: SLO

Leckrone Field
March 3, 1996

#296 Effingham, Illinois
Type: Paved Identifier: 1H2

Effingham County Memorial A/P
March 3, 1996

#297 Sandwich, Illinois
Type: Paved Identifier: Private

Woodlake Landing
March 22, 1996

#298 Aurora, Illinois
Type: Class D Identifier: ARR

Aurora Municipal Airport
March 22, 1996

#299 Plainfield, Illinois
Type: Paved Identifier: 1C5

Clow International Airport
March 22, 1996

#300 Romeoville, Illinois   Lewis University Airport
Type: Paved Identifier: LOT   March 22, 1996

By Lauren B.Kraft, Staff Writer
The Sun (Romeoville, Illinois) 8/2/02

You can almost hear the rumbling of planes while viewing a pictorial history of the Lewis University Airport.

OK, so if you do hear the engines it's because they're revving up right outside the exhibit. But the pictorial history tells the story of planes that have taken off from Lewis since the 1930s; airplanes flown by Gene Littleford and his wing-walker wife, Cheryl Rae; airplanes shuttling down the runway with Navy pilots behind the wheel; and others flown by Albert Luke, the first aeronautics instructor at the school.

Members of the Experimental Aircraft Association Chapter 15, which is based at Lewis, have put more than two years into the exhibit. The group scoured the university's archives, interviewed former instructors and pilots and came up with 20 panels showing the big events in the university's history. Small vignettes accompany each 2 by 4 foot panel.

"We started out just making stories about every picture we had" said John Bruesch, Chapter 15 treasurer. "Eventually we realized there were a lot more people in the area involved in aviation than we had realized.

The Lewis University archives held more pictures than the group originally thought, so a large part of the job became figuring out which pictures were most relevant. The two rooms full of pictures made an imposing project, but some of the choices were obvious.

The earliest picture found was one from 1931 at the school groundbreaking for. Bishop Bernard Sheil of Chicago, who founded the Catholic Youth Organization, got the idea for the school in 1930. Because of good circumstances - 160 acres had recently been donated by the Fitzpatricks of Lockport - and with Sheil's determination the first university building was erected and ready for business by 1932.

With help from local Philanthropist Frank Lewis, Sheil opened the Lewis-Holy Name School of Aeronautics for high school students. "His dream was to do something, to alleviate the effects of the Depression on the youth of Chicago," Bruesch said.

The technical school housed and educated high school boys until about 1939, sending about 17 students through the program each year, Bruesch said. In 1940, the U.S. military became interested in the school as a base and eventually commandeered the building. "It was a matter of convenience," Bruesch said. After the war, the school was opened to young ladies as well.

The history of Lewis University's airport from the first ground-breaking to the present is illustrated in the exhibit. So are the stories of local aviators. Each of the panels was put together after lengthy interviews and extensive research.

"We dug. We talked to people who had been Lewis alumni, who had been teachers at Lewis. We talked to Brother Bernard (Rapp, the Lewis archivist)," Bruesch said. "He's been around hearing the stories."

Some of the stories conflicted, but often the legends were easy to choose for the exhibit because of their significant ' contributions to aviation in the area, Bruesch said.

The biggest contributor to the project was Frank Goebel, to whom the display is dedicated.

"He had the most amount of time invested in the research," said Chris Lawson, director of aviation. "He worked tirelessly."

In addition to the Lewis archives, Goebel wrote to and visited the Joliet and Lockport Historical Societies, and area Navy and Air Force museums, Lawson said.

While the display - and one prominently displayed panel - is dedicated to Goebel, the other Chapter 15 members worked hard as well, Lawson said.

"The EAA group is the largest group of aviation enthusiasts that we have at the airport," Lawson said. "They're always bending over backwards for the airport."

#301 Wauseon, Ohio   Fulton County Airport
Type: Paved Identifier: USE   March 23, 1996

#302 Adrian, Michigan   Lewanee County Airport
Type: Paved Identifier: ADG   March 23, 1996

#303 Belvidere, Illinois   Poplar Grove Airport
Type: Paved Identifier: C77   June 15, 1996

A GREAT GENERAL AVIATION AIRPORT

ONCE BELVIDERE AIRPORT was found, it was hard to get in. Once I got in it, it was hard to understand.
Once it was understood, it was hard to forget.

There were many sources used to identify all the airports surrounding my home base of Gary - Griffith, Indiana. One nearby field was Belvidere, Illinois. Unfortunately, this airport was not on the most current Chicago sectional map. Scour the map as I did, there simply was no airport with the name "Belvidere." There was, of course, another field that I didn't know about before, called Poplar Grove airport.

Approaching Poplar Grove presented a vexing problem. Someone was shooting touch-and-go's in a Pitts Special. This is not usually a problem, except his patterns were extremely tight and his air speed was much higher than mine. I had a hard time getting into sequence with him. Compounding the problem, he was not radio equipped. I spotted my chance while I was a little north and he was on a speedy downwind leg. I could follow him on base leg and try to land quickly and clear the field before he came around again. I made the necessary announcements and managed to pull it off. On final, it became clear that I wouldn't be a factor to him on his next circuit, as he was landing on the grass strip that paralleled the paved runway to the north. I landed without complicating his life any further.

Even as I was getting out of the airplane, it was apparent that this was a very lively General Aviation field. There was activity everywhere. Pilots were everywhere. Engines were running in several areas at the same time. There were no less than three pairs of students with flight instructors in the FBO preparing for their early morning flights. Amazingly enough, the students were; a young man, a "slightly older'" woman and a much older man - a strong cross sectional representation. All of this flying energy brought a smile to my face.

Also in the FBO was a list of about 15 or 20 rentable aircraft. Amongst them was a Piper J-3 Cub. As with the first airplane I flew in early training, this one had no electrical system and had to be hand propped. There was a Cessna 140 with metal wings as well. This was an encouraging sight as training airplanes with tail wheels are becoming a very rare and much missed sight at airports around the country.

Alongside one of the runways was the start of a housing project. Many airports developed in the United States are owned and operated by home owners as private fields. Poplar Grove airport would have a rather unique concept: home owners (replete with their own hangars) on a public access field. That development became known as Bel-Air Estates. As I understand now, there are over 100 homes in Bel-Air.

The origin of the field was eventually revealed. The airport started in the late 1970s, when land owner Dick Thomas realized that Boone County was the only county in Illinois without an airport of any description. He soon developed his own farmland to make a runway and he called it Belvidere airport. Although his field was equidistant between Belvidere and Poplar Grove, Belvidere was the larger town.

As years went by, the population of Belvidere moved closer and closer to the airport. Predictably, the hue and cry went up to bulldoze the airport and relieve the growing town of the danger of airplanes falling out of the sky and landing on the innocent and unsuspecting populace. Meanwhile, the new owner, Dick Thomas's son, Steve, had developed a close relationship with Poplar Grove and, since Belvidere had fallen out of love with the airport, suggested that the field be annexed into Poplar Grove. The deal was done. Belvidere airport disappeared from the map and Poplar Grove airport made its debut.

Poplar Grove is very busy. Maybe "active" is a better term. There are enough pilots and flying students that the field added one more innovative feature: Each month, an FAA certified flight doctor sets up shop and conducts flight physicals. When I was there, at least a dozen pilots were there for their examination. She must do a good business there to leave her normal practice for a morning of tending to this bi-annual need of pilots.

Taxiing about the strip was a collection of beautiful airplanes including a Stearman and a WACO of some description. The Pitts, as gorgeous as it is, wasn't alone. It was hard to leave this hotbed of pilots and airplanes, but I had more airports to visit.

Belvidere (I mean, Poplar Grove) airport will be hard to forget.

#304 Greenwood, Illinois   Galt Airport
Type: Paved Identifier: 10C   June 15, 1996

I MEET ANOTHER MARATHON FLYER!

ONE CONSEQUENCE OF flying to so many different places is that it tends to make other pilots want to fly more. Since the sport aviation industry is in need of a little boost, I make sure that people at each field are aware of what I am doing. If they want to talk about it, I will take all the time they need so that they get the full impact of the adventure. Someone else may be doing the same thing, so I always ask about that also.

Sure enough, at Galt Airport in Greenwood, Illinois, I was talking with the FBO clerk about flying to various fields when she immediately recommended that I talk with Jeffery Brintton. Jeffery Brintton, she said, had visited more airports than any other pilot she knew. Obviously, we had something in common and should compare notes. Luckily enough, Jeff was on the field that morning.

Jeff is a young man in his late 20s. He flies a great looking Cessna 182.It is unclear how Jeff came to his decision, but his quest was just a little different than mine. He expected to fly to all the public access airports in Illinois and Wisconsin. So his initial effort was substantially more ambitious than mine. At the time we met, he had already been to 176 fields. One of his highlights was flying to 22 airports in one day. He explained the day as a perfect VFR summer day with plenty of daylight hours. He got a very early start and persisted into the late evening hours before coming home. I don't know how many hours he flew that day. When I fly all day and land at eight or nine fields, I come away exhausted, stiff and emotionally spent. Jeff must have been entirely depleted. His backside must have felt like it was glued to that left seat.

Jeff and I communicated with each other for a long time, mostly by e-mail. He sent a list of the airports he has visited. The similarity of our two lists and the sequence of our trips are impressive. In many cases, he visited the same fields in the same order I did.

Jeff's airplane is much faster than mine. The plane has about 10% more power. The extra power coupled with a controllable pitch prop and retractable landing gear gives him a substantial speed advantage. It takes a minimum of 2 hours for me to land at a field that is new. Other fields come easier, but then it is a long trip back home. With Jeff's airplane being (at least) 25 miles an hour faster than mine, he cuts down his "commute time" significantly.

We dropped out of contact with each other and I miss talking with him very much. Hopefully, Jeff will continue beyond the airports of Illinois and Wisconsin. Perhaps a goal of 1,000 airports for Jeff is not out of the question.

#305 McHenry, Wisconsin   McHenry Farm Strip
Type: Grass Identifier: Private   June 15, 1996

#306 Westosha, Wisconsin   Westosha Airport
Type: Paved Identifier: WI10   June 15, 1996

#307 Lake Geneva, Wisconsin   Lake Geneva Private Airport
Type: Paved Identifier: Private   June 15, 1996

#308 East Troy, Wisconsin   East Troy Municipal Airport
Type: Paved Identifier: 57G   June 15, 1996

#309 Rochester, Wisconsin   Fox River Airport
Type: Paved Identifier: 96C   June 15, 1996

CHAMPION AIRCRAFT COMPANY

RARELY DO I research a field prior to traveling to it, maybe because I am so anxious to get there or just lazy. This was the case with my call on Fox River Airport in Wisconsin. It was another bright and sunny spring day when I landed at Rochester. My surprise was discovering that I had just dropped in on the home of American Champion Aircraft Company. The airport is not a particularly modern strip. It's actually barren and in ill repair. The tenant's attention is focused upon something else.

The first things I saw were partially completed airframes being moved around outside the plant and one airplane being engine tested on the ramp. I wanted to see more. One of the people involved with the fuselage transfers directed me to a middle aged gentleman walking up the taxiway.

The man's name was Jerry Mehlhaff and he is the president of American Champion. Jerry was friendly and accommodating, answering my sophomoric questions about his operation. He had one of his employees take the time to conduct a tour for me. Jerry has a nice operation in Fox River.

While this is not a large organization, all work stations were active. He had done his industrial engineering work very well. He had done his staffing in fine style, also. His men and women were truly craftsmen. The work being done was of the highest quality. Jerry must have spent a lot of time training his work force. The product technology is of 1920-to-1950 type construction. These are not all metal aircraft but planes made in the traditional fabric, stretched and shrunk over a steel tube framework. The basic design is that of a tail wheeled airplane originally designed and built in the 1930s. The construction method used then is still being used today.

Jerry owns the type certificates for all of the old Champion line. His company now builds five major lines:

Model No.	Model	Power
7ECA	Citabria Aurora	118
7GCAA	Citabria Adventure	160
7GCBC	Citabria Explorer	160
8KCAB	Super Decathlon	180
8GCBC	Scout	180

The Decathlon is an all-out aerobatic aircraft, while the Citabria is the personal aircraft offering and has limited aerobatic capabilities with an O-360 of 160 horsepower. Remembering back to the early 1970s when the Citabria was introduced, its stunting capability was touted. You may recall that the plane was named Citabria because Citabria is "airbatic" spelled backwards? Of course "airbatic" itself is misspelled. Why would anyone want to fly an airplane called Citaborea?

The Scout is a 180 HP workhorse. It has the highest gross weight of the line at 2,150 pounds, and is equipped with flaps and a constant speed prop. The engine must be de-rated, as Lycoming O-360s with constant speed props are usually equipped with fuel injection and a slightly higher compression ratio which provides for a 200 horsepower rating.

Jerry is one of a few small manufacturers of general aviation airplanes. He had a dream of taking a well-established and respected design and returning it to production. He has turned his dream into a vision and is working hard to make it a reality. I think of him often and wish him success.

#310 Burlington, Wisconsin   Burlington Municipal Airport
Type: Paved Identifier: C52   June 15, 1996

#311 Beloit, Wisconsin   Beloit Municipal Airport
Type: Paved Identifier: 44C   June 15, 1996

THE WORLD'S PRETTIEST AIRPORT

TWO THINGS ARE noteworthy about Beloit. First, the airport has a sign that reads "Forty-Four Charlie, The Prettiest Little Airport Anywhere." Secondly, I believe it.

Beloit airport staff and friends have made a personal effort to ensure Beloit Municipal is a charming and attractive airfield. They have landscaped the grounds in an appealing fashion which compliments the natural terrain. Individuals have constructed rock gardens and flower gardens. The property is punctuated with swings and lawn chairs in shady places. Flowers have been selected with care blending complimentary colors and sizes. Areas surrounding the runway and the ramp are meticulously tended, as well.

When telling fellow pilots about my trips, I always encourage them to visit Beloit because of its beauty.

#312 Janesville, Wisconsin   Rock County Airport
Type: Class D Identifier: JVL   June 30, 1996

#313 Brodhead, Wisconsin   Brodhead Airport
Type: Grass Identifier: C37   June 30, 1996

PIETENPOL PUTS BRODHEAD, CHERRY GROVE ON MAP
By: Bernis Hoopman Finke, "Bernie's Pietenpol Mementos"

EACH YEAR FOR 21 years a Pietenpol Fly-In has been held at Brodhead, Wisconsin. If you mention Oshkosh, Wisconsin, it is readily recognized as the town that has a Fly-In. If you mention Brodhead most people ask, "where is that?"

Brodhead is close to the Wisconsin border, between Madison, Wisconsin, and Chicago. Each year during the Oshkosh Fly-Iin, loyal Pietenpol followers fly or drive to Brodhead for a weekend of reminiscing and catching up. It is a lot like a family re-union, only the talk is about airplanes instead.

The Brodhead Fly-In was started in order to recognize the popularity of a small, experimental recreational aircraft that was designed by Bernard Pietenpol and first built in 1929. There are several models; the Air Camper, an open cockpit two-seater that uses a car engine for power, is the most popular. Pietenpol, a self-taught engineer, designed a plane that was economical and simple enough for the average person to build and enjoy. After building and improving the design of different planes, Pietenpol concluded that this plane handled and performed in a manner that was safe and practical.

Orrin Hoopman, a friend of Pietenpol's, helped build and experiment with the different planes. When the design was completed, Hoopman decided that there should be plans or blueprints so that others could build the plane. Hoopman ordered a set of drafting tools from Sears and Roebuck and taught himself to draw the plans. Hoopman and Don Pietenpol still sell these plans to interested builders all over the world.

Brodhead is a small airport with grass runways, not unlike those at Pietenpol Field in Cherry Grove, Minnesota. There is usually 20 to 30 Pietenpol's flown in during the weekend. Other types of planes are flown in also, as the Pietenpol is not considered a long-range plane. Its speed is slow, 60 to 75 miles per hour, and many think the seats are uncomfortable. This year, one pilot flew by commercial airline from California to New York and then flew a Pietenpol from New York to Brodhead.

A number of years ago, some of the pilots sojourned to Cherry Grove landing at Pietenpol Field and camped overnight. They walked into Cherry Grove to visit the Pietenpol shop.

This year, the next generation revived the tradition with four pilots flying Pietenpol's and a fifth in a biplane. They flew into the Cherry Grove Airport and Don Pietenpol of Rochester met them there. They camped overnight at the airport and were invited to the Cherry Grove Mercantile for breakfast the next morning. They also checked out the Pietenpol Shop.

Pietenpol drove the group to Fountain where they visited the Fillmore County History Center. One of the Pietenpol hangars, a Pietenpol Air Camper and some Pietenpol memorabilia are on display there. After their visit to Cherry Grove, they returned to Brodhead.

About 300 people attend the Brodhead Fly-In each year. Most of the meals are planned, and there is room for campers or tents. Many of the pilots set up tents by their planes. Nearby towns have motels available. It is a very informal, educational and enjoyable event to attend. There are several other locations that are beginning to host Fly-Ins. Locations are scattered around the United States and one is in Ontario, Canada.

The interesting point of all this is that, if someone had not designed and built an airplane and someone else had not drawn the plans, Cherry Grove, population 50, would not be known around the world as the home of Bernard Pietenpol.

#314 Edgartown, Wisconsin   Jana Airport
Type: Grass Identifier: 58C   June 30, 1996

#315 Fort Atkinson, WI   Fort Atkinson Municipal Airport
Type: Paved Identifier: 61C   June 30, 1996

#316 Whitewater, Wisconsin   Gutzmer's Twin oaks
Type: Grass Identifier: 5Y3   June 30, 1996

#317 Palmyra, Wisconsin   Palmyra Municipal Airport
Type: Grass Identifier: 88C   June 30, 1996

#318 Delavan, Wisconsin   Lake Lawn Resort Airport
Type: Paved Identifier: C59 June 30, 1996

#319 Harvard, Illinois   Dacy Airport
Type: Grass Identifier: 0C0   June 30, 1996

SHOWMEN ONLY, PLEASE

DACY AIRPORT IS the home of the famous Dacy Air Show. Landing there is like landing in the middle of a rehearsal for an air show. Based here are scores of restored antique airplanes. Stearmans and Staggerwing Beechs are everywhere. Looking into a darkened hangar, I found a small biplane that had Hazel Sig's name on the side of the cockpit. It was in storage alongside a 1958 Packard Patrician!

The real thrill was when I talked with the patriarch of the Dacy Family, John F. Dacy. We talked for a couple of hours. It was a typical pilot's conversation at an airport. Whenever an airplane crossed low over the field or started up across the way, our talk would automatically stop while we watched what was going on. Pilots are easily distracted like that!

John told me he learned to fly in 1924, the same year he bought his first aircraft, an OX-5 powered Pheasant biplane. Dacy Airport, was the site of the original Dacy farm at the early part of the century. It was John who eventually turned it into an airfield.

During WW II, John served in the Army Air Corps as a B-24 crew chief in the European theatre - Italy, I believe. He told me that he also was a mechanic on B-29s stateside.

John and his wife Elsie are exceptionally proud of their daughter, Susan. Susan rebuilt her own Stearman as a teenager. I guess she flies the wings off it. But then, who in the Dacy family isn't flying the wings off of something!?! There are P-51 Mustangs, Pitts Specials and Super Stearmans, SNJ's (the Navy's version of the AT-6) and Super Chipmonks all over that field. After all, it is the home of Dave Dacy's Airshow troupe.

It appears that the name of Dacy, prominent in aviation since early in the 20th century, will remain so in the 21st. Flying has become part of the Dacy DNA chain by now. Having a chance to spend time with John F.Dacy at his field resides in my mind as a quality memory.

#320 Madison, Wisconsin   Dane County Regional
Type: Class C Identifier: MSN   July 4, 1996

#321 Madison, Wisconsin   Blackhawk Field
Type: Paved Identifier: 87Y   July 4, 1996

#322 Madison, Wisconsin   Waunakee Airport
Type: Paved Identifier: WI06   July 4, 1996

#323 Middleton, Wisconsin   Morey Airport
Type: Paved Identifier: C29   July 4, 1996

CESSNA MANUFACTURING COMPANY

WHILE ROAMING AROUND the FBO at Morey Airport, I was impressed with the volume of airplane parts on the shelves. Moreover, stacks of larger parts were in the back of the building. This was substantially more inventory of airplane parts than I have ever seen at an airport.

I remarked about this to the shift manager. He believed this was an offsite assembly point for Cessna Aircraft. His understanding was that Cessna has excess parts and component manufacturing capacity in Wichita, Kansas. He claimed that Cessna Skyhawks are assembled here to the same engineering and quality standards as they are in Wichita, Kansas. When the production output of planes at Wichita equates with the order book, Cessna stops production at Morey Field. In this way, production flow at Wichita is nicely smoothed. Wichita is protected from the disconcerting flood tides of product demands. Having been involved in production all my life, I seriously questioned the validity of his claim. There should be more cost effective ways of accommodating sales spurts. But then I build rail cars, not planes.

I flew off toward Prairie du Sac wondering how many Skyhawk owners are flying around in their Cessna 172s believing they came from Wichita.

#324 Prairie du Sac, Wisconsin   Sauk-Prairie Airport
Type: Paved Identifier: 91C   July 4, 1996

#325 Sextonville, Wisconsin   Richland Airport
Type: Paved Identifier: 93C   July 4, 1996

OUT OF GAS IN SEXTONVILLE

VISITING SEXTONVILLE, WISCONSIN on Independence Day, I was very low on fuel because not many FBO's were open on this holiday. Moreover, I wanted to stop at a couple of grass strips before going home. The fuel tank levels were too low to go on to Illinois and then to Indiana.

Richland Field in Sextonville was listed as having fuel service. Upon arrival, I taxied up to the fuel supply tanks. The fuel tanks were locked and only local club members could buy gas here. Fortunately, I met Vince Scarletti who was a member of the flying club. He had access to the gasoline and was willing to top off the airplane. The club was not used to selling to outsiders. They sent out statements to the members once a month and accepted cash or checks as payment. My credit cards were not going to work here. Vince Scarletti decided to trust me. He filled my tanks and accepted my promise to send him a check for the $60 or $70 worth of fuel. No small leap of faith here!

The flying brotherhood is a close knit group. There is an inordinate amount of mutual trust and understanding amongst pilots. Vince Scarletti is one of those men who easily demonstrated that trust - especially where it counts, in the wallet! Naturally, Vince was paid immediately, with a note expressing my heartfelt gratitude for his trust and confidence.

#326 Cedarville, Wisconsin   Dornink Airport
Type: Grass Identifier: C86   July 4, 1996

#327 Apple River, Illinois   Apple Canyon Airport
Type: Grass Identifier: C86   July 4, 1996

#328 Mt. Morris , Illinois   Bennet Memorial Airport
Type: Grass Identifier: C55   July 4, 1996

#329 Viola, Wisconsin   S & S Ranch
Type: Grass Identifier: Private   July 7, 1996

THE FIELD ON TOP OF THE HILL

THE S & S Ranch Airport is a private field. The owner is Vince
Scarletti who is mentioned above in the story about Sextonville,
Wisconsin. During my chat with him, he mentioned that he had
a private field on a farm he owned. While he spent some time on
his farm, it was not his primary place of residence. He occasionally
spent some weekends there. He gave me approval to visit his field.

After two and a half hours of flying, I reached Viola. The S & S
field was not hard to spot. The surrounding area was a vivid Kelly
green in color and the landing strip was set directly on a hill top.
Obviously, the strip had recently been blacktopped. With the jet
black appearance against the green grass, it stood out like a road
sign.

I had hoped that Vince Scarletti would be at the farm when I
visited, but no one was there. The whole hilltop was silent and serene
except for the scuffling of my feet. The view was magnificent in all
directions and it took a moment for the gloriousness of it all to sink
in. Then I realized that I have experienced such rare moments before.

It was the approach to grandeur felt at very few other airports. It is a feeling that I savor. I like Vince and it would have been good to see him again. It would have been even more wonderful to share this moment with him.

#330 Viroqua, Wisconsin Type: Paved Identifier: Y51	Viroqua Municipal Airport July 7, 1996
#331 Wonewoc, Wisconsin Type: Grass Identifier: 4D1	Three Castles Airport July 7, 1996
#332 Mauston, Wisconsin Type: Grass Identifier: 82C	Mauston-New Lisbon Union July 7, 1996
#333 Adams, Wisconsin Type: Paved Identifier: 63C	Adams County -Legion Field July 7, 1996
#334 Wautoma, Wisconsin Type: Paved Identifier: Y50	Wautoma Municipal Airport July 7, 1996
#335 Portage, Wisconsin Type: Paved Identifier: C47	Portage Municipal Airport July 7, 1996
#336 Watertown, Wisconsin Type: Paved Identifier: RYV	Watertown Municipal Airport July 7, 1996

I RATHER FLY THAN EAT!

MY WIFE NANCY rarely flies with me as she really does not like small airplanes. In fact, she is not too enthralled with jetliners. We are vastly different that way. Once I settle into a commercial aircraft, I always fall asleep before take-off. Nancy, on the other hand, worries about every odd noise, every random vibration or movement and the behavior of every passenger. Nothing escapes her attention or her deepest concern. It is a lot worse in the Cherokee. I swear the frame of the passenger seat is impaled by her fingernails.

She cares very deeply about the safety and well-being of her husband. She always inquires about the mechanical condition of the airplane, if there is any addition or modification that would make the airplane safer or more comfortable. She likes the fact that I call her immediately upon landing to let her know that "I am on the ground."

She worries that I don't eat properly when I'm away. Every time I come home and begin to tell her about the day's adventures, she will interrupt with "did you have lunch?" Keep in mind that she has prior knowledge of her husband's pathetic eating habits.

Too often I must admit that I haven't eaten since breakfast. With that she becomes annoyed. I get a comment or two about how my health relies on a good eating regimen. Lunch or a light snack garnered much importance in my flying scheme. Nancy even took to scolding me before the fact. As I left the house there would be non-too subtle reminders. Something must have taken root in my subconscious. Rather than lie to my wife, I would grab an occasional Milky Way bar and a Coke sometime during the day. A pilot's lunch, I called it. It cuts the edge off whatever hunger pangs might arise. She was not wild about that either.

Then came the realization that taking time for a sit-down lunch, took away from my flying time. That was indigestible! Great weather was going to waste; a love bird of an airplane would be sitting idle and anxiety growing within me. It was clear. I'd rather fly than eat!

#337 Athens, Michigan   David's Field
Type: Grass Identifier: 9C2   August 17, 1996

#338 Albion, Michigan   Midway Airport
Type: Grass Identifier: 35G   August 17, 1996

#339 Battle Creek, Michigan   W.K.Kellogg Airport
Type: Class D Identifier: BTL   August 17, 1996

#340   Parchment, Michigan   Triple H Airport
Type: Grass Identifier: 8MI3   August 17, 1996

#341 Kalamazoo, Michigan   Newman's Field
Type: Grass Identifier: MI83   August 17, 1996

A TRIP WITH BOB MYERS

BOB MYERS, OF Griffith Aviation, and I were flying around and visiting Michigan airports in the vicinity of Kalamazoo. We landed on a grass strip west of Kazoo: Newman Field. Newman is one of those fields where folks have built homes alongside the runway. As we rolled out on landing, we passed a lady sitting outside of her hangar after enjoying the day. She heard us land, looked and waved. That was all it took for us to taxi to her and start a conversation. Her name was Nancy Nagle.

We talked for a while. Before long, Nancy's husband, Bill Nagle, joined the conversation. We couldn't help but notice through the open hangar door that they had several Ercoupes. All of them are meticulously restored; one was as pretty as the next. Bill and Nancy Nagle are Ercoupe collectors. It seems that Bill goes about the countryside looking for Ercoupes that show evidence of being neglected or abandoned and buys them. He said that he paid less than $5,000 apiece for each of his planes. All of them needed to be taken down to their barest elements and thoroughly reconditioned. He spared no expense, and it appears the worth of each Ercoupe greatly exceeds the average or expected market value. Bill knows this, but rapidly adds that Ercoupes have always gained value. He expects to get all of his money back from each upon selling them.

Bill and Nancy also had a Meyers 260 in the middle of the floor. Like the Ercoupes, it was pristine.

#342 Paw Paw, Michigan
Type: Grass Identifier: 2C5

Almena Airport
August 17, 1996

#343 Watervliet, Michigan
Type: Grass Identifier: 40C

Watervliet Municipal Airport
August 17, 1996

#344 Zeeland, Michigan
Type: Paved Identifier: Z98

Ottawa Executive Airport
August 24, 1996

#345 Nuncia, Michigan
Type: Grass Identifier: 33

Jablonski Airport
August 24, 1996

#346 Grant, Michigan
Type: Grass Identifier: 01C

Grant Airport
August 24, 1996

#347 Kent City, Michigan
Type: Grass Identifier: 24M

Wilderness Airpark
August 24, 1996

#348 Ludington, Michigan
Type: Paved Identifier: LDM

Mason County Airport
August 24, 1996

#349 Baldwin, Michigan
Type: Paved Identifier: 7D3

Baldwin Municipal Airport
August 24, 1996

#350 Hart-Shelby, Michigan
Type: Paved Identifier: C04

Oceana Airport
August 24, 1996

#351 Rothbury, Michigan
Type: Grass Identifier: Private

Double J Resort
August 24, 1996

ANOTHER HARD FIELD TO FIND

OTTIGER AIRPORT IS a very small airport immediately north of the Muskegon, Michigan TRSA. As I flew south of Oceana Airport in Hart - Shelby, Michigan, I was carefully trying to make Ottiger without unnecessarily bothering Muskegon Approach Control.

Even with the airplane slowed to 90 knots, Ottiger was not where I thought it should be. As I was about to turn back north, an east-west grass strip appeared. In typical Michigan fashion, the edges of the strip were vividly marked with oversize yellow markers. These markers, about 4 feet in diameter, spaced down the two sides of a grass airfield, can be seen from miles away. For a guy who has always had trouble spotting a grass field, these are a Godsend. Using left hand traffic, the landing was as smooth as the runway surface, which was great.

Looking around, there was not much to see. The strip was not marked on the sectional chart so there was no way of telling where I was. Just then, two young men pulled up in a purple van. Both wore purple shirts, the same color as the van. They were here to pick me up. They were from the Double J Resort. The corporate color of the Double J must be purple.

I had no idea what was going on until the two men filled me in. It seems that someone heard my airplane in the pattern. At the Double J, the first one to spot an airplane about to land calls these two men. They, in turn, hustle to the airport to transport the guests back to the resort. These men pride themselves that no guests are kept waiting at the airport.

My stumbling onto this field had set an involved process in motion. The registration desk was notified that visitors were coming, as well. I told the two men that I couldn't stay and apologized for landing on a private strip and causing such commotion. I climbed back into the Cherokee and the men waited until I was gone to make sure that I wasn't going to change my mind. Later in the week, I sent them a short note thanking them for their care and hospitality. Enclosed in the note was a copy of the "Lunar Visit" airplane picture.

#352 Montague, Michigan Type: Paved Identifier: C26	Ottiger Airport August 24, 1996
#353 Grand Haven, Michigan Type: Paved Identifier: 3GM	Memorial Airpark August 25, 1996
#354 Evart, Michigan Type: Paved Identifier: 9C8	Evart Municipal Airport August 25, 1996
#355 Harrison, Michigan Type: Grass Identifier: 80D	Clare County Airport August 25, 1996
#356 Clare, Michigan Type: Paved Identifier: 48D	Clare Municipal Airport August 25, 1996
#357 Mount Pleasant, MI Type: Paved Identifier: MOP	Mount Pleasant Airport August 25, 1996
#358 Lake Isabella, Michigan Type: Grass Identifier: D15	Lake Isabella Airport August 25, 1996
#359 Mecosta, Michigan Type: Grass Identifier: 27C	Morton Airport August 25, 1996

JOHN AND EDITH'S FIRST AIRPLANE RIDE

AUGUST IN THE Midwest is as sultry as anywhere in the United States. This August 25th was one of the hottest and most humid in a long time. After visiting a half a dozen airports, I was sorely dehydrated. I had to get some liquid in me soon. Furthermore, I would have to slow the rate of dehydration. The opportunity to address both of these problems came about at Mecosta, Morton.

Both of the Mecosta fields are grass strips. The runways at Morton are east and west and northeast by southwest (3 and 21) orientation. The end of runway 21 ended at a crossroads. The end of the runway was less than 20 yards from the sidewalk. On the other side of the street was a convenience store. I parked the airplane and went across the street to get some fruit juice. An older couple had just gotten out of their truck as I arrived. They stood and watched me as I got out of the Cherokee and crossed the street. We walked into the store together. The husband said something about "pilots getting thirsty, too." We joked about the heat a little and went our separate ways.

We checked out our merchandise together and exchanged pleasantries again. Outside the store they asked what it was like to fly. Then it struck me: These two folks have never been in an airplane. They were in their 60s and had never been flying.

I tried to explain how great it felt and how easy it was. I told them that I would love to take them up, if for no other reason than to show them Mecosta as they had never seen it. They were reluctant for a minute, then, simply looked at me. I told them that the airplane held four people comfortably and the visibility was fabulous. With a little more coaxing, they walked across the street with me toward the Cherokee.

John sat with me in the front and Edith sat directly behind me. I showed John how it would be better if we left the door open against the prop blast for ventilation. It should have been longer. They were thrilled at being aloft. In span of a few minutes, many new understandings came to them. At first they gained confidence that the pilot knew what he was doing. Then they realized that no matter how hard they stared at the instrument panel, they wouldn't understand it. Then they felt at ease knowing that their partner was at ease. And then they enjoyed the sights of Mecosta. They pointed out to each other houses and farms that they recognized. They saw cars and pickup trucks on the roads with which they were familiar. They are even convinced that they recognized some of their friends and relatives from 2,000 feet up

I offered the controls to John, but he refused. He was too busy taking in all the sights. The flight lasted about 15 minutes and we landed back at the ramp across from the convenience store. The husband and wife, holding hands, stood away from the airplane as I started it. We waved good-bye to each other and I taxied off.

The sight of those two elderly folks with big smiles and loving eyes will remain with me for the rest of my life. The rest of the trip was nice, as well.

#360 Mecosta, Michigan
Type: Grass Identifier: 0C5

Canadian Lakes Airport
August 25, 1996

#361 Winn, Michigan
Type: Grass Identifier: MI53

Woodruff Lake Airport
August 25, 1996

#362 Elwell, Michigan
Type: Grass Identifier: 68R

Hamp Airport
August 25, 1996

#363 Grand Rapids, Michigan
Type: Class C Identifier: GRR

Kent County International
August 25, 1996

#364 Ligonier, Indiana
Type: Grass Identifier: Private

Motorola Switching Station
September 1, 1996

#365 Hillsdale, Michigan
Type: Paved Identifier:

Hillsdale Municipal Airport
Y85September 1, 1996

#366 Loars, Michigan
Type: Grass Identifier: 83G

Onsted Airport
September 1, 1996

#367 Brooklyn, Michigan
Type: Grass Identifier: 6G8

Shamrock Airport
September 1, 1996

#368 Napoleon, Michigan
Type: Grass Identifier: 3NP

Napoleon Airport
September 1, 1996

#369 Havana, Illinois
Type: Grass Identifier: 9I0

Havana Airport
September 29, 1997

#370 Beardstown, Illinois
Type: Paved Identifier: K06

Beardstown Airport
September 29, 1997

#371 Hillsboro, Illinois
Type: Grass Identifier: 3K4

Hillsboro Airport
September 29, 1997

#372 Rockford, Michigan
Type: Grass Identifier: 35C

Wells Field
October 5, 1996

#373 Greenville, Michigan
Type: Paved Identifier: 6D6

Greenville Municipal Airport
October 5, 1996

#374 Carson City, Michigan
Type: Grass Identifier: 47G

Mayes Airport
October 5, 1996

#375 Alma, Michigan
Type: Paved Identifier: AMN

Gratiot Airport
October 5, 1996

#376 Gladwin, Michigan
Type: Paved Identifier: GDW

Zettel Memorial Airport
October 5, 1996

#377 Houghton Lake, MI
Type: Paved Identifier: HTL

Roscommon County Airport
October 5, 1996

MY FIRST PASTIE!

HOUGHTON LAKE, MICHIGAN is just off the northern edge of the Chicago Sectional Chart. But I was hungry and it was about noon, I began to ask around if any restaurants were near the airports I planned to visit. No luck. All the fields were several miles away from an eatery. The farther north I went, the more I started to hear about 'pasties'. The pronunciation varied; the "a" could be either a hard or a soft "a" depending on the city. But everyone thought I should try them. The dish is of Norwegian origin. (Note: this part of Michigan and northward is copper country.) To this day, copper mining still takes place through the Upper Peninsula. Pasties were developed for copper miners to take with them for lunch. It provided a lot of nutrition in a very compact package. It was rich and filling. For someone who is really hungry, a pastie will fill the bill.

Finally, in Houghton, there was a restaurant adjacent to the airport. A short taxi down the periphery of the airport property and a short walk down the highway is all it took to get to Spike Horn Bar and Grill. The waitress recommended that I have the pastie with gravy and beer. I took her up with the only deviation being that the beer had to be non-alcoholic.

It was fabulous! Hot enough to burn the top of a person's mouth. But, like good pizza, it didn't matter. There was a professional football game on TV. It would have easy to sit there all day, drinking beer and watching sports. But I had airports to visit!

This book is about flying and it is intended for pilots and aircraft owners. This is not a book for recipes and home cooking ideas and household hints. Furthermore, with the following comes a pledge that there will be no other recipes in this book. It is not really pilot-like, but it isn't fair to go on about pasties and not provide some indication of how they are prepared. After that prelude, please look over the formulation of pasties as it was told to me. These little rascals are extremely tasty and hearty.

Pasties are like a beef stew wrapped in pastry dough. It is a natural leftover from a main course of Pot Roast or such as that. With the proper leftovers, pasties become a fast-fix meal that is easy for anyone. Here are the ingredients:

2 cups	roast beef cut into 1/4" to 2" pieces, cooked
1 2 cups	cooked potatoes; the same size as the beef
1 cup	beef gravy
2 cup	diced and cooked carrots

2 cup	diced and sautéed onions
2 tbls.	crushed dried thyme
2 tbls.	chopped parsley (cilantro is better)
2 tbls.	black pepper

Combine the above ingredients with about 3 cup of red wine; a hearty Cabernet or Merlot is best. Roll out an 8" circle of double crust pie pastry dough on a floured surface. Mound one cup of ingredients on half of the pastry circle. Moisten the edges of the pastry circle with water, then pull over the empty half and seal the dough pocket. Make as many pasties as the amount of stuffing will allow. Cut slits in the top so that it can breathe while baking. Some brush half-and-half cream on the pastie's top. Bake them in a 450° oven for about 20 or 25 minutes or until they are golden brown. Serve them as they come from the oven. The natives in upper Michigan serve them with hot gravy over the top and a cold beer alongside. Don't forget, if you're flying, make that an alcohol-free beer.

#378 St. Helen, Michigan
Type: Grass Identifier: 6Y6

St. Helen Airport
October 5, 1996

#378 St.John's, Michigan
Type: Grass Identifier: 7MI5

Schiffer Field
October 5, 1996

#379 West Branch, Michigan
Type: Grass Identifier: Y31

West Branch Community
October 5, 1996

#380 Standish, Michigan
Type: Paved Identifier: Y75

Standish Industrial Airport
October 5, 1996

FIRST, FLY THE AIRPLANE

THE FUN PART of this avocation is seeing lots of new things and also seeing things from a new perspective. The Standish Industrial Airport is exactly what the name says; it is located in the middle of an industrial park. The park is arranged so that all of the tenants have access to the runway.

Standish is a 2,500 foot long field that runs true east and west. While it is paved, I found that the ample length is not to be taken for granted. But I did.

While using a standard left-hand landing pattern, I was passing over a highly commercial area with a lot of traffic and activity. I got caught up in the swirl of motion around and directly below me, and it affected my attention of landing. Suddenly, I was too hot and too high. At first thought, the landing was worth trying to save, but that feeling didn't last long. There wasn't enough time and distance remaining to slip down. The runway was too short for the sloppy flying that I had done. I applied full power and pulled up and went around for another try. Only this time, I paid attention to what I was doing and safely landed the airplane. Another flying lesson learned!

#381 Pinconning, Michigan
Type: Grass Identifier: 52I

Gross Field
October 5, 1996

#382 Midland, Michigan
Type: Paved Identifier: 3BS

Barstow Municipal Airport
October 5, 1996

#384 Deshler, Ohio
Type: Grass Identifier: 6D7

Deshler Municipal Airport
October 19, 1996

#385 Sandusky, Ohio
Type: Paved Identifier: SKY

Griffing-Sandusky Airport
October 19, 1996

HARRY GRIFFING OF SANDUSKY, OHIO

GRIFFING - SANDUSKY Airport in northern Ohio remains a memorable stop. The weather forecast was for light rain. But the intensity of the rain was heavier than expected and the ceilings were also lower than predicted. I flew up close to the base of the clouds and calculated that the cloud cover was at 3,000 feet. It was a close call deciding if I would continue the trip. Flying low and slow under the weather is a bad practice known as "scud running". This type of flying is legal by FAA standards but it inherently is much more dangerous than normal flying. I would have called off the trip if the ceiling were lower than 3,000 feet.

Griffing - Sandusky was the most northern and most eastern field that I would visit that day. I wanted to fly to a few grass strips near there but I wasn't sure about what the rainfall would do the fields. This called for local knowledge. The fuel tanks would be topped off and then I could saunter back toward Indiana where the weather was much clearer. I asked the FBO operator about the grass strips and she told me to talk to the local pilots were in the adjacent restaurant. They were familiar with all the local landing areas. She pointed over my shoulder to a table in the corner.

No fewer than seven pilots were at the table. Each of them introduced himself and it was clear that this was a very friendly group. The last gentleman I met was Harry Griffing, the founder and operator of the field. It was not clear as to how involved he was in day-to-day operation of the field, given he was in his eighties. But he was spry and quick of mind; not much got past Harry. I asked about the various grass strips in the immediate area and everyone was very helpful.

After describing the landing conditions at one field that was close by, Harry pulled up a little closer to the table. There was the crack of a smile across his thin lips. "Bob," he said, "the owner of that field died last week. He used to be the oldest licensed pilot in Ohio." I asked Harry who the oldest pilot was now. The smile arched up both ends of his mouth now, revealing a little color of teeth. He simply came back with a low, calculated laugh, "hee,..hee,..hee,..."

Harry had become the oldest licensed pilot in Ohio!

#386 Norwalk, Ohio	Huron County Airport	
Type: Paved Identifier: OH21	October 19, 1996	
#387 Wakeman, Ohio	Wakeman Airport	
Type: Paved Identifier: I64	October 19, 1996	
#388 Willard, Ohio	Willard Municipal Airport	
Type: Paved Identifier: 8G1	October 19, 1996	
#389 Shelby, Ohio	Shelby Community Airport	
Type: Paved Identifier: 12G	October 19, 1996	
#390 Galion, Ohio	Galion Municipal Airport	
Type: Paved Identifier: GQQ	October 19, 1996	
#391 Forest, Ohio	Farm field	
Type: Grass Identifier: Private	October 19, 1996	

NO SANDWICH, STILL HUNGRY

THIS IS THE only private field that I visited without permission. The trip so far included visits to eight fields and the day was getting long. Since I hadn't had lunch yet, the folks at Galion Airport suggested dropping in at Forest, where there was a sandwich shop at the corner of the field. The shop was immediately across the street from the landing strip. Permission wasn't needed, since the restaurant was a natural haunt of pilots who used the field every weekend. I landed, but the little sandwich shop was closed. After taking a picture of the field, I left still hungry.

#392 Delphos, Ohio   Delphos Airport
Type: Grass Identifier: 09I   October 19, 1996

#393 Aledo, Illinois   Mercer County Airport
Type: Paved Identifier: C00   November 2, 1996

THE STEARMAN CORN BOIL

THE PRIOR VISIT to Aledo was pleasant, but I couldn't write a paragraph about it. However, some 10 months later was a different story.

Fellow pilot, ex-boss and old friend Bob Smith had his restored Stearman ready to fly for several months when he called on that Labor Day weekend. His question was simple. How about flying down to Galesburg, Illinois for the annual Stearman convention? Yes, indeed. Bob in the back seat and me up front on a trip of 130 miles….In an open cockpit airplane that shared the same birth date as me. It would be great.

The plan was a little involved. On Tuesday after Labor Day, I would fly the Cherokee to Plymouth, Indiana early in the morning. It was due for its annual inspection. The FBO there would accept the plane that morning. About the same time, Bob Smith would fly his Stearman from Elkhart to Plymouth, a distance of about 50 miles. From there, the two of us would be off to Galesburg. Later in the week, Bob would drop me off at the Griffith airport where my car was parked.

It all came together nicely. The crisp, clear morning did everything it could to enhance the beauty of Bob's pristine Stearman. Bob had his hands full landing the top-heavy Stearman on the paved runway at Plymouth Municipal, however. He taxied to the ramp in that beautiful blue and yellow PT-17. The sight of a World War II trainer with that barking radial engine can bring tears to the eyes of a grown man.

Bob had a flight suit, helmet and communications gear ready for me in the plane. He helped me into the front cockpit where I buckled in, hooked up and pinched myself. Yes, we were going to the Stearman Convention in a Stearman! Bob got into the rear cockpit and, within a few minutes, the R-670-5 Continental engine was blasting cool air onto my face. Shivers went up and down my spine but the cold air had nothing to do with it.

Bob didn't need much runway, so it was a "short-field takeoff". Within seconds, the stick was rapidly banging inside my thighs and Bob was yelling at me to take over controls of the plane. I flew N63301 to within three miles of Aledo, smiling all the way! This is still a sweet memory.

#394   West Amana, Iowa   Amana Airport
Type: Grass Identifier: C11   November 2, 1996

#395   Montezuma, Iowa   Sig Field
Type: Grass Identifier: 7C5   November 2, 1996

#396 Galesburg, Iowa   Sully Field
Type: Grass Identifier: 8C2   November 2, 1996

#397 Toledo, Iowa   Toledo Municipal Airport
Type: Grass Identifier: 8C5   November 2, 1996

#398 Traer, Iowa   Traer Municipal Airport
Type: Grass Identifier: 8C6   November 2, 1996

#399 LaPorte City, Iowa   Nichols Field
Type: Grass Identifier: 6C8   November 2, 1996

#400 Grundy Center, Iowa   Grundy Center Airport
Type: Grass Identifier: 6K7   November 2, 1996

#401 Allison, Iowa   Allison Airport
Type: Grass Identifier: K98   November 2, 1996

#402 Waverly, Iowa   Waverly Municipal Airport
Type: Paved Identifier: C25   November 2, 1996

#403 Postville, Iowa   Dale's Delight Airport
Type: Grass Identifier: Y16   November 2, 1996

#404 Monona, Iowa   Monona Municipal Airport
Type: Grass Identifier: 7C3   November 2, 1996

ON A CLEAR DAY, YOU CAN SEE...

FLYING FROM ONE airfield to another has been exciting. There seems to be no end to interesting people, enlightening history or random reminders to catch one's curiosity. True interest resides in little known aspects of the airport or area. But a person's attention can be lured to places other than those that have airports. I often wondered about these.

For example, my hometown of South Bend, Indiana has a relic from the past that is still visible from the air. It is about 8 nautical miles from SBN. When departing SBN, request a departure heading of 240 degrees magnetic to put you right over the old proving grounds of the manufacturer of fine, old cars as well as the Conestoga wagons of the 1800s. When built in 1926, the grounds were called the Million Dollar Outdoor Testing Laboratory. It is easy to understand how the more familiar "'Proving Grounds" caught on. In 1937 the company planted 5,000 pine trees to spell out the name "STUDEBAKER." The plat has been broken up and some of the letters are a little obscure, but the name remains readable. To do so, demands a 360 degree turn just to see the name as it is. Here are a couple of non-airport places I have over-flown with similar interest.

West of Dubuque about 20 nautical miles stands a recurring reminder of non-airport fascination. Several times I altered my course coming out of western Iowa to fly over Dyersville just to circle the baseball diamond that was built for Kevin Costner's 1989 movie, "Field of Dreams." It is pretty, from the air.

It remains a part of the Lansing family farm. Their farm house, featured in the film, is a prominent landmark. The field and the house are meticulously maintained. While there are no scheduled or organized activities, the field draws thousands of fans of all ages who walk onto the field popping a baseball into an old glove from high school days. Sometimes fans simply sit in the stands. Could they be waiting for Shoeless Joe Jackson to step out of the cornfield? Or, their fathers

That brings us to James Tiberius Kirk and Riverside, Iowa. Riverside is 10 miles south of Iowa City and 25 miles west of Muscatine. It is near the junction of Highway 218 and Route 22. They have no airport, but the town is mildly famous. Mildly as opposed to being <u>very</u> famous as they will be in the year 2233.

Riverside, Iowa was determined to make itself known in some form or fashion and they knew that growing corn or wheat or broccoli or whatever made their living it was not going to make Riverside famous. During one of the episodes of "Star Trek" it was mentioned that the captain of the starship Enterprise, a one James T. Kirk, was born in Riverside, Iowa on March 22, 2233. Clearly everyone knows this man, since he is the most famous starship commander of them all.

Well, not a populace to let grass grow under its feet, today's Riverside population took this opportunity by the horns. Within a very short time, Riverside changed its very being. They are living as if James Kirk is an actual person and has already been born.

A visitor to Riverside can buy a vial of local soil or "Kirk dirt" for a few bucks. There is a barbershop in town with a slab of concrete behind it. It looks like the remains of an old cement foundation of some sort. This marks the actual birthplace "to be" of James T. Kirk. By the way, to his friends like Bones McCoy and Mr. (No first name, no middle initial) Spock, he was frequently called "Jim." There is also a non-functioning model of a starship in the town square.

It is named Starship Riverside, since the Enterprise hasn't been constructed yet. You will have to fly low and slow to spot this stuff from the air.

I fully intended to take a car from Iowa City to Riverside and get a close look at all of this, but I resisted the urge. I have plenty of time.

Another non-airport town of interest is Fairmont in Grant County, Indiana, some 15 DME northeast of Elwood, Indiana and 20 DME south of Marion.

Fairmont has a very recognizable cemetery from the air, however. Every time I have flown over the site, I circled the graveyard at least once.

The town cemetery, wonderfully symmetrical and well-manicured, is Park Cemetery, the final resting place of James Byron Dean. That is James Dean, the man who invented "cool." Born in Marion, Indiana in 1931, the Dean family moved to Fairmont. James Dean grew up there through his high school years, Dean died tragically on September 30, 1955 after a movie career of only 16 months. His memory lives on in his hometown of Fairmont with annual pilgrimages, spontaneous festivities and celebrations to mark the pertinent dates in the life of James Dean. There are numerous locations to visit which James Dean "surely visited when he was alive." His home has been preserved and there is a movement on to save Fairmont High School. A fan can buy a dinner plate with a color image of James Dean almost anywhere. By the way, it is definitely "James" Dean; Jimmy Dean is the one who makes sausage.

With only three films to his credit (*East of Eden, Rebel Without a Cause and Giant*) and 50 years after his passing, James Dean's memory lives on with a loving fan base that seems to know no end. Even now, fresh lipstick prints appear on his tombstone every day.

Is a golden-ager alive today who was not influenced by James Dean? I think not. We still have a vision of James Dean in the scarlet windbreaker that he wore in "Rebel Without a Cause" in his role as Jim (Jimbo) Stark. As a restless, misunderstood, middle-class high school youth full of defiance he defined the tone for American adolescents in the middle 50s. I believe to this day that James Dean is the reason why I prefer to wear a red jacket.

There are a couple of other Indiana locations that inspire one to random thoughts; a couple in my home state of Indiana. There are two 'feel good' movies from the 80s. One is "Breaking Away" with Dennis Christopher and Dennis Quaid which was filmed at the annual site of the Little 500 bicycle race - the Bill Armstrong stadium on the Indiana University campus. That track is easily seen from the air to the ENE when departing from runway 35 at Bloomington.

The other movie location is Hinkle Field House on the campus of Butler University, a few miles east of Indianapolis International. It is also easy to spot from aloft. (But, you will be in "Class C" airspace.) This is where the annual high school basketball champions are played. This is the setting for the climactic championship game in the movie "Hoosiers" starring Gene Hackman and Barbara Hershey. By the way, there is no Hickory, Indiana. It was the Milan Indians, coached by Marvin Wood (not Norman Dale as played by Hackman) and the Indians won over the Muncie Central Bearcats (and not the South Bend Central Bears). Oh, one more thing: the final score was 32 to 30, not 42 to 40. With the score tied, Milan literally held the ball without play for five full minutes of game time interrupted only once when Muncie took the ball down court and missed the shot. Bobby Plump took the final shot for the win with a few seconds left. The Indians were never outclassed by Muncie in the game. Otherwise, the film was somewhat accurate.

#405   Lancaster, Wisconsin   Lancaster Airport
Type: Paved Identifier: 73C   November 2, 1996

There are a number of small grass strips around the southern periphery of Chicago. Until this time, I had simply over-flown them as I went to-and-from other fields. Bill Moran and I decided to visit them and get the required photograph of each.

Bill is a very special friend. A couple of years prior to this trip, my airplane was laid up with an engine overhaul. The overhaul and attendant work coupled with the attendant long lead time for parts was extensive so the total time that the airplane was out of service for three months. During this time, Bill saw to it that he afforded every opportunity to go flying with him. He didn't want to see me spend time on the ground while everyone else was flying. He has a compassionate and understanding soul.

All of the fields were in good shape and they presented no problem. One field, Grandpa's Farm in Mendota, Illinois, has a small rise in the middle. It isn't very high, but I made the mistake of taking it too slowly during landing. There was a little crosswind that day. At the approach end of the runway, trees are on both sides. The crosswind came over the trees and swept over the top of the wings. It caused some loss of lift at the moment of the airplane's flare; the most critical stage of the landings. It was pilot error; I should have kept up air speed in the mild turbulence. We checked the airplane for damage and, mercifully, there was none.

Bill was pleased to have been with me during the 500-airport quest. I was pleased that he could be part of it, too.

#406   Joliet, Illinois   Wilhelmi Field
Type: Grass Identifier: 0C3   November 3, 1996

#407 Leland, Illinois   Leland Airport
Type: Grass Identifier: E16   November 3, 1996

#408   Earlville, Illinois   Earlville Airport
Type: Grass Identifier: C94   November 3, 1996

#409 Mendota, Illinois   Grandpa's Farm
Type: Grass Identifier: 0C7   November 3, 1996

#410 Mount Morris, Illinois   West Grove Airport
Type: Grass Identifier: 28I   November 3, 1996

#411   Savanna, Illinois   Franklyn U. Stransky Airport
Type: Paved Identifier: SFY   November 3, 1996

#412   Chicago, Illinois   Meigs Field
Type: Class D Identifier: CGX   February 15, 1997

KRISTALLNACHT IN CHICAGO
AND WE WERE THERE!

MEIGS FIELD IS an important part of Chicago's history. Daniel Hudson Burnham, creator of the 1909 Plan of Chicago and designer of much of the city's lakefront park system, realized the importance of traffic management and the need for balance between commons and commerce.

Downtown Chicago and aviation go back to the very start of flight. The earliest flights in Chicago took place in 1910 in Grant Park, which is adjacent to Meigs present location. History holds that the pilot was Walter Brookins. Through 1911, flying continued at Grant Park with many flight records for altitude, duration and speed. Of course, this was going on all over the country.

Sporadic air mail flights to-and-from Chicago's Grant Park in 1918 were made by pioneer pilots Ed Gardner and Max Miller. Regularly scheduled air mail flights began in 1919.

Air traffic at Grant Park is no accident. Grant Park is the signature recreation and relaxation area of downtown Chicago, as it enjoys a central position in the city. It was the cornerstone of Daniel Hudson Burnham's 1909 Plan of Chicago which became the basis for rebuilding Chicago. Burnham also wanted a number of islands just off-shore for recreational use. One of the islands turned into the site for Navy Pier. Southward, he filled in a mile long spit and called it Northerly Island. Northerly was immediately adjacent to Grant Park and looked to be a safer but equally convenient place for a landing strip.

In 1922, money had been raised and they started building Northerly Island. Within a few years, the popularity and growing practicality of aviation caused civic leaders to look at Northerly as a possible place for all those airplanes that insisted on landing at the park.

In 1933, Chicago threw a party. Called the Century of Progress, it took place on Northerly and it was a celebration of Chicago's 100th birthday. The theme was Aviation. At this time, Italo Balbo, at the direction and with the support of Benito Mussolini, flew twelve Savoia Marchetti S.55X float planes to Chicago's shore line. He was welcomed like royalty by dignitaries. Balbo had all the honors heaped upon him. What was once 7th Street became "Balbo Drive". A monument to honor his feat stands now in Burnham Park across the harbor from Meigs Field. Once the fair was over in 1934, movement began to make Northerly an airport. We were, however, in a worldwide economic depression.

Good times returned after the war and work started on the Northerly Airport. The island was expanded to 1-1/3 its original size. Two years in the making, Northerly Airport was dedicated on December 10, 1948. There were 100 aircraft on the field during the grand opening. Only a year later, the name was changed.

In 1949, it became Meigs Field in honor of Merrill C. Meigs, the publisher of the Chicago Herald and Examiner newspaper. Merrill Meigs was an ardent promoter and supporter of aviation in Chicago. He fought hard to bring Northerly Airport into being. He worked equally hard to promote all three airports in Chicago. At that time, O'Hare was still named Orchard-Douglas and Midway was still called Chicago Municipal. It was fitting commemoration for the airport as well as a fitting honor for a true aviation enthusiast.

Through the years, Meigs Field only got better. With the advancement in aircraft, it was necessary to lengthen the runway to 3,900 feet. The passenger terminal was added in 1961. In terms of economic contributions, it is estimated that Meigs Field contributed 1,500 jobs and $60 million annually to the Cook county economy.

To everyone's surprise, Meigs was closed by Chicago Mayor Daley in 1996. Mayor Daley decided that the City of Chicago must have another park, and it had to be located exactly at the site of Meigs Field!

This compelled an immediate political response from Governor Edgar who claimed that Daley was being high-handed and irresponsible. Powerful support for Meigs came from the Aircraft Owners and Pilots Association and the Friends of Meigs Field. These two groups were relentless in their work to bring back the airport. If necessary, Edgar threatened to bring in the National Guard to take over Meigs and maintain operations. Daley countered that "by the time Edgar's troops get here, the field will be bulldozed into oblivion."

The rhetoric went back and forth for weeks. In some smoke-filled back room, a compromise was reached. The politicos were photographed smiling and shaking hands and Meigs Field reopened.

This was exceptionally good news for me. I had missed landing at Meigs prior to the shutdown. Well aware of the velocity at which politicians can make an airport disappear, Meigs had to be visited immediately. The weekend after reopening, I was there.

The uneasy truce between Daley and the rest of the civilized world and the continuing use of Meigs Field would last only to the evening of March 31st, 2003; the night when the bulldozers came.

Ironically, my wife and I were there the evening of the bulldozing. Meigs had a nice restaurant and it was a good place to eat. When we pulled up past all of the earth moving equipment, we were stopped at the gate by a Chicago police officer. (Nota Bene. We are not certain whether these were City Police Officers or privately hired guards.) He told us the field was closed, that we couldn't enter. We explained that we only wanted to go to the restaurant to which he replied that the whole field was closed. He persisted. We saw about a dozen or so aircraft spotted on the tarmac and questioned how these pilots and passengers were going to fare. The guard only repeated that the field was closed. We had no idea of what was about to happen.

The next morning, Nancy put the Chicago paper in front of me at breakfast. Staring at the front page photographs, I muttered under breath then what is still appropriate today; "The rotten sons of bitches."

Richard M Daley (son of Hizzoner Richard Joseph Daley, Democrat; 1955-1976) delivered the deathly blow to Meigs during the night of March 31. Like a sneak thief hiding in darkness, the city bulldozed the Meigs runway. With their powerful bulldozers and other earth moving equipment, they plowed a series of huge "X's" down the length of the runway. They did their dastardly deed at 1:30 AM with no advance warning. Daley never consulted with the city council. There was never a word to the FAA. Not even the tower controllers knew about this evil plan. Some 15 aircraft were left stranded on the Meigs tarmac. The destruction of Meigs occurred only fifteen months after Richard Daley's promise to the State of Illinois to keep the airport open 25 years. Obviously, Richard M. Daley made that promise in other than "good" faith.

In one despicable, autocratic move, Mayor Daley ended an incredibly remarkable history of flight in midtown Chicago. Gone forever is the great airfield that once graced Chicago's beautiful skyline. Daley said that he closed the field, not because his wife wanted a park, but for reasons of homeland security. The more skeptical believe that the airport island will soon be home to a gambling casino. The very skeptical believe that Richard M. will have a hand in it. And, the politically savvy will <u>know</u> he will.

The passion of pilots over their loss was illustrated beautifully by The National Air Tour of 2003. This Tour was organized to celebrate 100 years of flight by flying a 4,000-mile journey. The route was originally planned for the 1932 National Air Tour which didn't happen. The new 100-year tour paid a special salute to Meigs Field. On Tuesday, September 9th, 2003, dozens of vintage aircraft flew over the west shore of Lake Michigan from north to south along the Chicago skyline, over the closed Meigs Field. At the request of the friends of Meigs Field, the ships dropped rose peddles as they passed by.

Richard M Daley, the mayor of the Second City. King Richard, who does not need consensus or consent from anyone, but does as he pleases. King Richard, the Arrogant, those rose petals were for you!

#413 Moline, Illinois
Type: Class C Identifier: MII

Quad Cities International
March 2, 1997

#414 Cedar Rapids, Iowa
Type: Class C Identifier: CID

Cedar Rapids Airport
March 2, 1997

#415 Waterloo, Iowa
Type: Class D Identifier: ALO

Waterloo Flyers Club Field
March 2, 1997

#416 Charles City, Iowa   Charles City Municipal
Type: Paved Identifier: CCY   March 2, 1997

#417 Osage, Iowa   Osage Municipal Airport
Type: Paved Identifier: D02   March 2, 1997

#418   New Hampton, Iowa   New Hampton Municipal
Type: Paved Identifier: 1Y5   March 2, 1997

#419 Cresco, Iowa   Ella Church Field
Type: Paved Identifier: CJJ   May 10, 1997

#420 Austin, Minnesota   Austin Municipal Airport
Type: Paved Identifier: AUM   May 10, 1997

#421 Dodge Center, Minn.   Dodge Center Airport
Type: Paved Identifier: 87D   May 10, 1997

#422 Rochester, Minnesota   Rochester International
Type: Class D Identifier: RST   May 10, 1997

#423 Chatfield, Minnesota   Flying A Ranch
Type: Grass Identifier: MN22   May 10, 1997

IS THIS THE FUTURE OF SPORT AVIATION?

THE TRIP ON May 10th was designed to visit all the Minnesota airports on the Chicago Sectional. Only four remained. With some luck, I could get a story or two. The visit to Flying A Ranch proved that anticipation to be correct. Chatfield provided a good ultra-light story.

An organization of ultra-light flyers had started to congregate at Chatfield. I dropped onto this grass strip just prior to their meeting. Over a dozen flyers were available. The conversation was active and animated. I liked these guys a lot.

It is here that I began to believe that sport aviation will be reborn. What has been done to sport aviation is criminal. We have allowed it to become permanently paralyzed and unable to regenerate itself.

Take GPS systems, for example. A person can buy a GPS for $200 and it will save his life when he goes camping in the wilds. Put a GPS in an airplane and it will cost in excess of $3,500; even more because they must be IFR certified. We bought our airplane when it was 25 years old and paid more than what it sold for as brand new. That is crazy!

But that is not as crazy as buying a new airplane. Our Cherokee 180, an Archer from the New Piper Aircraft Company lists for well over $200,000! A Piper Arrow, the next step up from an Archer and, probably, the cheapest entrance for a pilot to enjoy retractable gear and a controllable pitch prop will come from the factory with a substantially higher price. From that point, consideration must be made for avionics and other accessories. Adding the proper IFR equipment with backups, a Horizontal Situation Indicator and a two-axis auto pilot will add another 25% to the price of an airplane. Rare is the person who can indulge a hobby that requires a cash outlay approaching a quarter of a million dollars. My sport is dying and we all know it.

The Statute of Repose, so long sought after to protect the industry from the evils of predatory lawsuits and multimillion dollar settlements, is certainly a step in the right direction but maybe it is too late to save the production lines of Cessna, Piper, Beech, Mooney, et al. Where, then, will be the growth of general aviation?

It just might be ultra-lights. Not FAA certified ultra-lights. We have already seen one model submit to FAA certification and the plane skyrocketed in price to above $30,000. No, it will be the unregulated by government, simple to build, cheap to buy and inexpensive to maintain versions of ultra-lights.

It will mark a return to basic flying, just as flying was affordable in the 1930s. Airplanes had 40 horsepower, weighed 800 pounds and had a maximum speed of 90 miles per hour

The men at Chatfield, Minnesota's Flying A Ranch were convinced of the above. With the talk now of $25 fees for filing a flight plan, they are more interested in getting $5.00 worth of automobile gasoline down to the air strip so they can spend the rest of the afternoon flying. Perhaps they won't be able to fly in weather or do the long distances like I do, but they will be the ones who perpetuate sport aviation.

The flyers at Flying A Ranch have vision for the industry and the desire for flight. It is on their shoulders that grass roots aviation will ride out this maelstrom of litigation and crippling insurance premiums. They will do it without the help of the FAA and the kerosene burning airlines. They are the tomorrow of general aviation. God Bless Them.

#424 Preston, Minnesota   Fillmore County Airport
Type: Paved Identifier: 49Y   May 10, 1997

#425 Rushford, Minnesota   Rushford Municipal Airport
Type: Paved Identifier: 55Y   May 10, 1997

#426 Winona, Minnesota   Winona-Conrad Airport
Type: Paved Identifier: ONA   May 10, 1997

#427   LaCrosse, Wisconsin   LaCrosse International Airport
Type: Class D Identifier: LSE May 10, 1997

#428   Chicago, Illinois   Midway Airport
Type: Class C Identifier: MDW May 26, 1997

#429   West Chicago, Illinois   Dupage County Airport
Type: Class D Identifier: DPA May 26, 1997

WHY I DON'T LIKE PAYING TAXES

BY ANY STRETCH of the imagination, the Dupage County Airport is the most shameful waste of tax payer money in aviation. The office building for the airport is a seven-story monstrosity in stone and masonry. The building rambles on for several hundred feet in length and has dozens and dozens of offices in it. In spite of the county's attempts for a couple of years to rent out the office space to private business, it has no tenants. Furthermore, the county went the extra step and built a golf course across the street from the building. What a waste!

#430   Rockford, Illinois   Greater Rockford Airport
Type: Class C Identifier: RFD   June 8, 1997

TWO AIRPORTS NOT VISITED

PULLMAN, MICHIGAN IS the home town of George Theodore Baker, a self-made man and multi-millionaire. While I never met Mr. Baker, I became very close to his beautiful National Airlines. He built this airline single handedly from nothing into the seventh largest carrier in America. My affiliation with National came later, after Bud Maytag bought out Baker's interest. I would love to have seen the little town from which George Baker sprang. I even tried it, once upon a time.

Hoskin Field is a 1,700-foot field which is well under my 2,000-foot minimum length. Nonetheless, on one hot summer day, I entered a left-hand pattern for a landing on runway 9. While still 400 to 500 feet above ground, I saw that the trees on the east end were a heck of lot higher than they seemed to be earlier! Furthermore, the Tana

Balls that highlighted the power lines rimming the west end of the runway now came into clear view. I felt that I could shoehorn the little Cherokee between them, but it would be a high risk proposition. I even doubted if I could get the plane out, no matter how much fuel was drained, no matter how low the temperature dropped. Landing at Hoskin would be a one-way trip. At 200 feet above ground, I applied full power and pulled up. Pullman passed below me becoming smaller and less important. It would simply be an airport that I missed.

The second missed airport is Chicago O'Hare International. It is an interesting airport and is the subject of the two stories that follow.

To get the full effect of the stories, please allow your mind to drift back to the early 1920s, when booze was illegal and the search for good times was unfettered. A socio-political void existed in Chicago and that haunting vacuum was filled by none other than Al Capone. Imagine being there in the mid to late 1920s when Johnnie Torrio's grip on Cook County was weakening and young Al Capone's skyrocket of life was about to captivate Chicago, America and the world. Capone's five years of influence and control would never be forgotten and forever be analyzed. With our present-day grip on reality, consider these two stories.

- - - - - - -

"Easy Eddie" was a man on the take and on the make. He was educated in Law, but had larceny in his heart. Starting his career in St. Louis in the early 1920s, he befriended Owen P. Smith who had invented the rabbit mechanism for dog races. Because dog racing was widely outlawed, the invention was worthless in most places except Chicago. Al Capone had the issue of dog racing tied up in the court system so the sport was popular in the Windy City. Until ruled otherwise in the courts, gambling on Greyhounds continued unrestrained.

Dog races were controversial because they were notoriously easy to fix. Simply feed 7 of the dogs a pound of hamburger before the race and bet on the 8th. The hungry dog will win the race every time. Perhaps, this was the case at the Hawthorne Kennel Club in Chicago, now Sportsman's Park, the track that was owned and operated by Al Capone.

Easy Eddie took Smith's invention to Chicago and sought out Capone who liked the mechanical rabbit. More importantly, Capone took a liking to Easy Eddie and gave him a position of power in his mob. Drawing on his legal training, Eddie kept Capone's thugs out of jail and ran the Hawthorne Kennel Club. Eventually, he became the President of both Hawthorne Dog and Horse Racing Tracks on the near south side of Chicago. Earning big money from his nefarious duties, Eddie could afford a mansion that filled an entire Chicago city block. The house was fenced; he had live-in help and all of the conveniences of the day. He even had a handgun range in the back yard.

Easy Eddie had two kids, Patricia and Butch. He loved them very much and gave them all any kid could ask for while they were growing up: clothes, cars, and the best possible education. His son Butch harbored a burning desire to attend a military academy; specifically, Annapolis. With the Feds and other special investigative units always in Capone's business, Eddie knew that a congressional appointment was out of the question. So Eddie put out feelers within the law enforcement circles and found an interest in gaining insider information and a series of clandestine meetings followed and a deal was made. Butch would get a pass into Annapolis and, in return, Easy Eddie would mole damning information to the Federal tax people.

Robert J. Schoenberg in his book, "MR.CAPONE" cites several examples of information leaked to Federal officers. The most critical was the information Eddie provided regarding the jurors for the pivotal tax evasion case which would eventually put Capone in jail for 11 years. He made the Feds aware that 10 of them were paid off. Specifically, jurors numbered 30 through 39 had been bought and would be the holdouts against conviction. Any one or more from this lot would guarantee a hung jury. The Feds advised the presiding judge, Federal Judge James H. Wilkerson, at the last minute. Wilkerson simply traded the jury selection list with a fellow judge on a case involving a first time offender with a minor offense. Capone didn't have a chance. He had to face actual justice and he knew who sold him out.

Within a week of Capone's release from jail in 1940, Eddie was shot and killed on Rockwell Street in Chicago. He was machine-gunned when a 7-passenger Cadillac touring car pulled up alongside his Jewitt. The finish was a shot gun blast to the face, a signature of an Al Capone hit. Easy Eddie, illicit liquor hijacker, corrupter of judges, policemen and politicians lay in a pool of his own blood. A .32 caliber automatic, a rosary and a crucifix were found in Easy Eddie's pocket.

- - - - - - -

This is well-known story to Chicagoans but it seems to be a mystery to everyone else. Paul Harvey occasionally tells the story of Butch O'Hare but even these reminders fail to gain much traction. I suppose it will continue to intrigue folks for many more years to come.

Butch's education at Annapolis and the beginning of his naval career overlapped his father's final years. He was trained as a fighter pilot, and was a skilled carrier pilot. He was an exceptional aerial marksman.

He distinguished himself in the early months of World War II while flying off the USS Lexington. On the 20th of February, 1942, three flights of enemy aircraft approached the American fleet. Butch commanded one of those flights of Grumman F4F Wildcats that pounced on nine Japanese twin engine (Mitsubishi Ki-21 "Sally") bombers. The book "ACE PILOTS", (author unknown) best describes the scene that Butch faced:

'Six Wildcats, one of them piloted by Butch, roared off the Lexington's deck to stop them. Butch and his wingman spotted the V formation of bombers first and dived to try to head them off. The other F4F pilots were too far away to reach most of the enemy planes before they released their bombs. As if this weren't bad enough, Butch's wingman discovered his guns were jammed. He was forced to turn away. Butch stood alone between the Lexington and the bombers.

'Butch didn't hesitate. He roared into the enemy formation at full throttle. While tracers from the concentrated fire of the nine bombers streaked around him, he took careful aim at the starboard engine of the last plane in the V and squeezed his trigger. Slugs from the Wildcat's six .50-caliber guns ripped into the Japanese bomber's wing and the engine literally jumped out of its mountings. The bomber spun crazily toward the sea as Butch's guns tore up another enemy plane. Then he ducked to the other side of the formation and smashed the port engine of the last Japanese plane there.

'One by one he attacked the oncoming bombers until five had been downed. The Executive Officer on the Lexington, Commander John S. "Jimmy" Thatch, (who had developed the Thatch Weave combat maneuver) later reported that at one point he saw three of the bombers falling in flames at the same time. By now, Thatch and the other pilots had joined the fight. This was lucky because Butch was out of ammunition. The Wildcats took care of several more bombers and the Lexington managed to evade the few bombs that were released. It was an amazing example of daring and shooting skill. Afterward, Thach determined that Butch had probably saved his ship. He was promoted to Lieutenant Commander and awarded the highest decoration of his country, the Congressional Medal of Honor. The official Navy presentation is recorded at the end of this piece.'

Chicago is very proud of its native son. Even though born of "gangster blood," they saluted him posthumously by naming its airport after him. Commander Edward H.O'Hare, son of Edward J.O'Hare, is memorialized in bronze in Concourse One of Chicago O'Hare International airport!" It reads as follows:

- - - - - - -

The President of the United States of America, authorized by Act of Congress, March 3, 1863, has awarded in the name of The Congress the Medal of Honor to

LIEUTENANT EDWARD HENRY O'HARE
UNITED STATES NAVY

Rank and organization: Lieutenant, U.S. Navy. Born: 13 March 1914, St. Louis, Mo. Entered service at: St. Louis, Mo. Other Navy awards: Navy Cross, Distinguished Flying Cross with 1 gold star.

Citation: For conspicuous gallantry and intrepidity in aerial combat, at grave risk of his life above and beyond the call of duty, as section leader and pilot of Fighter Squadron 3 on 20 February 1942. Having lost the assistance of his teammates, Lt. O'Hare interposed his plane between his ship and an advancing enemy formation of 9 attacking twin-engine heavy bombers. Without hesitation, alone and unaided, he repeatedly attacked this enemy formation, at close range in the face of intense combined machine gun and cannon fire. Despite this concentrated opposition, Lt. O'Hare, by his gallant and courageous action, his extremely skillful marksmanship in making the most of every shot of his limited amount of ammunition, shot down 5 enemy bombers and severely damaged a sixth before they reached the bomb release point. As a result of his gallant action--one of the most daring, if not the most daring, single action in the history of combat aviation--he undoubtedly saved his carrier from serious damage.

Butch O'Hare was lost in night action off the Marianas on November 26, 1943. He had 7 confirmed kills and 8 probable kills.

#431 Charlotte, Michigan
Type: Grass Identifier: 49G

Wend Valley Airport
June 14, 1997

#432 Sunfield, Michigan
Type: Grass Identifier: C43

Cure Field
June 14, 1997

#433 Eureka, Michigan
Type: Grass Identifier: 61G

Randolph Field
June 14, 1997

#434 St. John's, Michigan
Type: Grass Identifier: 2M16

Tripp Creek
June 14, 1997

#435 Chesaning, Michigan
Type: Grass Identifier: 50G

Nixon Memorial Airport
June 14, 1997

#436 Clio, Michigan　　　　　　　　Cagney Airport
Type: Grass Identifier: 51G　　　　June 14, 1997

#437 Frankenmuth, Michigan　　　William "Tiny" Zehnder A/P
Type: Grass Identifier: 66G　　　　June 14, 1997

#438 Saginaw, Michigan　　　　　Browne Field
Type: Paved Identifier: 3SG　　　　June 14, 1997

#439 Caro, Michigan　　　　　　　Caro Municipal Airport
Type: Paved Identifier: 78D　　　　June 14, 1997

#440 Sebewaing, Michigan　　　　Sebewaing Municipal Airport
Type: Paved Identifier: 98G　　　　June 14, 1997

#441　Bad Axe, Michigan　　　　　Huron County Airport
Type: Paved Identifier: 76D　　　　June 14, 1997

THE MCQUEEN FAMILY OF PIGEON, MICHIGAN

THE DAY HAD become very hot day and I was sweating rapidly. Dehydration was becoming a problem; I needed something to drink. The Fixed Base Operation at Bad Axe was unmanned and locked. There was no water fountain or soft drink machine to be found. There was, however, a family washing their Cessna 172. I walked up and started some small talk. After I mentioned that I was thirsty, they offered one of their soft drinks. Actually, it was one of those sport drinks that claim to replace vitamins and minerals lost during exercise. The drink was welcome and I was grateful.

This was the McQueen family. His business card says that he the Vice President of Thumb National Bank in Pigeon, Michigan.

It is quite common to geographically locate small towns and areas of interest in south Michigan by first envisioning the shape of the lower peninsula of Michigan to be a left handprint. This being the case, the area between Saginaw Bay and Lake Huron is usually referred to as the "thumb" of Michigan.

Jim's wife Kathy and his son Mike seemed to be a pleasant, contented family. They were genuinely happy to be with each other. It was really refreshing and, at the same time, reassuring. Jim McQueen is a relatively new pilot. He had the urge to fly since he was 10 years old but never could manage to take out time for flying lessons. Finally, once he was settled into his career with the family about raised, Jim started to satisfy his quest.

Nowadays, parents are all too often reduced to a taxi driver taking children to soccer and the mall only to come back in a couple of hours to pick them up again. Family members are often bitter enemies pitted against each other because of our lost ability to resolve issue through familial love and understanding. It was good to see the three McQueens together in a family activity.

Jim had been flying one year and accumulated only 85 hours before he ran into an obstacle: he needed a kidney transplant. He lasted long enough to satisfy the waiting list. The operation was a success and he regained his health. The FAA took away his medical status. All pilots must pass a bi-annual medical examination to certify their pilot's license. Jim was grounded. He had to sell his beautiful 1974 Cessna. He continues to work with the FAA in hopes of convincing them to reinstate his medical.

Jim has gone back to golfing and a little farming in his leisure time but he would rather be back flying.

It will be a steep uphill climb with the FAA to get his medical reversed. Once that agency moves in a direction, it is virtuously impossible to get them turned around. The FAA is intractable, immovable, rigid and uncaring. Hopelessly stuck in a bureaucratic morass, the FAA lives and thrives by causing problems for others. To solve problems gives the FAA (and other government agencies) less reason for being in business tomorrow. Good luck, Jim.

Back in Indiana, I sent a card thanking them for their kindness and hospitality, with a copy of "Lunar Visit". I think of them often.

#442   Deckerville, Michigan   Indian Creek Airport
Type: Grass Identifier: 56G   June 14, 1997

#443 Sandusky, Michigan   Sandusky City Airport
Type: Paved Identifier: Y83   June 14, 1997

A TRUE VACATION

JUNE 14TH, 1997 was a Friday. For the first time in 20 years, I had real vacation days coming. Until now, my work as a consultant meant keeping regular hours while the "billable time" lasted. No pay during national holidays, no pay for sick time and no pay for vacations. It was work, work and more work. But now it was different. Now I could take-off a day or two here and there.

With this newfound wealth of free time, a Friday soirée had to be scheduled. It would be during this long summer day that I could visit the "thumb" of Michigan. As I mentioned earlier, Wolverines will tell you that the lower portion of Michigan is shaped like a hand. The thumb is that area north of Detroit, east of Saginaw Bay and bordered on the west by Lake Erie. There are no major cities in "the thumb" and the airspace would be all mine.

#444 Waukegan, Illinois   Waukegan Regional Airport
Type: Class D Identifier: UGN   June 15, 1997

THE CLASSIEST FBO

IT WAS AN absolutely gorgeous summer day and I was getting in some instrument hours flying with my favorite CFII (Certified Flight Instructor; Instrument or, colloquially referred to as "Double I"), MS Laura Lichtel, now Mrs. Mike Jen. Neither of us had ever been to Waukegan Regional. The buildings were gorgeous. We were immediately struck by the richness of the decor. Typically, all soft appointments were in a deep forest green. The offsetting color was a light cream or eggshell. All the wood work was as handsome black walnut. None of the hallways were straight; everything was angled to prevent a sense of sameness.

Walking by the maintenance hangars, we noted that all the access doors had windows. This was obviously to show off the maintenance area. Hangar floors were painted a light battleship gray and kept immaculately clean. The floors actually sparkled!

Pilots lounge furnishings included several oversized Lazy Boy's with extra deep cushions. Entertainment equipment was built-in and operated by remote control. In keeping with the hallway design, this was not a square or rectangular room; indeed, it had eleven corners!

The staff was professional and cheerful. Their uniforms were extraordinarily designed and detailed. We were met at the plane by a smiling lineman, and a red carpet was spread before our feet. (He reappeared later to assist our departure and to say goodbye.) The desk personnel tended to our every need with an ever present smile. As we were leaving, they asked us to grade their service. Naturally, they earned an excellent grade. At the bottom of the form I wrote, "this airport has the classiest FBO I have ever seen!"

EDWARD W. SPENCER

THIS STORY ABOUT Waukegan Regional airport has nothing to do with its current status or a recent event. Rather, it goes back in time more than 150 years. Today, the Coast Guard maintains a staff and two Aerospatiale HH65 helicopters for air search and rescue work. Its team provides a valuable safety service for the boating and bathing public along the Milwaukee - Chicago shore of Lake Michigan. Long before helicopters, however, back in 1860, there was a lifesaving station on the Waukegan beach. It was located a short distance from the present airport. In golf jargon, it was probably a 3-wood from the end of what now is runway 5 or at the threshold of runway 23.

The lifesaving station was manned by the Northwestern University swim team, located in Evanston, Illinois. The trip from Evanston to Waukegan was as easy then as it is today. The Union Pacific rail line from downtown Chicago still runs very close to the beach location. One of the members of the swim team was a very powerful swimmer named Edward W. Spencer, a 19-year old sophomore enrolled in the Garrett Evangelical Theological Seminary on the Northwestern campus.

Early in the morning of September 8th, 1860, the schooner Augusta, under the command of Captain Darius Mallott, was six days out of Port Huron, Michigan with a load of timber bound for Chicago. Chicago in that era was devouring huge amounts of lumber, building and expanding into a major metropolis. The Augusta was 128 feet on the keel, displacing 266 gross tons and drawing just over 11 feet. She had good weather until she drew within 50 or 75 miles of Chicago. About 7:30 PM on the 7th, a heavy squall from the northeast caught the Augusta by surprise. All sailors know that Lake Michigan is a treacherous lake that turns angry very fast. With all the sail she carried and a heading of south by east, she was driving hard. However, danger lurked with each following wave. With the water beneath her confused, the Augusta broached and was set on her beam end. The cargo shifted when the ship slammed against the water, which reduced their maneuverability. The sail was lowered from the foremast, and the mainsail on the aft mast was heavily reefed. All the jibs were brought in to regain control of the ship. Running southward under desperately reduced sail, the lookout spotted the red lights of the wooden-side wheel steamer, Lady Elgin.

The Lady Elgin was north by east bound struggling with the high seas and taking them almost square on the bow. She was a stately, magnificent ship only nine years, 252 feet long with a 33 foot beam, and displaced 1,037 gross tons. On board were more than 485 passengers plus other cargo including 69 head of cattle. She was bound for Milwaukee under the command of Captain Jack Wilson, who knew very well the sly treachery of Lake Michigan.

The deck crew aboard the Lady Elgin could clearly hear the bellowing voice of Captain Mallot just off their starboard beam. She was close, much too close as Mallot barked out to his helmsman, "Hard up! For God's sake, man, hard up!" The Lady Elgin, after being sighted by the Augusta, had less than an hour to live.

The Augusta put her short prow squarely into the Lady Elgin, just aft of the starboard paddle wheel. When they separated, it was assumed that the Augusta had taken the worse of the collision, and both captains agreed that the Augusta should try and make Chicago without any delay. A lifeboat was lowered on the port side and dispatched around the aft end of the Lady Elgin to survey the damage. Once in the water, it was never heard from again. While some of the crew worked furiously to plug the hole, other crew quickly pushed the livestock overboard. The ship soon broke into two pieces and, within a few minutes, the pilot house broke away from the forward section.

Where there had been music and dancing, within seconds well over 400 souls were in the angry waters of Lake Michigan fighting for their lives - clinging to anything that floated, with Illinois shoreline in sight. But this tragedy was not over. Survivors were driven into the shore line with unbelievable ferocity by 10- and 12-foot waves and 70 mile an hour winds. Scores lost their lives at the edge of the water by being slammed into the beach or crushed beneath debris.

The lifesaving team could not see the wreck of the Lady Elgin, but they did see hundreds of people fighting for their lives. Edward W. Spencer threw himself into the fray with unbelievable determination. One-by-one he brought back storm-tossed souls only to go back immediately into watery turmoil. Those on the beach waded into waist-deep water to help Edward. As soon as one passenger was safe, Edward Spencer turned back for another, and then another. Without rest he drove himself, fighting the waves and exposure on unprotected bodies. Finally, after saving 17 lives, he stumbled out of the lake nearly in delirious exhaustion. Collapsing on the beach, he repeatedly called out, "Did I do my full duty? Did I do my best?"

The sinking of the Lady Elgin would mark the greatest loss of life on Lake Michigan until July 24, 1915 when the Eastland rolled over while loading passengers for a summer excursion at a Chicago River dock. Religious services were held at several Milwaukee churches for decades after the Lady Elgin-Augusta tragedy, in memory of the Milwaukee residents who lost their lives on that fateful autumn morning. To this day, St. John Catholic Cathedral holds a memorial service each September 8th in honor of its lost parishioners.

No one knows exactly how many people drowned as the ship's manifest went down with the wreck. The best estimate is that with a capacity of 485 persons, the Lady Elgin was slightly overloaded. The actual number of survivors is also lost to history, but best counts indicate that between 90 and 101 came ashore that night and lived. Seventeen of them owe their lives to one amazing, incredible man: Ed Spencer.

Many tales are told about Edward W. Spencer; some are true. He continued with his Divinity work. He did not suffer permanent nerve damage. Edward finished college with his class. He did not spend the rest of his life in a wheel chair, although he may have been confined to one in his later years. While some contend that he died on the beach that night, he lived to be 81 years old passing away in California in 1922. His spirit lives on at Northwestern University. A monument to his heroism was erected to his heroism at the university's gymnasium soon after his passing which describes his brave deeds on that September night long ago. The final line at the bottom of the stone is both an inspiration and a challenge to students who followed him at Northwestern: "Did I do my best?" The question provides thoughtful soul-searching for students and pilots as well.

#445 Kenosha, Wisconsin   Kenosha Regional Airport
Type: Class D Identifier: ENW   June 15, 1997

#446 Sturdevant, Wisconsin   Sylvania Airport
Type: Paved Identifier: C89   June 15, 1997

#447 Racine, Wisconsin   Robert H. Batten Field
Type: Paved Identifier: RAC   June 28th, 1 997

#448 Lyons, Wisconsin   Wag-Aero Private Field
Type: Grass Identifier: Private June 28th, 1997

NOT AGAIN!

ALL PILOTS RECEIVE the standard aviation equipment catalogs through the mail. There is a very active mail order business due to the thin structure of general aviation. That is, there is no heavy concentration of pilots in America. Pilots represent less than 1% of the American public. Compounding this lack of concentration is the fact that they are scattered all through the population without bias for personal income, gender, occupation or geography. There are organizations such as the Flying Doctors but there is also the Flying Farmers. While the Ninety Nines represent the women flyers, there is no specific organization for men. In other words, a flyer could be anyone, anywhere.

What has been described above is a marketing nightmare for retailers. Since only 1 percent of the audience is a flyer, advertising in the mass media is not cost effective. Television, radio, mass mailings are all cost prohibitive. Retailers have concluded that distribution of their catalogs to currently active pilots is the best way of putting their promotional effort in front of the correct audience. Such is the case with Wag-Aero out of Lyons, Wisconsin. They have a nice mail order business based on the periodic mailing of flyers and catalogs. Wag-Aero has a private air strip and Lyons, Wisconsin is only 75 miles away. A visit was in order.

The trip on July 5th, 1997 took me northward on the VFR route up the Chicago lakeshore. I first visited Robert Batten Field in Racine, Wisconsin on the shore of Lake Michigan. Since Wag-Aero was not in my LORAN C data base, I had to set up some intersections with the VOR system. The air navigation went well, but the pilot's execution was faulty. I missed the field.

I flew over a field that had a very rough looking surface. It could have been either a paved or hard surface strip, or one that had deteriorated badly and is referred to as an unimproved runway. I have been to a couple like that in Illinois and Indiana. I entered the pattern and landed without incident. Except... I had missed Wag-Aero by about one mile! I was now firmly planted on the Burlington, Wisconsin airport.

The folks at Burlington remembered me. They tried to make me feel better by saying how easy it is to mistake Burlington for Wag-Aero. Because they are so close and somewhat similar, anyone can make the same mistake. They were being kind. The fact is, the two strips are not similar, they run in different directions and one is really grass while the other is really paved. I screwed up, pure and simple.

I got back in the plane and headed for Wag-Aero again. The field was less than a mile away. This time, I made it. I still feel embarrassed about having landed at the wrong airport.

#449   Lake Geneva, WI   Lake Geneva Estates
Type: Paved Identifier: Private   June 28th, 1997

#450 Waukesha, WI   Waukesha County Airport
Type: Class D Identifier: UES   June 28th, 1997

#451 Hartford, Wisconsin   Hartford Municipal Airport
Type: Paved Identifier: HXF   June 28th, 1997

#452 Sheboygan, Wisconsin	Sheboygan County Memorial
Type: Paved Identifier: SBM	June 28th, 1997
#453 Manitowoc, Wisconsin	Manitowoc County Airport
Type: Paved Identifier: MTV	June 28th, 1997
#454 Appleton, Wisconsin	Outgamie County Airport
Type: Class D Identifier: ATV	June 28th, 1997

ANOTHER FIRST

THERE ARE SEVERAL firsts on my list. There is the first airport where a landing fee was assessed, the first where I landed by mistake, and so on. Then there is the story where ... Well, it goes like this.

I called in a position report and reported my intention was to land at Outgamie Regional Airport Appleton about 15 miles east of Appleton, Wisconsin. The radio traffic was very low and the tower was very helpful so the talk between us was easy and casual. The landing, as I recall, was on runway 21. The Tower Operator was also filling the role of Ground Control. At roll out, I asked to be spotted somewhere near the on-field restaurant. As Ground Control, he was very accommodating and told me exactly where to park and how to get to the café. I followed his instructions, but as I walked from the Cherokee along the fence, there was no way to get to the pedestrian side of the airport. All the gates were locked all the way to the terminal. I tried all the doors at the terminal. Most of them were placarded with signs that only air crews were allowed or entrance was not permitted or some type of warning. Regardless of the warnings, they were all locked. I circled the whole terminal and could not find an open door until the last one.

I opened the door and walked in. The little wind outside was whipping around the corner of the building and the door slammed shut behind me. Walking up a ramp I realized that it was a passenger loading - unloading ramp that connected the passenger gates with waiting aircraft. This is a standard arrangement, so it was immediately familiar. The interior door at the other end of the ramp was locked tight.

This is too difficult. All I wanted was a sandwich and this was too much work. I turned to leave. Now I had a problem: The door to the outside which had slammed itself shut was now firmly jammed. I was caught between two locked doors in the passenger ramp!

I half-ran up the ramp to signal someone, but I could see no one. There was no one inside the terminal to signal. I tried knocking on the interior door, and could not attract anyone's attention. I felt trapped. Then I spotted a telephone on the wall. Alongside the phone was a list of airline gates and ticket counters; next to each listing was the phone number of the corresponding gate or ticket counter. The phone I was on was listed, too. It showed the gate number plus passenger ramp. I could see through the window, the gate was empty. I called the ticket counter. A woman answered.

I explained that I was caught on the ramp. She became furious. She wanted to know whose authorization I had to be there. Who let me in? What was my purpose there? I explained that I was a private pilot trying to get some lunch. She cut me off and asked what airline I flew for. Why didn't I call my own carrier? The more she spouted off questions, the less she waited for an answer and the angrier she became. This was getting ugly. Here I was - all alone, trapped between locked doors and I had a woman yelling at me.

Finally, she paused to catch her breath. I edged in a comment that all I wanted was to get out of here. She said that she would be down very soon. She hung up and I waited. Within a couple of minutes, the ramp phone rang. I figured it was for me. Again, it was my new-found friend. She began to pose challenging questions about my reason for being caught on the ramp. Now she was even more furious. She allowed less time for answers on this call than she did during the previous encounter. Now I was frustrated. I wanted out and this was going nowhere. She threatened to send the police. I really didn't care who came. Anyone else would be more understanding than this woman.

After she hung up, obviously in a snit, I could only wait. A young man showed up within a few minutes and peeked into the window. I made myself visible to him. He tried the door from the outside, but it still wouldn't open. He pulled harder and I began to push from the inside ...still nothing. As my lifesaver was tugging on the door handle, I began to lunge with all my weight at the door from the inside. It finally gave way. Free at last, free at last. Thank God Almighty, free at last!

My young lifesaver was much more polite and coherent than the woman on the phone. In fact, he was downright friendly. He quickly grasped my situation. He advised me that this was a high security area and that I had to leave. FAA regulations were clear about that. I understood and began to retrace my steps back to the Cherokee. I wasn't as hungry as when I had landed. He walked with me and we enjoyed a pleasant conversation. The young man continued to walk with me even after we left the terminal area. I started to feel odd. The Cherokee was only 100 yards away. I pointed out my airplane and told him that I could make it from here but he continued with me. Then it struck me. Stopping in my tracks I turned to him and asked if he was escorting me off the property. He smiled and answered in the affirmative. He had no choice. Airline policy and FAA regulations dictated that he had to see me off the field.

I told him that it wasn't necessary, but he was just doing his job. He stood next to the Cherokee even after I got inside and started the engine. We both smiled to each other. He waved good-bye when I taxied away. I waved back.

After 40 years of flying and hundreds of landings at hundreds of airports, this was the first time I was thrown out of an airport.

#455   New Holstein, WI   New Holstein Municipal Airport
Type: Paved Identifier: 8D1   June 28th, 1997

EASTWARD BOUND!

IT WAS OBVIOUS that if I wanted to land at 500 airports, I would have to go east as well as west. Looking at the map marked with all the airports that have been visited so far, the majority of my flying was to the west with most eastern travel limited to some Ohio fields. I would have to go farther east. A small sliver of West Virginia peeks through between Ohio and Pennsylvania. It was only for a few miles but there were a couple airports, and they could be reached in one day's travel. But if only one were gained, then it would have to be Wheeling, West Virginia. Yes. Wheeling is a very recognizable, steel producing West Virginia city. A trip was planned for an eastward excursion.

Weather in the Midwest that day, was clear with only the mildest of disturbances likely in eastern Ohio. An early start on Saturday morning during the longer days of summer would almost guarantee the possibility of a round trip that included Wheeling, West Virginia.

The first stop was in excellent VFR weather, but it quickly deteriorated. Within 50 miles, the ceiling had dropped to 3,000 feet although visibility remained above 10 miles. It was a lot like flying in an Oreo cookie. For the next 150 miles, the ceiling and visibility held at those levels. While I didn't like it, it was still plenty safe.

After stopping at the two Coshocton fields, I decided to press on to West Virginia. Cadiz, Ohio was the final checkpoint. I wanted to spend some more time with the folks at Cadiz but they were busy with other things. Some 50 miles later, I was at Wheeling, West Virginia. The airport at Wheeling merits a story of its own.

#456 Bucyrus, Ohio
Type: Paved Identifier: 17G

Port Bucyrus Airport
July 5, 1997

#457 Coshocton, Ohio
Type: Grass Identifier: 80G

Tri City Airport
July 5, 1997

#458 Coshocton, Ohio   Downing Field
Type: Paved Identifier: I40   July 5, 1997

#459 Cadiz, Ohio   Harrison County Airport
Type: Paved Identifier: 8G6   July 5, 1997

#460 Wheeling, West Virginia   Wheeling - Ohio County Airport
Type: Class D Identifier: HLG   July 5, 1997

OLDE STIFEL FIELD

THE CITIZENS OF Wheeling have a true sense of history. Originally named Stifel Field, Wheeling-Ohio County Airport was dedicated on November 1, 1946. The first commercial flight into the field was Pennsylvania Central's DC-3, NC49553. City officials were counting on a more modern DC-4, but it went down for maintenance and the Goony Bird was a last minute substitution. Hurriedly painted on the nose was "Capitalliner City of Wheeling." Later in the day, a TWA Constellation landed in Wheeling. While the airport has undergone improvements and modernization, (there are a number of approaches including a ground-based ILS system for Runway 3) the field has retained the old terminal building and has maintained its original 1940's configuration. All the advertising is for products that are recognizable but in the theme of the thirties. The old wooden ticket window with vertical bars and a small opening at the bottom where money could be slid in and tickets can be slid out is still there. The bars appear to be varnished white oak. The floors and ceilings are one-inch square black and white tiles. There is an old rotating beacon in the middle of the lobby. A three-bladed Constellation prop hangs on the wall. The terminal is, in effect, a small aviation museum.

A substantial amount of credit goes to Dr. Charles C. Quarles

(DDS, retired) for his outstanding work in preserving the historical preservation of the terminal interior as well as his contributions of airline memorabilia.

Wheeling, West Virginia wins the award for the Most Charming Airport visited.

#461 Steubenville, Ohio
Type: Paved Identifier: 2G2

Jefferson County Airpark
July 5, 1997

#462 Carrollton, Ohio
Type: Paved Identifier: TSO

Carroll County Airport
July 5, 1997

#463 Atwood, Ohio
Type: Grass Identifier: OI56

Atwood Lake Resort
July 5, 1997

#464 New Philadelphia, Ohio
Type: Paved Identifier: PHS

Harry Clever Field
July 5, 1997

#465 Beach City, Ohio
Type: Grass Identifier: 2D7

Beach City Airport
July 5, 1997

#466 Ashland, Ohio
Type: Paved Identifier: 3G4

Ashland County Airport
July 5, 1997

#467 Hinckley, Illinois
Type: Grass Identifier: 0C2

Hinckley Glider Field
August 23, 1997

#468 Maquoketa, Iowa
Type: Paved Identifier: OQW

Swift Field
August 23, 1 97

SAY WHAT?

THE NAME OF this field can only be correctly pronounced by the natives: MA CO KID AH. That is, MA as in "When do we eat, Ma?" Then CO as in coincide or coincidental. Then KE as in "kid" and TA as in "duh". Emphasis is on the second syllable. Ma COKE e dah!

I must have sounded like a total foreigner when making radio announcements coming into the field. But then, the names of many airfields in Wisconsin, Iowa and Illinois, are mispronounced!

#469 Marion, Iowa   Marion Airport
Type: Grass Identifier: C17   August 23, 1997

#470 Waukon, Iowa   Waukon Field
Type: Paved Identifier: Y01   August 23, 1997

#471 Black River Falls, Wisconsin   Black River Falls Area Airport
Type: Paved Identifier: BCK   August 23, 1997

#472 Sparta, Wisconsin   Sparta\Camp McCoy Field
Type: Military Identifier: CMY   August 23, 1997

#473 Tomah, Wisconsin   Bloyer Field
Type: Paved Identifier: Y72   August 23, 1997

#474 Necedah, Wisconsin   Necedah Airport
Type: Paved Identifier: DAF   August 23, 1997

#475 Baraboo, Wisconsin   Wisconsin Dells Airport
Type: Paved Identifier: DLL   August 23, 1997

#476 Juneau, Wisconsin   Dodge County Airport
Type: Paved Identifier: UNU   August 23, 1997

DO YOU HAVE 100 LOW LEAD AVAILABLE?

AFTER SPENDING 15 years as a consultant without paid holidays or vacations, having a real job was different. For one, a vacation allowance meant that I could take a day now and then. This was the case on July 5th, 1997. With the rest of America working, I could have the air to myself. Besides, it was a beautiful, sunny day.

Having visited more than more than 450 airports, I realized that, except for about 15 or 20 fields, my journeys had led me to all the airports on the Sectional map. With some effort, my goal of 500 airports could be met with a visit to the rest of the airports on the Sectional map. I set aside this day to fly to many of those airports that remained unvisited. A few were in Iowa, several around the Chicago area and a handful in Wisconsin.

The trip was uneventful until I started to run low on gas at Waukon. The left tank (capacity of 25 gallons) had less than five gallons in it. The right tank indicated less than half full. I was getting worried. No fuel was available to the public at Waukon. There was a fuel supply, but only club members with special keys could turn on the pumps. No fuel was available at Black River Falls either. Surely, Sparta, a combination military base and public access field would have gas. They did, but it was not sold on weekdays. I'm 300 miles from home, almost out of fuel and see no indication that aviation gas is sold in this part of Wisconsin during the week.

Tomah or Necedah were very close but no fuel for sale. Now I was worried; this had never happened before. The thought of three or four gas guzzling takeoffs were etched in my conscious. It wasn't until I reached Baraboo that I could fill the tanks. But, I called in first to check availability. Maybe having the air to one's self has its drawbacks. Who is going to staff fuel pumps for only one guy who is flying around on his vacation day?

#477   Fond du Lac, Wisconsin   Fond du Lac Skyport
Type: Paved   Identifier: FLD   December 13th, 1997

#478   Oshkosh, Wisconsin   Steve Wittman Field
Type: Paved   Identifier: OSH   December 13th, 1997

#479   West Bend, Wisconsin   Kettle Moraine Airport
Type: Paved   Identifier: ETB   December 13th, 1997

#480   Green Bay, Wisconsin   Austen - Staubel Airport
Type: Paved   Identifier: GRB   April 10th, 1998

#481   Sturgeon Bay, Wisconsin   Sturgeon Bay Municipal
Type: Paved   Identifier: SUE   April 10th, 1998

#482   Ephraim, Wisconsin   Ephraim - Fish Creek Airport
Type: Paved Identifier: 3D2   April 10th, 1998

#483   Menominee, Michigan   Menominee Municipal Airport
Type: Paved Identifier: LUM   April 10th, 1998

#484   Oconto, Wisconsin   Oconto Municipal Airport
Type: Paved   Identifier: OCQ   April 10th, 1998

#485   Shawano, Wisconsin   Shawano Municipal Airport
Type: Paved   Identifier: 3WO   April 10th, 1998

#486   Clintonville, Wisconsin   Clintonville Municipal
Type: Paved Identifier: CLI   April 10th, 1998

#487   Waupaca, Wisconsin   Waupaca Municipal Airport
Type: Paved Identifier: PCZ   April 10th, 1998

#488   Goshen, Indiana   Eby's Pines Private Air Strip
Type: Grass   Identifier: Private   May 17th, 1998 Grass

ME AND COUSIN BILL

OUSIN BILL AND I became much closer after meeting the way we did in Plymouth. We talked on the phone quite a bit and exchanged e-mails often. It was a good relationship. His spelling of our last name was more Anglicized. That is, the family changed the spelling to make the second "h" a "k". Both versions of the name are pronounced alike; but the new spelling is easier for people to pronounce correctly the first time.

Bill's brother Clarence, who lives in California and I share a common interest: we actively pursue our genealogy. Bill put me in touch with Clarence and, before long, the three of us were exchanging family data and other information over the internet. We were making phone calls to other relatives and creating a very complete picture of the Hechlinski family. Only one Hechlinski came to America: Jacob, my great grandfather. He migrated to the United States about 15 years before the Civil War, well before the Potato famine and the flurry of European border wars in the late 19th century.

During one of these calls, we heard that a young woman in the Fort Wayne area, Patty Ritter, was also very active in our family's history. She was married and had two young boys. It became evident that Patty had done some scholarly work on the family tree. Bill and I decided it was time to meet her.

I flew the Cherokee to South Bend Regional and picked up Bill early in the morning of May 17th. It was another great Hoosier day for flying. Patty and her kids met us at Smith Field, north of Fort Wayne at noon. Adding to the fun was the fact that we had come across an old wedding picture of her grandparents. (See genealogy story at Airport #78.) We also persuaded her and the kids to take their first airplane ride. After several hours, Bill and I said our good-byes and headed home.

Enroute, we talked with the folks at Eby's Pines. They graciously gave us permission to land at their private field and take a photograph. I told Bill that he was going to a part of Indiana history by being a passenger on one of my 500 airport visits. He seemed genuinely pleased (maybe even excited) at the prospect. That is, until we saw the field. It was 3,000 feet long, but it was grass. Bill didn't like it. He was convinced, considering the warmth of the day, 3,000 feet wasn't not enough to get off the ground once we landed. He cautioned me all the way up to a short final approach. Within 500 yards of landing, he was still saying that it wasn't too late to abort. I countered that I've been to a hundred of these grass strips on hot days and had not had a problem yet. I urged him to please be confident in the pilot and the equipment. He wasn't.

The landing was uneventful and we found a cool shade tree to ease the heat of the midday sun. Bill could not relax. He paced and fretted and I could see his frame of mind was not going to improve as long as we were there.

The wind at the time could be generously described as "light and variable". It was too light to measure and too wispy to determine its direction. It really did not have an impact on our take-off although pilots religiously take-off into the wind. With 3,000 feet of runway and a negligible wind, I suggested taking off in the opposite direction of how we landed. Bill snapped back at that idea. He strongly recommended that we taxi back down the runway so we could use the wind to our advantage. This was no time to attempt to convince Bill otherwise. I taxied back the entire length of the runway. As we did, I watched the GPS indicate the changes in our position.

By the time we got to the other end, all pre-takeoff checks were complete. I spun the airplane around 180 degrees and advanced the throttle. After the little Cherokee rolled only 500 feet or so, the airplane was soft on the struts and spongy in the nose. A little back pressure on the control column and she wanted to fly. Well before we had eaten up 1,000 feet of the runway, the Cherokee was established in a satisfactory climb rate with 100 mph air speed. Bill seemed to breathe a little easier and allowed himself to sink back into the seat. I love you, Cousin Bill!

#489   New Carlisle, Indiana   Kenny Houston's Air Strip
Type: Grass   Identifier: Private   June 6th, 1998

A FRIEND OF DAD'S

DAD'S CONDITION WAS getting worse with each day. He was 81 and everything was becoming more difficult for him. He had suffered a series of small strokes, including one which hospitalized him for 10 days. During examinations, they found lung cancer and had to remove his right lung. His feet were in terrible condition and a constant source of pain.

We knew that his hunting days were over and he said that his condition would not allow him to fish. It appeared that he would spend the rest of his days watching the Chicago Bears get beat, the Cubs lose their pennant chances earlier and earlier in the season and the Bulls make a mess out of their roster for reasons only their management knew. Now and then, the two of us would fly over the different places where he had fished with his friends and we'd hunted together. It would never be the same.

Then, he got the idea to visit Kenny Houston. Kenny had been dad's foreman at work. They developed a very close friendship in the 10 years they worked with each other. They also retired about the same time.

Kenny always talked about his plane and the grass strip he had alongside the barns. He told Dad about his many adventures with his Cessna. Dad had never seen it and, because it was on the way home this day, we decided to stop and see if it was still there.

We did and it was. Only now the Kenny Houston that owned it was his son. Kenny Senior had died some time ago and Kenny Junior took over working the farm. The airplane was a beauty, a Cessna 175. This rare bird had a 220 horsepower engine with a controllable pitch propeller. Kenny (either senior or junior, I'm not sure which) modified the airplane with fancy high lift wing tips and gap seals - the tricks to make the aircraft jump off the ground faster and handle easier. Kenny Junior flies it regularly.

Dad was sorry that he couldn't see his old boss again and expressed his condolences to his son and family. The fellowship with Kenny's son was important to dad.

#490   Chesterton, Indiana   Bodin's Strip
Type: Grass   Identifier: Private   June 6th, 1999

#491   Geneseo, Illinois   Gen-Air Park
Type: Grass   Identifier: 3G8   June 28th, 1998

#492   Marseilles, Illinois   Spring Brook Marina
Type: Paved   Identifier: Private   July 5th, 1998

THE FUNNY TAILED AIRPLANE CLUB

EVERY SUNDAY MORNING, a group of pilots meet for coffee and donuts at the Griffith airport. They are older and more mature than most pilots. Each owns his own plane; one of them, Corliss "Corky" Beck, owns two.

They are good men who have a reputation for helping at the field. Corky is one heck of an avionics specialist and, necessarily, a darned good electrician. Chris Karabatsos, Ercoupe owner, is a good mechanic who knows his way around airplanes. He is wickedly adept in tight places. Ed Roden is a practical man who can see the short way to do every project. These and a couple of other men are joined at a common point: they all own Beech Bonanzas or Ercoupes. That is, they all own V-tailed or split tailed airplanes. Together they constitute the "Funny Tailed Airplane Club."

TO SPRINGBROOK MARINA

CHRIS KARABATSOS LOVED to fly with someone younger than himself. Chris is not certain of his ability to react in an airplane anymore, but then he was near 80 at the time. This day, we both knew that we would make a little aviation history. During this trip he would tell me a spellbinding story about events that happened in 1934.The day started like this.

We took off in mid-morning on a beautiful, sunshiny day into a 30 minute flight to Spring Brook Marina in Marseilles, Illinois. The approach over the Illinois River is very deceiving and tricky as there is a deep and abrupt embankment at the very beginning of the runway. It is best to be a little high and carry a little more air speed to the threshold. There is a great restaurant at the field but it is not for fliers but rather for the marina crowd. It may have looked a little awkward but it was a good landing. There were hundreds of power boats berthed there and they look like so many water bugs on the river. They knew we were pilots (meaning, not boaters) but we didn't care. Chris and I settled in and ordered our "$50 hamburgers".

Chris is a retired police officer from East Chicago, Indiana; his tour of duty extended back into the 1940's. One of his earliest partners was Philip Dewar, an older and more experienced officer. Early in their relationship, Phil revealed to Chris that he was the true killer of John Dillinger. What a revelation! So much so that it had to be included here. Chris went on to describe the story told to him by Dewar.

It is general knowledge that Dillinger was an Indiana born desperado and he mostly held up banks all over the mid-west. It is also well known that he spent the last several months of his life in northwest Indiana, specifically, Lake County. Chris related that Dillinger relied on the incredible inner workings of the underworld element of Lake County, Indiana to protect and sustain him. Those associations supported Dillinger as he roamed the county night by night in that famous, red panel truck for months on end. It is told that not all of these relationships were from the underworld and this put a serious shadow on his capture. If Dillinger were brought in alive, the damage would be wide and deep. Surely it would not only be Dillinger going to jail. The answer - he could not be taken alive.

F.B.I. agent, Melvin Purvis knew of Dillinger's whereabouts and set up his operation in Chicago. The only federal connection to Dillinger was a federal warrant for transporting a stolen car across a state line which is a violation of the Dyer Act, hardly a life or death offense. It was a personal vendetta for Purvis. As long as Dillinger was at large, or alive, it would be a festering wound between them. There was also a tremendous personality conflict between Purvis and J. Edgar Hoover. His career teetered on his ability to bring Dillinger to justice or, as it would really turn out, bring justice to Dillinger.

There was a meeting between Melvin Purvis and the East Chicago police to discuss how to trap Dillinger. Together, they arranged the well-known ambush of John Dillinger, Anna Sage and Polly Hamilton outside of the Biograph Theater in downtown Chicago. This was all being done with the total exclusion of any the Chicago police, Cook County Sheriffs or Illinois State Police law enforcement officers.

The six East Chicago police sent were Captain Tim O'Neil, Sergeant Martin Zarkovich (who would become the East Chicago Chief of Police), Walter Conroy (later to be East Chicago's Chief of Detectives), Officers Glenn Stretch, Peter Sopsic and Phil Dewar. Phil Dewar would fire the first and fatal shot. All these men were trusted to do the job at hand and keep their mouths shut.

As the threesome left the Biograph, it was obvious that Dillinger sensed something in the air. He became nervous and cautious almost immediately. He made an abrupt left turn off Lincoln Avenue into the dark alley heading northeast toward Halstead Street. Anna Sage was tightly on his left arm and Polly Hamilton was close on his right. Phil Dewar came running up from behind with his .38 Special in his outstretched hand. Dillinger knew he was in desperate trouble. He shed the two women and broke into a run. As Dewar closed in on John Dillinger, he fired a shot into the back of Dillinger's head at point blank range. The bullet exited just under Dillinger's right eye and he fell dead to the ground. That was not the end of the gun play as all the officers wanted part of the action. Dozens of shots were fired but not very many were discharged in the alley. Unfortunately, civilians were injured. In the melee, Dewar continued with another shot to the left side of Dillinger's head as he lay on the ground. It was the capper bullet to make sure.

With a dozen law officers standing over his corpse, John Dillinger lay dead in a narrow, obscure alley having been fully denied any due judicial process. Summarily, there was no full disclosure and cross examination of witnesses in front of a jury of his peers. Sentence was pronounced but withheld from his plight was an opportunity to appeal to a higher authority. The execution was a cold blooded ambush. It denied John Dillinger "due process" or an opportunity to make peace with this Creator.

Capitan O'Neill and Sergeant Zarkovich would share in the Federal reward money. Zarkovich relieved Phil Dewar of his service pistol that night explaining the Chief wanted it. It would later be sold at auction.

The most important point is Chris was finally an integral part of my odyssey. May God bless his soul.

#493   Park Forest, Illinois   Meadow Creek Private Strip
Type: Paved   Identifier: Private   July 5th, 1998

BY THE WAY

THERE IS NO airport visit to be discussed here. This is only a good airport story that starts with the flight entry in my log book It looks like this:

Date: Sept 27, 98
Plane: Piper PA-28-180 8369W
Flight: Griffith, Local
PIC Time: 0.9 hours

Souls on board: 2 Remarks: Met Mac Halewicz,- 16th birthday, his first flight

There is a classic picture or scene of some young boy, or girl, hanging over an airport fence watching airplanes come and go. I'm sure that Norman Rockwell did one of these. Their thoughts are about flying and it is all wishful. I met one of those kids on this day.

I had just landed from a local flight whereas I got airborne just to enjoy flying for its own sake. I was up for an hour or so. Afterwards, I pushed the Piper into the hangar and started for the parking lot. I saw this kid right away. Yes, he was hanging over the airport fence just as one would suspect. I knew what was going through his mind. He wanted to be a pilot. I struck up a conversation with him and he validated my suspicion, he was smitten with flight. He further told me that this was his 16th birthday; the youngest a person could be to fly.

I liked him; he was well-mannered, polite and an overall nice kid. I asked him if he wanted to go flying for a little while. I don't recall what he said but his one-step leap over the fence remains vivid in my memory.

All the duties were assigned to Mac; push aside the hanger doors, hook on the tow bar and pull the Cherokee out onto the taxiway. He followed me around the airplane as I went through the pre-flight inspection. We left the door open while we taxied out; it gets stuffy on the ground. After our ground checks were satisfied, we claimed runway 26 and lifted off into a southerly heading.

We climbed to an altitude of about 1,500 feet and flew past Cedar Lake for some maneuvers. His eyes were looking everywhere at once. I gave him control of the airplane early on in the flight. He had a good feel for airplanes right from the start. We flew for a while and passed the control back and forth some. My memory is that we first tried a banked turn to the right. Mac was the only kid I took flying that had his feet on the rudder pedals right away and used them. It wasn't the best turn in aviation but this guy was close to being a natural. The more we flew, the smoother he got. When I was flying he followed me on his controls. It was heartening to watch him in his first minutes of controlled flight.

We flew for almost an hour. Then, we returned to Griffith and put the airplane away. We talked for a few minutes and went our separate ways. I wished Mac a "Happy Birthday".

Time slipped by rapidly. In the process of compiling this gathering of stories, I happened upon that entry of September 27th of 1998. His family still lives in my home town. A simple telephone call to them netted Mac's cell phone number. The next morning, I caught up with him in El Paso, Texas. Lo and behold, Mac is now a DC-9 pilot for USA Jet. He has 4,000 flight hours; most of it as Pilot in Command. Expectedly, his memory of that afternoon is a lot more detailed than mine but then, I'm old! The important thing is, we never forgot that summer day in 1998. Good heavens, I love this sport!

WITHOUT PERMISSION

MEADOW CREEK IS only 7 or 8 miles from Griffith-Merrillville Airport. It is difficult to come home from the southwest without seeing that long, white paved runway. I tried hard to find out who would give permission to land there. In fact, the word was that the neighborhood was so exclusive that no one was welcome there. Membership is for the wealthy only and only with the consent of the neighborhood can outsiders land there.

All that talk only made me more determined. If I can't obtain the necessary permission, then I will go in with brass.

Bill Moran and I took off from Griffith with only that airport in our sights. We were going to give the impression that we belonged there. The first step was to circle the field at a low level and low speed. We figured at least two circuits would make it appear as if we were looking over the place with some investment intent. Then we broke off our circling and entered a landing pattern. The landing roll was slow and continued clear to the opposite end of the runway.

Both of us got out of the airplane and spent considerable time on the ground; perhaps 20 minutes. We tried to look like we were picking out the lot we wanted. Once we thought we had convinced anyone who may have been watching that we were "one of them", we got back into the airplane and back taxied on the runway. After a leisurely run-up, we lined up on the runway and took off. We again circled the field, then went home.

We made no attempt to conceal our "N" number or to let anyone think we did not have every right in the world to be there. We thought we pulled something off because there were no repercussions from our cheap, unauthorized visit.

Do you think anyone cared? We don't think so, either!

#494   South Bend, Indiana   Chain O' Lakes Airport
Type: Grass   Identifier: Private   November 28, 1998

A REUNION WITH RONNIE POLCYN

RONNIE IS MY cousin. In our loosey- goosey family, it was no wonder that I had not seen him in forty years. That is an embarrassment throughout my family because, like Ronnie and me, we all live in the same town or very nearby.

South Bend is only 70 miles from my home. Chain O' Lakes airport is very special in my heart because it was the first Indiana field from which I took off and landed an airplane.

According to my log book, an instructor named Hank Gores went with me in a Champ 7AC for an hour and a half of familiarization flying. We concluded the flying lesson with a half hour of touch and go's, the date was September 3rd, 1961.

It was time to go home and place this little grass field, now more and more surrounded by homes, into my book of memories.

This was a cool, blue, pretty day in northern Indiana. I had already talked with South Bend's ARSA and they told me to use caution at the field. It seems that Chain O' Lakes has been getting less and less traffic and maintenance is less and less frequent. The winds dictated a northwest to southeast landing. SBN was right about the field, it was rough.

The principal users of the airport were model airplane flyers. Ronnie was one of them. In fact, he has earned acclaim in the hobby. There have several modeling magazines where his picture appeared in several with articles describing his proficiency at handling model airplanes in contests.

Flying models is an art requiring dexterity, adroitness and of hand-to-eye coordination. I know this from (expensive) firsthand experience. These flyers only have one sense to determine the next flight control input to a radio control model, and that is sight. No flying by feel here.

The visit was good. It was warm and reassuring to see Ron again and to bring each other up-to-date on family developments. Moreover, we renewed our friendship.

#495   Milwaukee, Wisconsin   Lawrence J. Timmerman Airport
Type: Class D Identifier: MWC   March 18, 1999

A VISIT TO NORTHERN RAIL CAR COMPANY

JERRY HANAS AND I have been friends for over 25 years. We met in 1982 when he headed up the Northern Indiana Commuter Transportation District, or N.I.C.T.D. This is state operation working with the Chesapeake and Ohio Railway. The Chessie, at that time owned and operated the old South Shore Railroad; a commuter rail service operating between South Bend, Indiana and Chicago. The state, in the form of N.I.C.T.D., would provide capital funds for the purchase of new cars and the Chessie would provide management, maintenance and operational manpower.

Eventually, Chessie wanted out of the commuter business completely. In 1999, Indiana bought the assets of the commuter Rail Line. Jerry was installed as the General Manager and has been at the helm since the state took over the rail road. The rail road runs to this day; the last interstate, interurban passenger railroad.

I worked with the company that built the new cars for N.I.C.T.D. I enjoyed working with Jerry Hanas and his staff for several years. Then I learned that, after 17 years N.I.C.T.D was about to begin a "midlife" overhaul of the cars. This would be a massive undertaking. Jerry was working very hard to get this project going and I wanted to be a part of it. Jerry and I came to an agreement and he hired me into the Northern Indiana Transportation District.

Soon after, there was an unfortunate accident and some cars were nearly destroyed. The repair of the cars would be more than our meager work force could handle. Jerry sent the car to Northern Rail Car in Milwaukee. Jerry wanted to visit the shop prior to final bid approval and, since I would get the car for overhaul after Northern Rail Car completed their structural repairs, Jerry wanted me to accompany him. Jerry is also a private pilot. Why not just fly to Milwaukee?

The morning of March 18th was cold and blustery. Actually, it was damned windy! A take-off in windy conditions is a piece of cake in a Cherokee. However, the landings can be treacherous. I flew to Valparaiso (20 miles away) to pick up Jerry. The winds favored no runway and blessed no pilot. I fought the airplane to the ground.

We decided to take the VFR route up the east side of Chicago to Milwaukee. This is flight over Lake Michigan shoreline; perhaps 2 miles out. The maximum altitude allowed is 2500 feet MSL to avoid for approaching aircraft into Midway and O'Hare airports. We notified all the controlled fields along the way for clearance, including Gary Regional, Meigs Field on the Chicago shoreline,

Waukegan and Kenosha. Finally, Milwaukee radar vectored us inland to Timmerman.

Timmerman tower cleared us for a straight-in approach. From the ATIS, we thought we had a favored runway that would put us right down the throat of the wind. It should be a piece of cake. Wrong! The wind was still shifty. As we came within 25 feet of the deck, the wind took a 30 to 45 degree shift to our left. It was a strong shift, as well. Again, I fought to keep control of the plane and pushed the controls forward to pin the nose wheel to the pavement. At rollout, I showed Jerry the control column: the aileron control was fully against the left stop. We flew it all the way down to taxi speed.

As the day went on, the winds subsided. The excitement was over, allowing us to have more casual conversations on the way home. All in all, it was a good trip with a good friend on a pretty (albeit windy) day.

#496 Cloverdale, Indiana
Type: Grass Identifier: 78I

Pam's Place
October 15, 1999

#497 Lowell, Indiana
Type: Grass Identifier: Private

Dave Sutton's Airfield
October 31, 1999

#498 Milwaukee, Wisconsin
Type: Class C Identifier: MKE

Mitchell International Airport
November 28, 1999

#499 Crystal Lake, Illinois
Type: Paved Identifier: 3CK

Lake in the Hills Airport
November 28, 1999

#500 Lansing, Illinois
Type: Paved Identifier: ICQ

Lansing Municipal Airport
April 30, 2000

CAN WE MAKE 1,000 FIELDS?

L ANSING MUNI IS an interesting field. It was born of the forward thinking mind of none other than Henry Ford. Mr. Ford was at the forefront of aviation as he was at the leadership of all new and meaningful technology. With flight, he was of the opinion that there should be an airfield no farther away from another field than 20 miles in several directions. Charles Lindbergh also had the same idea. It is easy to imagine a spider web of routes across America which would appear as aviation's version of a Bucky Ball.

One of these early airports would be on farm land which straddled Indiana and Illinois just south of Homewood, Illinois and Hammond, Indiana. It would be called Chicago-Hammond airport. The principal purpose for this field would allow Ford planes to transport executives and haul high priority freight to and from Ford's Illinois facility immediately north in the Village of Hegewisch. Not only did Henry and Edsel Ford fly into Hammond-Chicago but so did such notables as Charles Lindberg and one eyed-Wiley Post.

Ford management lost interest in Chicago-Hammond when the Interstates and air freight operations at O'Hare, Midway and Gary Regional came into their own. The field continued to be a major general aviation airport supporting several hundred planes. Once Lansing became a city, the city politicos renamed it Lansing Municipal.

Chicago-Hammond Field offered geographical advantages to all flyers. It was situated between Chicago business on the northwest and Indiana's industrial regions to the east. It continues to grow and prosper even to this date.

Ford is gone but the original yellow brick hangar is still here. The 1,000 acres on the Indiana side, once known as Maynard, Indiana, virtually melded into the city of Munster; no one remembers Maynard. The airport continues to get larger as it has acquired considerable acreage to the south - enough to support a north-south runway. The aircraft manufacturing plant that was supposed to be built across the street to the north, never materialized, but sport aviation flourishes. Much of the traffic from the deposed Chicago lakefront airport, Meigs Field, has nested in Lansing. I was proud to make it my 500th field.

#501 Stevens Point, WI   Stevens Point Municipal
Type: Paved Identifier: STE   August 18, 2000

THE CIRCUMNAVIGATION OF LAKE MICHIGAN

THIS IS A trip I wanted to take for many years - into northern lands of Wisconsin and Michigan. But, I was unsure how to do it. A series of trips would always result in long, droning flights home. Then, as I reached for more northern fields, there would long-legged flights inbound as well. Clearly, the best approach would be a multi-day itinerary around Lake Michigan.

Wherever I ended up for the night, so be it. No matter where I was, the next field was only a small distance away. It appeared to be a day-long leg over Wisconsin toward Lake Superior's south shore and Remain Over Night (RON) there. The following day would take me across the Upper Peninsula, or, The U.P. It is better known, in these parts, as 'da you pee'. The route home would be south through the Lower Peninsula of Michigan. It would three days away from home, but I could see more fields and spend more time at any of them without being concerned about getting home at a reasonable hour.

Weather for the 18th, 19th and 20th of August was predicted to be dominated by a high pressure area. Once a slow moving crud system passed, it would be at least three days of beautiful flying weather.

After a couple of hours of waiting, Radar showed that the crud system was moving slower than anticipated. Currently, the weather was at minimums. A change for the better was eminent. I was going to take off in anticipation of improvement. The best I could hope for was about 1,700 feet of altitude. Proceeding west and a little north would skirt me around the O'Hare Class B airspace. Remember, O'Hare's cylinder of air does not stop at 8,500 feet or so as do most Class B's. Rather, it stretches to the moon.

After a couple of hours of flying, I was about three or four miles dead east of Mineral Springs. I was still holding at 1,700 feet beneath the cloud deck, but the ground was coming up to meet me. Where my home field is 640 ASL, this territory averages about 1,000 feet. The visibility was just as good now as it was when I first took off. I was flying at 700 AGL and it was becoming uncomfortable. I was ready to bank west when the cloud cover opened enough to reveal Steven's Point dead ahead. I'd just gotten lucky.

#502 Marshfield, Wisconsin   Marshfield Municipal Airport
Type: Paved   Identifier: MFI   August 18, 2000

At Steven's Point, #501 above, I asked about a courtesy car for lunch. The FBO operator furled his brow and told me their only car had been taken out early in the morning by some travelers from an insurance company. They were going to have it all day. He decided to let me use his company car, if I was going to be gone for an hour or so. Just as I was about to leave to get a bite to eat, a call came over the Unicom. A pilot about 10 south was inquiring about a courtesy car as well. I assured the desk guy that I would wait and have lunch with the late arrival.

A Cessna 182 came up on the horizon. The pilot in command was a Mr. William H. Roddis, a distinguished looking gentleman in his 80s. I smiled. Older men are full of great aviation stories and memories. How little did I know.

Bill Roddis and I drove to the strip mall which had the local Sears store. Bill owned the shopping mall building; he could take care of his business there and catch another ride back to the airport. We spent the next 2 hours chatting about aviation.

The Roddis family purchased the Hatteberg Veneer Company in Marshfield, Wisconsin. This was in the late 1890s. Subsequently, the company was renamed Roddis Plywood Corporation and it became renowned world-wide as a supplier of specialty and high quality plywood. Roddis did significant work with the British during World War II. They supplied the base material for the de Havilland Mosquito Fighter/Bomber in the early 1940s. This aircraft, able to fly faster than a Spitfire and higher than any German aircraft at its time, was a huge success. And it was constructed from Roddis-manufactured butternut plywood.

An even more interesting aspect of his company's activity is that.Roddis was the prime supplier of veneers and plywood for the Hughes Flying Boat, the HK-1 or Hercules. Roddis Plywood worked very closely with Howard Hughes and his engineering staff throughout the development and construction of the Spruce Goose. Bill looked at me over his sandwich and asked if I had been to Marshfield, Wisconsin yet. He said it was the home of Roddis Plywood and there was a letter on the wall of the FBO that I would be interested in reading.

Bill had immediate business to attend to and I really wanted to get to Marshfield, so we parted company. I felt extremely fortunate to have had lunch with the man whose company made the plywood for the Howard Hughes Flying Boat. The text of Bill Roddis letter follows.

- - - - - - - -

Milwaukee, Wisconsin 53211
January 8, 1997

"Dear Dan,

"In reply to your inquiry regarding the H-4 Hercules, - yes, I can confirm the (sic) The Roddis Plywood Corp made plywood for this plane. I was the Chief Inspector at the time and was responsible for the tests and certification of the plywood being made. There are still people living that worked in the plant during the war. One of my assistants was Shirley Gray who, many years later, was a check-out girl at Wings. There is a Lentz family from Marshfield, whose son Daryl Lentz is Maintenance Manager for the EAA in Oshkosh. He told me his mother worked for us in WW II. There must be more.

"Our story about the Spruce Goose is briefly this. We made plywood for the British (5V3-specification), for the gliders and for a Cessna trainer, all to U.S. military specs. However, Howard Hughes made up his own specifications because of the size of the plane. He wanted to save as much weight as possible. Aluminum was in short supply, so that plywood was not a critical material at the time. He included Basswood as one of the species we could use as a core (inner ply) material. Without exception, Birch was used for the outer ply. Because of the size of the plane, much of the plywood was 3/4" thick, sometimes more. Basswood is quite porous and relatively light in weight, compared to Birch, for example. Also, basswood is abundant in Wisconsin and we used a lot of it in our commercial plywood.

"In gluing the U.S. and British plywood, most of it ran to thinner veneer which was more delicate and could not be run through a glue spreader. The thicker plies for the Spruce Goose could be run on conventional roller spreaders, which are quite accurate; but the Basswood and Birch combination created quite a problem for us. The Birch being a dense wood did not absorb the glue. On the other hand the Basswood was light and porous. The result was that the glue would soak into the Basswood and not enough would remain on the surface for a good glue bond. Our own strength tests were marginal, even though we were doing our best.

"For all these years I've been meaning to see the Spruce Goose. But I never made it. Its' been moved to Oregon to be displayed but the people doing this ran out of money, so it is no longer on display. So far as I'm concerned, I was so happy has to hear that it flew.-since if it hadn't, we would have been in "big trouble." It is a great credit to Howard Hughes to have assembled the people who masterminded this project. It still is a mind-haggling airplane! Except when it was test flown by Howard Hughes there was not much publicity at the time. Except when Howard went before Congress to get the project approved.

"Let me add that when the Spruce Goose was on display, they arranged the tours so that people could walk inside the wings. Our plywood was all stamped with batch numbers and dated so that for quality control we could identify the time it was glued and who was operating the press. We kept these records for a while, but now they are all gone. It is a tribute to our employees that they so diligent and cooperative, realizing the importance of quality control on such a project.

(Signed)
William H. Roddis"

I left Bill Roddis at the restaurant. He had some business with the Sears store manager and told me that it would be easy to get a ride back to the airport. But I thought deeply about what just happened. The man with whom I had lunch with a few minutes before was a business acquaintance of Howard Hughes who was the most mysterious, misunderstood, and strangest millionaire in our history. At one time, he was the richest man in the world. All of this and I had spent a couple of hours with a man that knew him personally. The closeness of this brought a strange thought to mind.

In the early 1900's a Hungarian writer by the name of Frigyes Karinthy wrote a novel called "Chains." In this she proposed that anyone in the world can be connected to any other person in the world through a chain of acquaintances that has no more than five intermediaries. This theory is called "Six degrees of separation" with each intermediary being a degree of separation. (I know a guy who knows a guy ...) By knowing Bill Roddis, I was one degree away from Howard Hughes. It became a little mind boggling.

With a smidgen of imagination, this clearly meant that if I were one degree of separation from knowing Howard Hughes, then I was only two degrees of separation from knowing:

Jacqueline Cochrane	Jeanne Crain
Linda Darnel	Bette Davis
Marlene Dietrich	Billie Dove
Joan Fontaine	Zsa Zsa Gabor
Ava Gardner	Paulette Goddard
Kathryn Grayson	Jean Harlow
Olivia de Havilland	Susan Hayward
Rita Hayworth	Katharine Hepburn
Janet Leigh	Hedy Lamarr
Gina Lollobrigida	Carole Lombard
Ida Lupino	Jayne Mansfield
Marilyn Monroe	Terry Moore
Jean Peters	Ella Rice
Ginger Rogers	Jane Russell
Yvonne Schubert	Norma Shearer
Elizabeth Taylor	Gloria Vanderbilt
Mamie Van Doren	Shelley Winters

....and countless, nameless others!

#503 Mosinee, Wisconsin   Central Wisconsin Airport
Type: Paved   Identifier: CWA   August 18, 2000

#504   Antigo, Wisconsin   Langlade County Airport
Type: Paved Identifier: AIG   August 18, 2000

#505   Rhinelander, Wisconsin   Oneida County Airport
Type: Paved Identifier: RHI   August 18, 2000

#506 Hancock, Michigan   Houghton County Airport
Type: Paved Identifier: CMX   August 18, 2000

QUALITY FRIENDS, TO BE SURE!

NIGHT WAS APPROACHING rapidly. I had a mental schedule for the day that was too ambitious for my late start this morning. Knowing Houghton County airport was some distance from Hancock, I called the FBO and asked if there was local transportation to the city. Since it was very late in the day, the radio operator has serious doubts that transportation could be arranged.

After a few minutes, a call came in from another airplane. Whoever it was told me that he was about 10 minutes behind me and his wife was supposed to meet him at the field when he landed. If I could wait the 10 or so minutes, he would be happy to offer a lift. As a man who is without options, I accepted graciously.

The first of my two great memories of this layover was the town of Hancock itself. Hancock is old fashioned in appearance. It looks like the set for a 1950s movie, and it has not changed in 50 years. I thought that some 1953 Fords and Chevy's (and a few Studebakers) in the street would have looked very appropriate and right at home. Hancock still remains a very charming town in my mind.

My new friends and benefactors, Pete and Trudy, were magnificent. Pete, a dentist, offered help based solely on the fact that I was a fellow pilot in need. He was a true gentleman and that help was forthcoming almost immediately. With our gear in hand, we talked side by side waiting for Trudy. She pulled up in a white Lincoln. Trudy is a very pretty lady. She has soft red hair and gentle features. She also had the radio tuned to classical music and it was loud. These two together were like Ken and Barbie dolls, made for each other. They lived near Grand Rapids, Michigan, but spent as much time in Hancock as their lifestyle permitted. They kept the Lincoln there year round.

They were not comfortable with me being alone in Hancock. They did their best to persuade me to join them and their family for dinner. They promised to provide the transportation, and, they would pick me up the next morning to go to the airport, if I so desired. I was overwhelmed. While I really enjoyed their company,

I needed some down time to collect my thoughts and put together notes before the next day of flying.

I got out of the Lincoln in front of the hotel and we said our goodbyes. Watching as they pulled away, I knew that I had just spent quality time with some quality folks.

#507 Ontanagon, Michigan	Ontanagon Airport
Type: Paved Identifier: OGM	August 19, 2000
#508 Ironwood, Michigan	Gogebic Airport
Type: Paved Identifier: IWD	August 19, 2000
#509 Land of the North, MI	Land O' Lakes Airport
Type: Paved Identifier: 4Y4	August 19, 2000
#510 Marquette, Michigan	K.I.Sawyer International
Type: Paved Identifier: SAW	August 19, 2000

In 1954, the government entered into a 99-year lease, officially signed on January 24, 1955, with Marquette County for the site of K.I. Sawyer Air Force Base. Construction started almost immediately.

On January 24, 1956 Lt. Colonel Blocklehurst became the first commander of K.l.Sawyer AFB. The runway was completed in 1957 and in 1958, 25 F-102 Aircraft were sent TDY from Kinross AFB at Sault St. Marie to operate out of Sawyer for several months while the runways at Kinchelo were being repaired and extended.

The 62nd Fighter Interceptor Squadron from O'Hare Airport, Chicago was transferred to Sawyer and became an operational F-101 "Voodoo" squadron in 1959 after the runways at Sawyer were extended to 12,300 feet.

The Strategic Air Command became operational as a tenant unit with the assignment of a KC-135 Air Refueling Squadron - first the 923rd ARS, which was soon replaced by the 46th Air Refueling Squadron The first B-52H arrived at Sawyer in August 1961, along with the 410th Bomb Wing.

#511 Munising, Michigan   Hanley Air Field
Type: Grass Identifier: 5Y7   August 19, 2000

#512 Manitque, Michigan   Schoolcraft County Airport
Type: Paved Identifier: ISQ   August 19, 2000

#513 Newberry, Michigan   Luce County Airport
Type: Paved Identifier: ERY   August 19, 2000

#514 Grand Marais, Michigan   Grand Marais Airport
Type: Paved Identifier: Y98   August 19, 2000

A BEAUTIFUL VISIT GONE BAD

GRAND MARAIS FROM the air is like so many other northern Michigan airports: from five miles out, it emerges as a brown smudge in a sea of deep green forests. There is no tilled farmland and none of the usual lacing of streets. The few roads are hidden by the tall trees. As I drew near the airport, I could see that it was a two-runway field, "X" in shape. I had no Flight Guide diagram, but it appeared that the runways were true NE - SW and SE - NW in headings. The ground looked smooth and the region had been without measurable rainfall; nevertheless a soft field landing would be prudent. Grand Marais Airfield was rough. Typically these seldom-used fields really get torn up during the winter and receive very little maintenance in the summer.

Once on the ground and immediately after opening the cockpit, the beautiful scent of cedar and pine was instantly apparent. No one was there, so I walked about enjoying the wonderfully quiet solitude and the lingering aroma of the north woods. It was great!

After 10 minutes or so, the blissful quiet was disrupted by the sound of a badly tuned car engine with a blown out muffler. I started to walk toward the road when a very old and rather beat up station wagon came onto the field. The car stopped about 50 yards away from the Cherokee. It was an older, full size car; from the middle '80s, I think. Two men were inside, about 30 to 35 years old.

They were big, swarthy and drunk. The stink of beer and sweat overwhelmed the previously sublime and fragrant atmosphere. These guys were blitzed and they were profane! Every four-letter word imaginable began to pour from that car. It was a non-stop blustering stream of foul language. They had the roughest appearance and my sense of serenity was displaced by serious apprehension. It was quickly evident that they had either heard or seen my arrival and they wanted me to take them somewhere south in Michigan. This was not looking good at all.

When packing for this around-the-lake trip, I knew there would be some rough terrain to over-fly. After all, this was the wilderness part of northern Michigan. I packed a little kit in the event I went down in the wild. It contained, among other items, a shelter cover, a space blanket, waterproof matches, string, some rations, aviation band radio with extra batteries and a .45 automatic with a spare clip. This kit was handy on the back seat of the airplane.

The more the profanity spewed forth, the more I backed up to the airplane. I put on my friendliest face and begged off from these men with every excuse that came to mind. They didn't seem too interested in the fact that I was "behind schedule and had to get going." After the fact, I figure that a "schedule" meant nothing to these gorillas. It was, however, the best I could come up with at the spur of the moment!

As I got onto the right wing of the airplane, they were stumbling out of their station wagon still swearing. They were in a foul mood when they arrived and their attitude was getting worse by the minute. They were outright angry and belligerent.

In the left seat, I manipulated the controls to start the engine with my left hand. My right hand reached over the seat back and into the survival kit. The cool touch of the Kimber .45 automatic on my fingertips began to soothe my frazzled nerves. The odds of this incredible scene were beginning to even-out.

Of course, this was not the reason I included the gun in my kit. It was, however, entirely appropriate to have it on the front seat at this time. The two brutes never saw the gun; they had no idea I was armed. I slid it under the sectionals and open Flight Guide book. The engine started. No time for niceties such as yelling 'clear', checking oil pressure and other routine things. Moving forward quickly was more in order.

The brakes were released before the engine caught so, with ignition, the plane jumped forward. As the airplane rolled out, my two "friends" stumbled after me. Their swearing became more animated. No sweat. I can taxi much faster that they can stagger.

At the center crossing point of the two runways, I applied more throttle and right brake. With about 2,500 feet of runway, I went as far to the northwest as needed and spun the aircraft around on the left main gear, keeping as much motion as possible, and steadily pushed the throttle to the panel.

By that time, my friends had gotten back into their wagon and were rumbling to the midpoint of the field leaving a cloud of brown dust behind them. They had ugliness on their mind. Clearly, they intended to ram the airplane.

The more I rolled and the closer they got made no difference; we were on a collision course. On my last look at the air speed indicator, the plane was past 65 mph. It was time to horse it into the air. Smooth handling will earn style points, but it would not win the contest at hand. As soon as the Cherokee broke ground I let the nose level out to gain as much air speed as possible. The blur of their old car flashed past the peripheral vision of my left eye. They passed under me. Air speed and attitude were increasing but slower than I ever saw it before. Past the substantial overrun, the trees stood tall and imposing. With a little push on the control column, the plane leveled out at about 50 feet above the tops. This is where I should be.

There could still be trouble. For example, I found it easy to imagine that everyone in this area had a 30-'06 rifle with him at all times, probably be equipped with a telescopic sight. All I could do was stay low and keep moving east as fast as possible. After a little while, I dared to breathe normally....then slumped in the corner of my seat against the side window. I didn't know if I overreacted to their fearful presence or if there really was a danger. I still don't. The good news is that I am here to write about it.

#515 Sault Ste Marie, MI   Chippawa County Airport
Type: Paved Identifier: CIU   August 19, 2000

#516 Hessel, Michigan   Lindberg Field
Type: Paved Identifier: 5Y1   August 19, 2000

#517 Sault Ste Marie, MI   Sanderson Field
Type: Paved Identifier: ANJ   August 19, 2000

THE PRIEST FROM SAULT STE MARIE

SANDERSON FIELD IS the original Sault Ste Marie Airport. And a great one it is. It is paved, but the hangars and small, fixed base operations offices are old and decrepit. The offices are sorely in need of paint and maintenance, and not all of the hangar doors close. There are heaved portions of the parking ramp and grass grows through cracks in the concrete at every step. The field showed its age and wear and tear from years of exposure to the harsh northern Michigan winters.

Yet, it is a cozy field and because of its age and condition. In short, it is quite charming. What's more for a transient pilot, it is convenient. I could see several good restaurants within walking distance, a block or two away. There was a nationwide chain hotel just two blocks away where I would spend the night. Taking a few minutes to tie down and lock the Cherokee, I unloaded my stuff and started walking. The survival kit, except for the .45, was left behind with the dirty laundry. I took the flight bag with all the charts and approaches that pilots tend to accumulate and a light carryall for my clothing changes. It had been a long day of flying, but it felt good to sit and relax over a small filet and a couple glasses of scotch.

The hotel desk people helped me find a Catholic Church the next morning, but it was a mile or better away - too far for toting my gear so they graciously called a cab. The cab driver was a young girl named Jolie. She was very familiar with the church because it was her parish as well. In fact, when she pulled up she spotted her father's car in the parking lot. He always went to 8:00 AM Mass she said. I asked to her to pick me up after Mass for a ride to Sanderson, and she guaranteed to be waiting for me.

The priest celebrating Mass was of foreign descent. His service was highly respectful and the homily after the gospel was excellent. He may have been a little hard to understand, but that was because I was in the back pew. Less than an hour later, Mass was over and we all took time to greet and shake hands with this warm and personable priest.

My lady friend the cabbie was not there yet. To make it easy for her, I stood immediately in front of the church and right on the curb. She couldn't help but see me. Fifteen minutes, then twenty minutes went by. Everyone else was gone and still no taxi. The priest had turned out the lights, locked the doors and came out the front entrance. We looked at each other. He got my most pathetic look. He knew I didn't have a ride, so he offered to drop me somewhere. When I told him that I needed a ride to the airport, he became reluctant because he thought it was the large airport 30 miles outside of town. I told him that it was not Chippewa County airport but Sanderson. I added that I was going to a private plane, not some airliner. That changed everything. His eyes lit up and a broad smile came across his face. Now he was excited. I believe he was pleased to help me, but going to a small airplane is what really got his juices up.

On the way to Sanderson, I tried to keep the conversation on matters of religion and the Catholic Church. The priest would answer my questions or comment then, quickly turn the discussion back to private flying. He could not get enough about small airplanes. I liked this guy.

My new friend parked outside the chain link fence immediately adjacent to my Piper. With the field at his footsteps and the airplanes in sight, he began to get a little giddy. I offered my hand to say goodbye. It was too late. He had turned off the engine and was already getting out of the car. I gathered my things and got out of the car, he was already at the airplane.

The cool night had made the plane all dewy so I had a little job to do getting it wiped down as well as doing the pre-flight inspection. I unlocked the door so the priest could see in; he clambered onto the wing and slipped into the left seat. His eyes were darting all over. In a few minutes, he got back on the ground and blessed me. Then he blessed the airplane. Then he blessed the ramp and the flight and turned and blessed the airport and all the other planes. He blessed a few more items but I didn't catch them all. This was a really great priest!

Then it dawned on me. "Look Father, I am only going to Drummond Island which is about 15 minutes away. If you aren't doing anything for an hour or so, why not come along with me and I'll bring you right back?" I added, "probably within an hour."

Now he really lit up. He started blessing the plane, the flight, the ramp and everything in sight all over again. This was getting to be a very holy airport. He zipped back into the plane and I had to ask him to get out so that I could sit in the left seat. "Oh, yes. Of course, of course", he said through the biggest grin I have seen in years, and he scampered out of the airplane. He came back in directly behind me and started to bless the instruments and radios. Now he was getting <u>really</u> happy.

Departure from Sanderson is tricky, in that Canadian air space is just off the north end of the field and avoiding it requires an abrupt bank to the south. To accomplish this, the airplane was brought level and trimmed at 2,000 MSL. The priest's eyes were darting everywhere and taking in everything. With my feet on the rudder pedals, I eased back into my seat and folded my arms. I looked at the priest and said, "One of us should be flying the plane." He turned and saw my yoke without hands on it and instantly grabbed his control column. His first flying lesson had started.

He learned how to initiate and neutralize a turn. He caught on quick. In a few minutes, with reduced power, he had us on a downwind leg for Drummond's Runway 27. I took over and let him soak in the landing experience. Once on the ground and out of the airplane, he blessed Drummond, he blessed both Runways 9 and 27. He blessed everything. Another pilot sauntered toward us with a big welcoming smile on his face. The priest wheeled and blessed him as well. There was no escaping that holy water!

#518 Drummond Island, MI   Drummond Island Airport
Type: Paved   Identifier: Y66   August 20, 2000

#519 St. Ignace, Michigan   Mackinac County Airport
Type: Paved   Identifier: 83D   August 20, 2000

THE MIGHTY MAC

ST. IGNACE (PRONOUNCED 'ig niz') is a charming little community with an equally charming airport. The management at the field catered to the Mackinac Island trade in a number of different ways. There was regular air taxi service as well as ad hoc trips for those who couldn't wait. This was managed by a great pilot and gentleman named Pete Fullerton. He developed the over-flight business with commentary from the well versed pilots. When I was there, it looked as if they had a good business. Pete confirmed that when he told me his pilots were getting 50 landings a day; most of them to Mackinac Island. It was heartening to see so much air traffic to and from the island.

I had no serious intention of landing at Mackinac Island. Upon approaching St. Ignace, the traffic at Mackinac seemed too busy for my taste. There seemed to be too much variance in aircraft in the pattern, ranging from two place Cessnas to larger and faster business twins. And there were a lot of them. I decided to over-fly the island and return another day.

Upon departing St. Ignace, the famous Mackinac Bridge became visible. What a wonderful sight it is. Then, it was the engineering marvel of the world. The five-mile long bridge had been designed by the great engineer Dr. David B. Steinman. Then, it was the longest bridge in the world with a span of 3,800 feet between towers. Started in early May of 1954; the bridge finally opened for traffic on November 1st, 1957. At last, St. Ignace on the upper Michigan peninsula and Mackinaw City on the tip of the southern peninsula were permanently linked.

But Engineer Steinman perceived his steel and concrete work as not only a long awaited utility but an object of sheer beauty. A lover of music, he saw a romantic resemblance to one of his favorite instruments, the harp. And he had his beautiful bridge painted accordingly. The Golden Gate Bridge is the color of rust. This bridge would be soft forest green and pale ivory. And it does, indeed, look like a harp!

Viewing the bridge from any angle is enchanting, but it is even more so from a low flying airplane. The bridge is truly magnificent. I throttled back the engine and lowered the nose in order to see this piece of work close up. At just above deck level, I slowed the airplane even more to 65 knots with a notch of flaps. Even then, it was too fast. At Mackinaw City I brought up the nose, banked left heavily and leveled out parallel to the road on the east side of the bridge. Now, I was a lot closer to the traffic. I could see the occupants in the cars, some were waving. I could not reduce speed any more so the view was not prolonged. It was nevertheless, truly exhilarating!

Now, there are longer and more modern bridges, such as the Akashi-Kaikyo Bridge in Kobe, Japan and the Great Belt Bridge in Denmark. But none is more beautiful than the Mackinac Bridge.

One more thing: A particularly nasty rumor is going around about me flying illegally near the bridge on August 20th, 2000. I categorically deny that I flew under the bridge from the west to east (with 10 degrees of flaps and an air speed of 75 knots.) This is a malicious tale that has no basis in fact. However, there is plenty of clearance for a Cherokee to fly between the water and the underside of the bridge....155 feet, to be exact. The field elevation is a critical: Maximum altitude under the bridge is Field Elevation plus 75 feet.

Regardless; this action would be illegal and could cause a pilot to lose his license.

#520 Cheboygan, Michigan   Cheboygan County Airport
Type: Paved   Identifier: CVX   August 20, 2000

#521 Bois Blanc Island, MI   Pointe Aux Pins
Type: Grass   Identifier 6Y1   August 20, 2000

WARREN AND DELANE

AFTER ENJOYING SOME great flying camaraderie with the pilots at St. Ignace, it was time to head south for home, landing at a few airports on the way. It had been a great trip so far. There were two solid days of flying, thanks to the huge high pressure area that still lingered in the Midwest.

I would not be going to Mackinac Island. The CTAS frequency was monitored all the way from Sault Ste. Marie and the traffic at the resort island was hideous. Mackinac was attracting all sorts of airplanes, from turbo jet twins to Cessna 150s. As each landed, others would announce at 10 DME miles out. Probably more than a dozen aircraft were continuously zeroing in on Mackinac; a dicey situation that did not seem to slacken. There would be low time pilots waddling around in the pattern in slow aircraft along with serious iron at twice the approach speed of a Cessna 150. It would not be prudent to enter into that fray. Better to over-fly Mackinac and leave that visit for a quieter moment.

Traffic at Cheboygan City-County Airport offered a much more serene atmosphere. While refueling, the line boy asked if I was returning from Mackinac. That must be a common occurrence since Mackinac is a million miles from everywhere and they don't sell avgas there. He understood why it was over flown, and but quickly enlightened me on Bois Blanc. Its runway was long, wide and smooth as a pool table. He thought it was a better island to visit than Mackinac. The FBO manager sauntered into our conversation and he, too, sang the praises of Bois Blanc. The island had a good place to get a sandwich, everything was close in, and the beaches were spectacular. A flight instructor nearby added that she took her students into the Bois Blanc airfield quite often. A little over-water flying seemed to add to a student's flight maturity and confidence, she said. Bois Blanc was so close that the Hobbs Flight Hour meter wouldn't even move. It had to be less than a six minute flight. I'd heard enough. My Cherokee's nose was turned back to the north.

The folks at Cheboygan were right about the field; it was in excellent condition. Considerable rain through the summer had turned the field and surrounding vegetation brilliant green under the extraordinarily clear, blue sky. The island was gorgeous from the air and the air strip was a snap to find.

Bois Blanc Island (usually referred to as "Bob-Lo") is southeast of Mackinac Island and dead north of the Cheboygan airport. The south shore of the island lies in the Straits of Mackinac which connect Lake Huron and Lake Michigan. All water traffic between Lake Michigan and Lake Huron passes south of the island through the straits. In the winter, all traffic for Lake Michigan and Lake Superior is routed north of the island. This allows the straits to freeze, thereby enabling an ice bridge to form between Bois Blanc and the southern Michigan mainland, providing a great traffic route for light vehicles such as snowmobiles.

Without tying down or even locking the airplane, I ambled over to a sort of oversized, door-less garage, where someone had thoughtfully pinned maps of the island on the wall. There aren't that many roads and streets on the island; getting lost was out of the question. The beach would be easy to reach.

About 20 bicycles were scattered in and around the garage. Some had two wheels and a few of those had air in the tires. All were more than 50 years old. I picked out the most roadworthy. With map in hand, I pedaled toward the Hawk's Landing Restaurant recommended by the guys in Cheboygan.

The short trail from the field put me on Lime Kiln Point Road. By the looks of the map, I guessed that Hawk's Landing was about a 10- minute bike ride away. Bicycling was a favorite sport of mine as a child; this would be enjoyable.

The late morning bike ride was refreshing. Once off the airport the surroundings were all forested. The mature trees arched over the road forming a majestic, cooling canopy. The road was unimproved with pea gravel surface and only a few water puddles. This should be an easy ride.

I had not been on a bicycle for years, however, and my legs were beginning to burn. Even after slowing down, the burn did not diminish very much. I did not recall a bicycle seat being this small, either. With stinging, salty sweat pouring into my eyes I began to wonder if any sandwich was worth all this.

Within minutes, I came upon a County Sheriff's vehicle. As is typical in Michigan, the Sheriff, Graham Whipple, was driving a SUV type truck. His radar unit hung outside the door of his Explorer, which struck me as odd. This was a country road and I had seen only one car in the 15 or 20 minutes. Sheriff Whipple was friendly enough. With a knowing smile, he said "You are tuckered out, aren't you?" I gave him a grin. He was right. Judging from his comments, I was only about half way to the sandwich shop and his directions were welcome.

I asked about his speed trap. He said that there had been complaints about cars tearing down the road far in excess of the 25 MPH speed limit. Whipple's handling of speeders was refreshing. As he clocked one car doing about 45, he showed an expression of indignation and signaled a palm down hand movement repeatedly. The driver seemed to respond immediately. Whipple offered to take me to the sandwich shop. With as gracious a refusal as my burning calves allowed, I wheeled down to the beach.

Hawk's Landing is a café, a notions shop, a general store, a video rental shop and a great place to catch up on the latest island news. Owned and operated by Sheila and Jeff Godbold, they encourage patrons to linger and chat with them when customer traffic permits.

As soon as I sat down, people in the adjoining table included me in their conversation. Before long, another couple, Warren and

Delane Vanderbeck, sat down across the aisle. These two folks knew everyone in the café and they lit up the place. Conversations became more interesting and lighthearted; laughter came easily. Friendships are close on Bois Blanc, probably deeper than most communities. The Vanderbecks are deeply loved and, despite being a newcomer, I became closer to them. I didn't feel like a stranger.

Comments, discussions and jokes came from all corners even after the sandwiches were long gone. Eventually, someone asked where I came from? They all laughed sympathetically about how my bike trip from the airport affected me. I think they had seen this before and realized it is much more difficult than driving a car around the isle. Warren and Delane insisted that I put the bicycle in the back of their van; they would drive me to the airport.

The trip (in a motor vehicle) was very short and the sparkling personalities of Warren and Delane continued to buoy the conversation. We joked about me being unable to fly if returned on the bike. They had serious doubts.

We continued to converse during the pre-flight, and then said our good-byes. Warren and Delane wanted to stay for my takeoff so I did most of my check list while taxiing from midfield to the southeast end of the runway. The run-up was quick and uneventful which permitted me to roll off without unduly delaying my new friends.

The Cherokee was airborne before midfield. I waved furiously to Warren and Delane and gave them a little wing waggle. Then I spotted Deputy Sheriff Graham Whipple on the road at the end of the runway. He was standing outside his Explorer and waving. I responded with a very pronounced wing waggle. After all, who knows what I'll be driving the next time I visit Bob-Lo.

Thus, I left Bois Blanc, - its smallish post office, the solitary tavern, one-room schoolhouse, two chapels and little café named Hawk's Landing – put a smile on my face. There were other towns and fields to visit before the day was over but the warmth of these new friends lingered. Now, years later, pleasant memories of Warren and Delane Vanderbeck remain in my heart.

#522 Indian River, MI   Campbell Municipal Airport
Type: Paved   Identifier: Y65   August 20, 2000

#523 Boyne City, Michigan   Boyne City Municipal Airport
Type: Paved   Identifier: N98   August 20, 2000

#524 Boyne Falls, Michigan   Boyne Mountain Airport
Type: Paved   Identifier: BFA   August 20, 2000

#525 Gaylord, Michigan   Otsego County Airport
Type: Paved   identifier: GLR   August 20, 2000

#526 Gaylord, Michigan   Lakes of the North Airport
Type: Paved Identifier: 4Y4   August 20, 2000

CLIPPED WING PILOT

WITH THE CAMPING facilities, riding trails and beautiful golf course alongside the airport, it was easy to spot Lakes of the North Resort from the air. The championship level golf course and the well laid out vacation housing was a beautiful sight. Although the field's home town is Gaylord, it is much closer to Mancelona, Michigan. In fact, the Mancelona volunteer fire department maintains firefighting equipment there.

After shutting down the Cherokee, I ambled around in the sunshine and worked out a few kinks. A gray haired gent peddled up on a bicycle. Ken Smith, the golf course ranger, said as soon as he saw me in the pattern, he started toward the field right away.

Ken is a pilot whose wings have been clipped. He told me he had a stroke about 1992 or '93. It left him with a serious, speech impairment and the FAA pulled his license. He flew a Cessna 172 for 13 years and his love for that airplane, flying and the joy of being in the air was apparent. As he talked, his eyes looked outward. His every word forged a single thought in my heart: Goodness, this man was passionate about flying! This also convinced me to grab every bit of enjoyment that flying can afford, as soon as possible. The freedom of flight is available only to the physically fit.

#527 Roscommon, Michigan   Roscommon Conservation Club
Type: Paved Identifier: 3RC   August 20, 2000

LOOKING BACK

ROSCOMMON COMPLETED MY aerial circumnavigation by air of Lake Michigan. I love that lake and, as a sailor with years of experience on it, I have the utmost respect for it. All of the Great Lakes share the one tendency, they are fast. Weather develops over them quickly turning them from placid to ugly to deadly. For the last three days, the lake was lovely to look upon, almost hypnotic. I was now proud to spend the three days becoming more familiar with it and making new friends. The stories I gathered are well worth the trip.

#528 Ottawa, Illinois   Bourne Country Club
Type: Grass   Identifier: Private   November 11, 2001

#529 Ottawa, Illinois   Prairie View Country Club
Type: Grass   Identifier: Private   November 11, 2001

WHERE IS PRAIRIE LAKE?

EVERYONE AT GRIFFITH airport knew about my ongoing quest. Once in a while, a pilot would make a recommendation. Usually, folks just got tired of hearing the same reply that I have "been there." Until later in year 2000, that is. That is when Lou Sertich and Bob Sealscott told me about a nearby place to get a sandwich that I may not have visited. It was a private strip at some golf course near Ottawa, Illinois. The golf course was Prairie Lake County Club. They were right. It was virginal as all get out. I wanted to know as much about the field's location as possible.

Private strips are not assigned three- or four-character identifiers, so Loran and GPS would not work. It was less than 80 miles away. Lou's description was very detailed. It was a grass strip, 2,600 feet long and ran north and south. The airfield was in the middle of the golf course with a lake just off the north end. There were trees east of the north end and a radio tower immediately to the west of the north end. Some buildings were at the midpoint of the field on the east side. Lou said he always came in from the south and, because it was short, he came in low and slow. Lou flies a great looking Partnavia. If he could get in there with his twin, the little Cherokee would have no difficulty whatsoever. The following Sunday, I set out to visit Prairie Lake CC.

The flight was beautiful. With a bright sun, coolness in the air and only slight northerly breezes, the weather was perfect. I came in at 3,000 feet MSL right down the 241° radial out of the Joliet VOR. The mileage measured about 18 or so from the VOR and, the spot Lou had depicted was approximately 3 miles this side of Ottawa. I figured finding the field would be easy. The season was in my favor, with the grass turning brown and the crop stubble a golden hue against the rich color of well watered fairways. The golf course would be a cinch to spot from almost any altitude.

Ottawa appeared on the horizon sooner than expected. About five miles out, I slowed to 90 knots, a good solid approach speed. Ahead, I could see the horizon looked brown from the harvested crops and the onset of winter but there was no sign of a golf course, with or without a landing facility. Since sky diving was very active at Ottawa, going over the field and coming back to the northeast would be a dangerous route. At the slow speed, a 60-degree bank to the right was much safer. Just as the wing dropped down low, I spotted the rich, Kelly green sod of an 18-hole golf course. It had to be Prairie Lake.

To make sure, I dragged the field coming out of the south as if to land. Sure enough, it looked just as Lou described it: a north-south grass strip with a lake at the north end. There were trees east of the north end and some buildings just south of them. This runway was identical to dozens of grass runways 2,000 to 2,500 feet in length that I had visited over the past 10 or 12 years. There was no radio tower at the northwest corner of the field but that mattered little. Towers come and go, unlike trees and lakes, which stay put from week to week, towers are a lot more tentative.

I had this one wired. My 528th field was right beneath me. I pulled the Cherokee into a left turn, entered a left downwind leg southbound at about 800 feet AGL and started making landing announcements on 122.9 MHZ. No real need to be concerned, as there was any other traffic.

Respecting the length and unknown condition of the surface, I held my over-the-threshold speed to exactly 80 mph and the nose was pulled back for a slow, 'soft field landing'. The field was in excellent condition - not exactly the top of a pool table, but very good, nonetheless. As the airplane slowed, I passed a small sign on the right. It read "Welcome to James Wehrli Airport." Not exactly what I anticipated.

I walked south toward to the buildings on the east side of the field glancing at the James Wehrli sign every few steps. A young lady emerged from the Pro Shop coming toward me in a golf cart at a full speed. She was smiling; so was I.

Her name was Brenda. She welcomed me to Bourne Country Club. I must have had an awful look on my face as I asked her "Where am I? With her smile at full tilt, she told me we were at Bourne Country Club, the prettiest and best 18-hole golf course within 50 miles. Maybe so, I acknowledged, but where in the in the dickens is Prairie Lake? Well now, she said, Bourne is a far better course than Prairie Lake. I should be glad to be here, rather than there.

How do I tell her that I was aiming for Prairie Lake and hit Bourne by mistake? I simply asked, "If this isn't Prairie Lake, where is it?" The golf cart came trundling to a stop and Brenda spun out from behind the steering wheel. With a furrowed brow, she pointed southwest west and said " about a half mile that way." It was more a question than an answer: she didn't seem certain which.

With her brow still furrowed and my look bordering on bewilderment, we went to the clubhouse for a soft drink. Brenda did not feel much like to talking to me by this time. Obviously, I was not a potential customer. I didn't seem too bright, either.

With what little of my dignity remained, I headed back to the plane. It was a long walk in the bright sun and, by that time, four or five sets of eyes were burning holes in my back. I didn't turn around. The pre-flight was brief and cursory. Climbing into the cockpit, I determined that a downwind takeoff in a 5 to 8 knot breeze was far better than to taxi back past Brenda and the small band of golfers around her. No need for a run-up and power checks. As the Cherokee drew abreast of my new friends, she was already airborne.

At 300 feet, I banked heavily to the left. Immediately, I saw Prairie Lake where Brenda said it would be. I came in on a left base and lined up for the landing. There ahead of me was the north-south grass strip, about 2,500 feet in length. At its northern end was the small lake. There were buildings to the east and trees farther to the north.

And on the west side of the runway was the radio tower.

Like Bourne, Prairie View had a grassy ramp area to park airplanes. Unstrapping from the cockpit, I climbed out of the Cherokee and walked into the clubhouse.

"Just fly in?", someone asked, smiling.

I smiled back and nodded.

"Where did you come from?"

"Indiana."

#530 Chariton, Iowa   Chariton Municipal Airport
Type: Paved   Identifier: CNC   October,14 2002

#531 Osceola, Iowa   Osceola Municipal Airport
Type: Paved   Identifier: I75   October,14 2002

JOHN R. BARCUS, 100% PILOT

To MOST PILOTS, airplanes are an avocation. We enjoy airplanes and flying and brag about it at every opportunity. It is great sport to let slip the fact that we are flyers at cocktail parties, church socials and PTA meetings. The raised eyebrows, the "oohs" and "aahs" are priceless. What pilot doesn't remember when his Airman's Certificate was new, and how he couldn't wait to use it for identification verification when cashing a personal check at the local super market?

We participate in piloting. But rarely do most of us get more than 50 hours in the air each year. Airline pilots are different, of course. Most of them have a private plane in addition to their professional flying, truly the "Bus Man's holiday". When airline pilots are not flying for their airline, they are at the local airport with their plane. They are close to 100% but not quite. Some people are 100% aviation. I believe John R. Barcus is one of them.

John R. Barcus is the Manager of Osceola Municipal Airport in Osceola, Iowa. John's interest in and pursuit of flying was traditional: he was the kid at the airport trying to get rides in anything with wings. When World War II began, John enlisted in the Army Air Corps. Soon, he was in bomber training and was commissioned an officer. He flew B-24s in European theater. Sixty years later, his eyes became sad as he recalled the low level raid over Polesti. It was like the enemy had a shooting gallery. His unit lost 35 airplanes in just 3 minutes and he lost a lot of friends.

Upon leaving the Army Air Corps, John bought his first airplane, a BT-13 at a military surplus sale. With his heavy aircraft experience, he was quickly hired by Braniff Airways and he flew DC-3s and DC-4s for a living.

Over cookies and coffee, John related that he holds Experimental Aircraft Association membership #14. His 50 year-old membership card is signed by Howard Paul Poberezny, whose nickname at the time was 'Howie.' John told me that the next number to be assigned was #13 but John did not want it so Don Kames took it leaving #14 for John. John use to fly into Midway Airport for Braniff and that is how he was able to make the meetings of the fledgling Experimental Aircraft Association. They used to drive from Chicago to Milwaukee and back when there was no I94 and the road was only a two lane highway.

John, Howie and 21 other people met regularly, but there was no money to fund an organization. They agreed to have annual dues, then could not agree on the amount, vacillating between $3.00 and $5.00. Eventually, they each kicked in $5.00. John is of the opinion that his presence began to add momentum to the organization. Probably so, after all he was an airline pilot.

For the first conventions, they had Fly-Ins at Curtiss-Wright Field (now Timmerman Airport) in Milwaukee. Much to their discouragement, only 15 to 20 airplanes would show up. They knew other people were out there building their own airplanes or clipping the wings of J-3 Cubs or playing around with larger, more powerful engines. They thought it might help if the Fly-In was moved to Rockford, Illinois. They did and things changed.

Rockford is only about 40 west of the Fox River Valley. Nestled in this valley are some of the moneyed suburbs of Chicago. These folks can afford flying and airplanes, and they showed up at the convention in great numbers. They provided huge amounts of support in both attendance and money. Annual attendance at the Fly-In consistently hit 20,000 and more.

John tells an incidental story about the first Rockford show, that attendees were very sloppy, leaving papers and garbage all over. No one was pleased with that. There was even talk of not letting the EAA back into Rockford.

The EAA's own Nick Rezich, "The Voice of EAA" solved the problem. Nick was the announcer at the convention and he took every opportunity to warn the crowds of the danger of foreign object damage to airplanes from trash and clutter on the ground. His constant chatter over the public address system included reminders to "Pick it up! "Don't throw trash on airport property" and "Don"t litter the aircraft area". It stuck and cleanliness improved. Today, fifty years later, people notice how spotlessly clean the EAA Convention is despite the huge crowds. In fact, first time visitors are immediately made aware of three things at the gigantic Fly-In now known as "EAA AirVenture"; the tremendous number and variety of airplanes on the field, the orderliness and friendliness of the crowds - and that there not one speck of paper on the ground.

Nick Rezich continued his work with the Experimental Aircraft Association as a founder of the EAA's Antique\Classics division. He wrote monthly articles for Sport Aviation magazine and tirelessly worked as the "Voice of EAA" in describing the nonstop activities at the Oshkosh convention into 1980. At age 61, Nick Rezich succumbed to esophageal cancer in 1981. He was admitted to the EAA's Sport Aviation Hall of Fame in 2003.

During my visit, John gave me a copy of the 1st issue of EAA's newsletter, the "Experimenter." This was done on the cheap. Howie Poberezny approached Ray Scholler who had a one-man print shop. Ray did the first issue of 100 copies at no charge. After that, Howie and the EAA would pay as they could, and Ray kept his prices low. Today, Ray prints monthly issues of Sport Aviation, official magazine of the EAA. He also employs over 200 people. The EAA wouldn't think of having anyone but Ray do the work.

Not surprisingly, some members thought there should be an EAA Museum. Poberezny and the board of directors put the arm on 100 or 200 members for donations, including John. After about $150,000 was collected from 75 or so members, they broke ground. Once the museum was a visible entity, the big money came in. Heavy donations from radio personality Paul Harvey, actor Cliff Robertson, Miller Beer and others then made the museum a reality.

These days, John is happy running the airport for the city of Osceola. He is surrounded by pilots, especially on weekends. He also is the Flight Instructor for the field which means he gets to associate with the new blood coming into the sport. Youngsters who intend to go on to obtain their Air Transport Rating and subsequently find work in the airlines, are probably well served by John's remembrances of his past experience with Braniff.

John is full of stories. He caresses his memories with the tenderness and fondness of a baby's touch. I could have stayed with him for a long time. But, the cookies and coffee were gone; it was time to leave. There were more fields to visit. By the way, we shared those cookies and coffee in a comfortable apartment ...adjacent to the back of the FBO office. That should do it. As I said, John R. Barcus is a 100% pilot. He lives, eats and even sleeps aviation.

ANATOMY OF A TRIP

THIS PROMISED TO be a great trip. Three or four days of perfect weather, nothing pressing at home and new adventures ahead. I thought it would be fun to trace the flights with small notations such as departure bearings, mileage between fields and fuel stop data. In this way, all the flights could be retraced easily at a later date. I had thought about doing this before but never had. We were airborne at 6:00 AM on the 23rd of September and headed right for the Omaha Sectional.

#532 Newton, Iowa   Newton Municipal
September 23, 2003   Type: Paved Identifier: TNU

From Griffith to the first stop in Iowa took 2.6 hours. Actually, Knoxville was my <u>intended</u> first landing. At 15 miles out, I tuned into the AWOS frequency (Automated Weather Observing System) to get the current weather at the airport. At the end of the report, a recording indicated that runways 15 and 33 would be closed from Monday the 22nd to Saturday the 27th. The very airport I had picked as the kingpin of the trip was out of service. To make sure, I called on Knoxville Unicom and the man who responded verified that construction was underway. I have got to learn to read NOTAMS!

The Cherokee's tanks were down to about an hour and a half. North to Newton was the most reasonable alternative. It was a field that was not yet visited although it was an "entry field"; one that would later be used as an initial landing point in Iowa. Newton was right on the eastern edge of the Omaha Sectional and that made it a good field to visit for the first time and refuel at the same time. Knoxville would again serve as an "entry airport" another time. A call to Newton Unicom confirmed that fuel was available; it would only be a 25 mile diversion.

At Newton, I found not only fuel but an unexpected flattering. As soon as I entered the FBO, the manager of Johnson Aviation and chief pilot, Ethan Nasalroad met me at the door. He immediately asked if my airplane was for sale. He had an immediate buyer looking for a Cherokee like mine. I told him that selling 69W was really out of the question; still, he looked it over and asked about the extent of the apparent upgrades. He even named his price. Nasalroad was very personable and the offer was flattering, but I thanked him for his interest and told him there could be no sale. I had a trip to complete.

Refueling: 32.9 gallons at $2.82, $92.78

Departure heading, distance: 206 degrees, 310 miles

#533 Lamoni, Iowa   Lamoni Municipal
September 23, 2003   Type: Paved Identifier: LWD

SUSPICIOUS NOISE FROM BELOW

NO ONE WAS around when I arrived at LWD. This is not surprising since GA airfields busiest times are Saturday and Sunday. The strip seemed to be a good concrete runway, although there were weeds galore.

When I was ready to leave, however, I heard a loud howl on the taxi back. It sounded as if a wheel bearing was ready to go. I came to a complete stop on the runway and, sure enough, the noise stopped. Resuming the taxi, the noise came back with a vengeance. At the run up area, I shut down the airplane and got out. I moved the plane manually and found no unusual noise or drag and the main wheels were all cool. In walking down the runway, I concluded that the runway grooving was the source of the racket. This airplane has been on grooved surfaces before without any noise like this, so I deduced that it had to be the specific groove pattern that was the culprit. I never heard the howling noise after leaving Lamoni.

Departure heading, distance: 281 degrees, 75 miles.

#534 Mount Ayr, Iowa   Judge Lewis Field
September 23, 2003   Type: Paved Identifier: 1Y3

Departure heading, distance: 256 degrees, 15 miles.

#535 Bedford, Iowa   Bedford Municipal
September 23, 2003   Type: Grass Identifier: Y46

FLYING IS A FAMILY AFFAIR

THIS AIRPORT CONFIRMS my belief that the most memorable people are in aviation. Immediately after landing, I met an older man by the named Jerry Swietzer who was cutting grass in the taxiways and hangar aprons. Within 10 minutes, we were joined by Chad Willie and his lovely wife, Betty, both flyers. Betty routinely flew her Corbin Baby Ace and, according to Chad, "...she really throws that airplane around the skies." Chad had just finished restoring his Waco, replete with an OX-5 engine. It was beautiful. I have seen many Wacos, but this one was distinctive in that it had highly varnished walnut chocks. My Cherokee is held in check with a couple of pine chocks that I stole from the Griffith FBO.

Chad makes his living by re-manufacturing antique airplanes and assisting with home-built airplanes. His specialty is the design and manufacture of custom wooden props. Chad and Betty live in nearby Corning, just three stops farther in my odyssey.

Departure heading, distance: 282 degrees, 23 miles.

#536 Clarinda, Iowa   Schenck Field
September 23, 2003   Type: Paved Identifier: ICL

Departure heading, distance: 271 degrees, 14 miles.

#537 Shenandoah, Iowa   Shenandoah Municipal
September 23, 2003   Type: Paved Identifier: SDA

Refueling: 20.5 gallons at $2.30, $47.15
Departure heading, distance: 57 degrees, 18 miles.

#538 Corning, Iowa   Corning Municipal
September 23, 2003   Type: Paved Identifier: CRZ

Departure heading, distance: 266 degrees, 37 miles.

#539 Red Oak, Iowa   Red Oak Municipal
September 23, 2003   Type: Paved Identifier: RDK

Departure heading, distance: 296 degrees, 18 miles.

#540 Council Bluffs, Iowa   Council Bluffs Municipal
September 23, 2003   Type: Paved Identifier: CBF

Refueling: 13.18 gallons at $2.50, $32.64
Departure heading, distance: 31 degrees, 27 miles.

#541 Harlan, Iowa   Rushenberg Municipal
September 24, 2003   Type: Paved Identifier: HNR

OLLIE PASH

MY FIRST STOP of this morning was a little, lazy field about 15 minutes northeast of Council Bluffs. Nothing spectacular, then I met Ollie Pash. He is the airport manager

Ollie kept me spellbound for well over an hour with tales of Alvin and Lawrence Rustenberg who founded this field in the 1930's. Alvin made flying history when he flew his 1946 Piper PA-12 to every state in the union west of the Rockies,

Then Ollie started to drop names like Patty Wagstaff and Lieutenant Jerry Deren. Patty Wagstaff flew her first professional aerobatic show in Harlan. The show climaxed her one month stay in Harlan where she practiced her trade in a rented Pitts Special just before her first national win. It seems that Ollie and Patty grew very close to each other, and Ollie was very proud that he was able to teach Patty a little something about aerobatic flying.

Lieutenant Deren, on the other hand, owed everything he knew about stunt flying to Ollie Pash; Ollie was his primary aerobatic teacher. Jerry Deren went on to fly with the Navy Thunderbirds. His position in 2004 was left wing to his flight leader, Commander Russ Bartlett.

ANOTHER ONE OF THOSE COINCIDENCES!

FAST FORWARD TO July 4th, 2007. In the spring of 2007, my beautiful bride of 45 years, and I had decided to retire. Clearly, it was time to leave corporate America to the younger, more energetic citizens. We would devote our first free summer to sailing. That is, we would sail around Lake Michigan in our beautiful sailing vessel, "Etc." Talk about life in the slow lane, 120 days of sailing is certain to lower anyone's blood pressure!

This took place while we were visiting Ludington, Michigan. We had been there for a day or so when we were assisting in new comer to the dock by lending a hand with his docking. Lines were tossed and tied and the new arrival was well secured. We had a little discussion and the skipper told me that he was from Iowa. I believe his first name was Jim. His last name was certainly "Mitchell." I mentioned back to him that I did a lot of flying in Iowa for a few years. He responded by asking if I had ever been to Harlan, Iowa. Emphatically, I told him that I had most assuredly had been there because I had spent several hours with one of the most fascinating men in aviation while I was there. In fact, the man I was talking about, Ollie Pash, had got his pilot's license when he only 13 years old and such. I continued on to tell some highlights about Ollie's life and how he trained the Air Force Thunderbirds in aerobatics as well as teaching advanced aerobatics to Patty Wagstaff who would go on to capture the women's world title in stunt flying. He said, "Yeah. I know. I married his daughter. She's below." He turned and called below. "Hey Jolene, come topside and meet this guy. He knows your father!"

Departure heading, distance: 068 degrees, 27 miles.

#542 Audubon, Iowa   Audubon County Airport
September 24, 2003   Type: Paved Identifier: ADU

Departure heading, distance: 192 degrees, 20 miles.

#543 Atlantic, Iowa   Atlantic Municipal
September 24, 2003   Type: Paved Identifier: AIO

Departure heading, distance: 120 degrees, 18 miles.

#544 Creston, Iowa   Creston Municipal
September 24, 2003   Type: Paved Identifier: CSQ

A FRIEND IN NEED

FLYING BECAME DECIDEDLY more difficult after Creston. Just before noon, the bug population of Iowa held a reunion on my windshield. These are huge bugs probably about 1 2" to 2" long and light brown. They plastered the whole airplane. Thanks to the short duration of the flights, I was able to maintain some degree of visibility. At Creston, Larry West became an immediate friend. While Larry did not know what these bugs were, he knew the best way to clean them off. He gave me a bottle of glass cleaner sold locally. It was very effective. I have lost the name, but it kept me flying on that day and I owe Larry a debt of gratitude.

Refueling: 20 gallons at $2.50, $50.00

Departure heading, distance: 029 degrees, 38 miles.

#545 Winterset, Iowa   Winterset-Madison County
September 24, 2003   Type: Paved Identifier: 3Y3

Departure heading, distance: 310 degrees, 38 miles.

#546 Guthrie Center, Iowa   Guthrie County Regional
September 24, 2003   Type: Paved Identifier: GCT

Departure heading, distance: 049 degrees, 28 miles.

#547 Perry, Iowa   Perry Municipal
September 24, 2003   Type: Paved Identifier: PRO

COL. WILLIAM TAVINGTON =
LT. COLONEL BANASTRE TARLETON

THERE WAS VERY little activity at Perry when I landed, but my
attention heightened as I taxied up to the hangar. Specifically,
an orange and black sign on a side wall caught my eye. It advertised
the business as "Tarlton Flight Service", a very familiar name to
me. It is my wife's maiden name. Both of us are heavily involved in
researching our family tree. Our research has been very intense for
several years and has involved a lot of travel.

My wife's maiden name is "Tarleton." We had found two Tarleton
families in New Hampshire and three Tarleton families in southern
Maryland (St. Mary's county); all from the late 1770s. Many of these
families have dropped the "e" in the name, so chances are he came
from one of these and if it were Maryland Tarletons, he would be
very close kin to my wife.

I walked into the hangar and was greeted by two men. I knew that Randall, the tall, slender fellow was a Tarlton; it was like was looking at my brother-in-law.

I introduced myself and asked a few leading questions. Did he see the movie "The Patriot" starring Mel Gibson? Randall smiled and nodded yes. Did he understand the role of the character Colonel Tavington in the picture? Now, sheepishly, Randall hung his head and scuffled his feet. Yes, he knew who that character portrayed. Clearly, Randall had a sense of his family's history. He was aware that "Patriot's" Colonel Tavington who was, in real life, none other than Banastre Tarleton of the British army. He was better known as the Green Dragoon, which in fact is the title of Banastre Tarleton's biography. We have an old copy of it and it has been a good reference for family research. Randall and I continued to discuss our families and ancestors as best we could recall them. Randal felt that his people came from the St. Mary's county branches also. Nancy came from the Thomas branch but that didn't sound familiar to Randal.

It would have been easy for us to talk all day, but he had work to do and this unexpected interruption, while fascinating, was interfering with his schedule. He gave me the name and address of his father, Richard Tarlton in Clive, Iowa. Richard was the genealogist in the family and he would be much better source of information and a superb collaborator. I tucked the address away and made a mental note to contact Randall's father as soon as possible upon returning from this trip.

Departure heading, distance: 315 degrees, 14 miles.

#548 Jefferson , Iowa   Jefferson Municipal
September 24, 2003   Type: Paved Identifier: EFW
Departure heading, distance: 275 degrees, 13 miles.

#549 Carrol, Iowa   Arthur E. Neu Municipal
September 24, 2003   Type: Paved Identifier: CIN

Departure heading, distance: 290 degrees, 21 miles.
#550 Sioux City, Iowa   Sioux City Gateway

September 24, 2003   Type: Paved Identifier: SUX

Refueling: 26 gallons at $2.99, $77.74
Departure heading, distance: 014 degrees, 74 miles.

#551 Lemars, Iowa   Lemars Municipal
September 25, 2003   Type: Paved Identifier: LRJ

Departure heading, distance: 022 degrees, 23 miles.

#552 Orange City, Iowa   Orange City Municipal
September 25, 2003   Type: Paved Identifier: ORC

Departure heading, distance: 317 degrees, 15 miles.

#553 Sioux Center, Iowa   Sioux Center Municipal
September 25, 2003   Type: Paved Identifier: SOY

Departure heading, distance: 358 degrees, 11 miles.

#554 Rock Rapids, Iowa   Rock Rapids Municipal
September 25, 2003   Type: Paved Identifier: RRQ

Departure heading, distance: 095 degrees, 19 miles.

#555 Sibley, Iowa   Sibley Municipal
September 25, 2003   Type: Paved Identifier: SBM

Refueling: 15.4 gallons at $2.50, $38.50
Departure heading, distance: 197 degrees, 38 miles.

#556 Sheldon, Iowa   Sheldon Municipal
September 25, 2003   Type: Paved Identifier: SHL

Departure heading, distance: 135 degrees, 11 miles.

#557 Primghar, Iowa   Primghar Municipal

September 25, 2003   Type: Grass Identifier: 2YO

Departure heading, distance: degrees, 12 miles.

#558 Hartley, Iowa   Lambert Fechter Municipal
September 25, 2003   Type: Paved Identifier: OY4

FECHTER ATCAA

LAMBERT FECHTER BECAME synonymous with Northwest Iowa aviation in 1942. Lambert started flying from Sheldon, Spencer and Hartley in Taylorcrafts, Aeroncas, and a Curtiss Wright Jr.

In 1940, he received his private pilot's license at Sioux City, which was then the Rickenbacker Airport. By 1941 he had earned his commercial, instructor, and secondary flight instructor ratings. He was a flight instructor during 1942 at Iowa City, and in 1943 he taught future Army and Navy pilots. Then he joined the Navy and graduated at the top of his pilot training class.

During 1944 and 1945 he instructed at Norman, Oklahoma, New Orleans, Louisiana, and Dallas in many types of Navy aircraft including the Stearman. In 1946 he started a flying service at Sutherland. In 1948 he gave flight instruction from the Spencer, Iowa airport. In 1949 he gave up flying to become a farmer. However, this lasted only a year; 1950 he became a flying-farmer near Hartley, Iowa.

By June of 1959 he was a flight instructor, charter pilot, FAA examiner and also the personal pilot for several local executives. He inspired an extraordinary number of people to learn to fly. Some people say that because of him, there were more pilots per-capita in Hartley than any other city in the nation. He had logged close to 10,000 flying hours before being fatally injured in an aircraft mishap. The town of Hartley named its airport in his memory and the Fechter Military Operating Area used to overlay many of the airports he used during his 21-year flying career.

The Iowa Air National Guard Headquarters changed the name from Fechter to Crypt Military Operating Area. There is, however, a Fechter ATCAA to the north of the Military Operating Area.

Departure heading, distance: degrees, 8 miles.

#559 Paullina, Iowa	Paullina Municipal
September 25, 2003	Type: Paved Identifier: 1Y9

Departure heading, distance: degrees, 15 miles.

#560 Cherokee, Iowa	Cherokee Municipal
September 25, 2003	Type: Paved Identifier: CKP

Departure heading, distance: degrees, 16 miles.

#561 Storm Lake, Iowa	Storm Lake Municipal
September 25, 2003	Type: Paved Identifier: SLB

Departure heading, distance: degrees, 16 miles.

#562 Ida Grove, Iowa	Ida Grove Municipal
September 25, 2003	Type: Paved Identifier: IDG

AN OASIS IN IOWA

THIS LITTLE TOWN in Iowa has the neatest approach for its airport. At the edge of town and the end of the runway lies a little lake with the prettiest green embankments around it. In the lake are a smallish lighthouse and a scaled down three-masted ship. Castles and castle-like buildings surround the airport as well as on the airport grounds. The bank facing an approaching pilot is spelled out in brilliant white stones reading "Welcome to Ida Grove." I came to find that all of this was the responsibility of one man, Byron Godbersen, who passed away in 2003.

Godberson was the founder and owner of Midwest Industries in Ida Grove. Midwest manufactures marine and small farm equipment, and employs approximately 300 people. Mr.Godbersen liked the castle design and implemented it into the buildings built for him by his employees.The privately owned structures are beautiful and help to promote our community, but few tours are given of the interior.

The man-made 10-acre lake is named after Byron's wife, LaJune. Apparently, this lake (or perhaps "pond" is more appropriate) was intended for their marine interests, but it serves no real purpose now. The ship is a half-scale replica of the HMS Bounty.

Along the property, a stone towered suspension bridge spans the Odebolt Creek. Less than a thousand yards from the bridge is a tower marker on an adjacent golf course.

The hangar at the northwest end of the airport was built in 1973. It is privately owned by Midwest, and houses their corporate plane and a completely restored WACO biplane. The hangar also is used for marine and farm equipment dealer demonstrations and sales presentations, as well as many civic and political meetings.

In 1975 a second newspaper, Ida County Courier took root in Ida Grove.Their building is also an ancient castle design.. I am told that there is one of the most modernly equipped weekly newspapers inside the building. What a contrast!

One of Byron Godbersen's most recent projects was Lake LaJune Estates, a housing development. The development is an antique arch, old style streets, small lakes and Byron's castle-type homes. His own home has a moat, a drawbridge and a watch tower.

From the air, the town looks like a lush, wooded park from the air - in stark contrast to the surrounding area, which is completely dedicated to farming.

I wanted to see this little town in detail but considering that I was afoot and saddled with a totally different agenda for the week, so I reconciled myself to returning to Ida Grove another time. The self-made promise included bringing my wife to enjoy this architectural oasis with me.

Departure heading, distance: degrees, 17 miles.

#563 Wall Lake, Iowa	Wall Lake Municipal
September 25, 2003	Type: Grass Identifier: 3YD

Departure heading, distance: 100 degrees, 16 miles.

#564 Sac City, Iowa	Sac City Municipal
September 25, 2003	Type: Paved Identifier: SKI

Departure heading, distance: degrees, 9 miles.

#565 Rockwell City, Iowa	Rockwell City Municipal
September 25, 2003	Type: Paved Identifier: 2Y4

Departure heading, distance: degrees, 16 miles.

#566 Pocahantas, Iowa	Pocahantas Municipal
September 25, 2003	Type: Paved Identifier: POH

Departure heading, distance: degrees, 22 miles.

#567 Emmetsburg, Iowa	Emmetsburg Municipal
September 25, 2003	Type: Paved Identifier: EGQ

Refueling: 23.6 gallons at $2.50, $59.00
Departure heading, distance: 347 degrees, 21 miles.

#568 Estherville, Iowa	Estherville Municipal
September 25, 2003	Type: Paved Identifier: EST

Departure heading, distance: 126 degrees, 19 miles.

#569 Algona, Iowa   Algona Municipal
September 25, 2003   Type: Paved Identifier: AXA

Departure heading, distance: 140 degrees, 30 miles.

#570 Eagle Grove, Iowa   Eagle Grove Municipal
September 26, 2003   Type: Paved Identifier: EAG

Departure heading, distance: 080 degrees, 26 miles.

#571 Hampton, Iowa   Hampton Municipal
September 26, 2003   Type: Paved Identifier: HPT

Departure heading, distance: 185 degrees, 31 miles.

#572 Iowa Falls, Iowa   Iowa Falls Municipal
September 26, 2003   Type: Paved Identifier: IFA

Refueling: 16.5 gallons at $2.50, $41.25
Departure heading, distance: 030 degrees, 15 miles.

Rain ahead but it seemed to be on the left side of the course. Almost to Ottumwa, we would run into more rain but that only bracketed me on the left side. The route to OTM VOR was relatively clear. The speed over the ground picked up to just under 150 knots. Because of this speed, I was once again catching up with the edge of the rain. Over OTM, the skies were clear but in addition to the weather systems hovering immediately behind the airplane was a second front coming directly from the west. The course to the east was starting to look dicey with cumulus build-up. None of these clouds could be called "towering cumulus" or anything near so devastating a system. Nonetheless, they were significant and flying near them or under them would be unwise. This complicated weather scheme had to be approached with caution.

Flying around them seemed to be a practical option. It was still early morning, so I decided to pick my way through the weather. Moreover, with several good airports en route, I could identify and select all fields within 10 miles of my position as preferred landing spots. Any sign of high winds, lightening or anything else presented a danger, I could land immediately.

The first field was Aledo at Mercer, Illinois. I know this field well. It is north-south and I have landed there a couple of times - once in November, 1996 and again in September, 1997. The '96 visit was in the Cherokee. The'97 landing was in a PT-17. Aledo presented itself as a good fallback position with clear weather around it. If I could not spot Galesburg in the building weather, I would do a 180-degree turn back to Aledo for the duration.

The weather soon changed to scattered rain systems. One was dead ahead, and about a mile in diameter. A similar rain event was a mile or two eastward and a mile more north. If I could get past these, Galesburg would be right the area when I break clear of these two rain areas. This is dicey flying. Every step forward was tentative with careful awareness for an increase in turbulence or harsh bouncing; either being a certain indicator that a hard bank to the left and downward towards Mercer County Airport. At times like this, pilots scoot their rears into the seatback and lean forward to heighten sensitivity to every nuance if the goings on around them.

The short flight north of the first rain cell was uneventful. As I drew away from it and the distance to the second cell also grew without signs of roughness, strengthened my resolve and confidence grew, too. It took only a few seconds to fly around both rain cells and under the moderate cumulus clouds was almost past tense. Then, Galesburg appeared on the right. There was clear weather all around the airstrip as well. I could still see Aledo behind me but now Galesburg became my next landing area.

Beyond that, the weather looked much clearer. I could relax again, having passed the third and last line of weather. The final 60 or 70 miles would be a ski run downhill.

So that was my trip: four full days of flying with 20.1 hours in the air, forty one airports were visited and the fuel burn was 196 gallons of 100 octane fuel at a cost of $439.09. I made dozens of acquaintances, captured several good stories and gained enough memories to keep me warm all winter. I can't wait to do it again next year.

"Griffith traffic, Cherokee 8369 Whisky is 10 West and comin' home."

#573 Noblesville, Indiana	Noblesville Airport
August 6, 2004	Type: Grass Identifier: I80
#574 Middletown, Ohio	Hook Municipal Airport
August 14, 2004	Type: Paved Identifier: MWO
#575 Hamilton, Ohio	Butler County Regional
August 14, 2004	Type: Paved Identifier: HAO
#576 Lebanon, Ohio	Warren County Airport
August 14, 2004	Type: Paved Identifier: I68
#577 Waynesville, Ohio	Red Stewart Airfield
August 14, 2004	Type: Grass Identifier: 40I

THE MISSION OF STEWART FIELD

I T IS EASY to smile as I recall such grass fields as Wheeler's in Westfield, Indiana (October 10, 1990,) the Flying "A" Ranch in Chatfield, Minnesota (May 10, 1997) and Wyncoop in Mount Vernon, Ohio (July 8, 1995). There are few pretenses at grass strips. IFR ratings, constant speed props and retractable landing gear are not important. Steel tube airframes, doped fabric and the love of flight are cherished. This is the reflection of Red Stewart Field in Clinton, Ohio.

Stewart Field's founding premise of is grass-roots flying. Like

Wheeler's in Indiana, there was only one tricycle gear airplane to be found: an elderly "V" tailed Bonanza - obviously abandoned - with a multitude of parts and panels missing, either salvaged or vandalized. The working planes at Stewart include an Aeronca Champ, a couple of J-3 cubs, a couple of crop-dusting planes to tow several gliders that frequent the field and a beautifully restored 1942 PT-17 Stearman.

It is an active field, but the instruction there is not necessarily designed to shepherd a student through his commercial training on to his ATP certificate. Here, the introduction to flight is in one of the yellow airplanes up to and including training in a Pitts Special at $288 per hour.

Writer Steve Hanshew is a frequent flyer at Stewart Field. His account of its development is rich with the history and accomplishments of the Stewart progeny.

The History of Red Stewart Field
The Red Stewart Family History
(Written by Steve Hanshew)

Many people are born to live a normal life, work a normal job. Red Stewart was not one of these people. Red was the last of a dying breed. He was a Barnstormer. To Red Stewart, the Piper Cub would become an extension of his personality. He went beyond what any factory test pilot at Piper thought possible and did what many would never dare. In flight, he would disconnect the control stick, throw it out of the door. He would proceed to land the airplane using power, elevator trim and rudder. While in flight he would sit on the wing strut outside of the airplane, flying the aircraft from there. When doing loops, he would touch his landing gear on the ground at the bottom of the loop. While working for Frigidaire in the mid 1940's, Red would fly to work and land in the parking lot instead of drive.

There are many other similar feats that were testaments to Reds' prowess with the yellow Piper. These feats are not just myths, either. There is actual news footage of some of these "maneuvers". His famous statement was "Don't ever do this, but if you do, here's how".

Late in 1945, Red invested with his father in the purchase of a

108-acre farm two miles south of Waynesville, Ohio. Red bought in with the understanding that the 40 acres of the wooded, non-tillable portion would be deeded to him separately. If Red was going to do what he loved doing, he was going to need an airport. When the plant manager at Frigidaire told Red to stop landing in the parking lot with his airplane, Red quit the plant, got a box of dynamite and a bulldozer, and started clearing that 40 acres. It was 1946. With the help of his wife Irene and some friends, the airport was completed by the end of the year.

Red bought a brand new Piper Cub from the Lock Haven factory at a discount and became a certified Piper dealer. The airport, his business, and his superior skill with the yellow Piper grew, as did his sons Emerson Jr.(nicknamed "Cub", of course), Steve, and David. All of Red's sons began flying in their early teens. Red flew an amazing 18,000 hours teaching, cajoling, eating and breathing flight.

Cub Stewart is an accomplished pilot and flight instructor. He has over 10,000 hours of flight time in a variety of aircraft. A substantial amount of his time is in aerobatic flight, vintage aircraft, and war birds. He is also a corporate pilot for Gosiger Tools in Dayton; a supplier of high performance machines for the metalworking industry.

Cub's main claim to fame, however, is as an Airframe and Power plant mechanic (now called Aviation Maintenance Technician) and Airworthiness Inspector, with a specialization in older style fabric covered airplanes. He was voted Aviation Maintenance Technician of the year for the whole country in 1991. The restored L-4 and L-6 Observation planes from WW II that are hanging in the U.S. Air Force Museum were restored by Cub and his wife, Cathy. Cathy is also a certificated AMT and a wizard on fabric covered aircraft.

Emerson III, Cub's son, now in his thirties, is the Chief Flight Instructor and also an AMT. Flying since he was 13, Emerson has over 6500 hours, mostly in tail-wheel aircraft. He has been flying aerobatics for over 14 years and has flown in air shows for five. His wife Kim is a commercial pilot who tows gliders, gives rides, monitors training fleet airworthiness, and is learning how to work on fabric covered aircraft. Cub's daughter Sara is an accomplished pilot and airplane owner, who also has a business degree. She is married to a corporate pilot and is the flight school office manager.

Red's kids and grandkids are continuing the dream he began 50 years ago, flying Cubs out of what is now Red Stewart Airfield. He was a Barnstormer in the truest sense of the word, and although he has taken that flight west to be with the Lord, his presence is still with the pilots at his field. We all miss him.

#578 Wilmington, Ohio   Clinton Airport
August 14, 2004   Type: Paved Identifier: I66

#579   Greene County, Ohio   Lewis A. Jackson Regional
August 14, 2004   Type: Paved Identifier: I19

A GIANT OF AVIATION

Lewis A. Jackson was born in Angola, Indiana on December 29, 1912. By any measure, his is an impressive resume. He earned a B.S. degree in Education at Indiana Wesleyan University in 1939. In 1948, Jackson obtained a Master's Degree from Miami University, Oxford, Ohio and in December 1950 a Ph.D. in Higher Education from Ohio State University.

Dr. Jackson's career history further indicates the quality of this man. He advanced from Graduate Dean to Dean of Students, Vice President for Academic Affairs, Acting President and President of Central State University, then Acting President and Vice President for Administration at Sinclair Community College. He was also the Director of Flight Training at the Tuskegee Institute and trained nearly thousand pilots during World War II.

Within his community, he contributed time and effort as a member of the Greene County Regional Airport Authority, and served as a Director on the board of the Xenia (Ohio Area Development Corporation.

Lewis Jackson's passion was, of course, flying. Early on, Lewis Jackson was involved with aviation. He barnstormed the Midwest in the 1930s. With his proficiency as an aviator growing, he gained a Commercial License with an instrument rating and then a Transport Pilot's license. He also managed to acquire a mechanic's Airplane & Engine license, as it was known then. He ventured into business, forming an aerobatic flight school in Chicago with Cornelius Coffey. The Coffey & Jackson Flying School is alleged to have been located at Chicago's old 57th Street airport.

Always an experimenter, the most accurate count of airplanes that he is said to have home-built is put reliably at 10 although it could have been more. As an inventor, Dr. Jackson designed and flew the 'Versatile I' an airplane that could be driven on the road as a car. Soon after, Lewis Jackson continued with another automobile\airplane which folded its wings for surface travel. Neither could be economically developed for the marketplace but both flew successfully. Not surprisingly, Lewis was President of the local chapter of the Experimental Aircraft Association for many years.

Many awards honor his achievements, including:

- The Distinguished Alumnus Award, Indiana Wesleyan University Alumni Association
- The Frontier Award, First Frontier Inc.
- The Pioneer, Achievement and Trail Blazer Awards presented by Links Inc. Special Recognition, Ohio Department of Transportation, Division of Aviation and Federal Aviation Administration
- Certificate of Appreciation, Xenia Area Development Corporation

Clearly, dedication of the Greene County airport, to the memory of Lewis A. Jackson, was a fitting memorial to a champion of aviation.

One accomplishment was not written on a brass and walnut plaque or etched on a crystal vase. Heralded almost immediately as a genuine success story of the black man's achievements, the Tuskegee program was not intended to be. Rather, there were dark intentions to scuttle the Tuskegee program in failure.

It was revealed to me by Bennie McRae of Trotwood, Ohio was personal friends with Lewis A. Jackson in Ohio and C. Alfred Anderson in Alabama for 25 years. Bennie prefaced his discussion with me by saying that neither of these two men, who distinguished themselves in American flight history, ever wanted or sought notoriety. The story concerns the (ultimately) famous Tuskegee Institute and combat flight training for black men.

Jackson moved to Tuskegee in 1939, where he received additional flight training in the Civilian Pilot Training program. He soon became head of training at the Army Air Force 66th Flight Training Detachment in Tuskegee Institute, a state coeducational school for black youths, founded by none other than Booker T. Washington.

Training black men to fly high-speed, complicated aircraft in combat did not sit well with the military establishment. The Army Air Corps, the War Department and the South East Air Corps Training Command wanted the black experiment to fail. They inserted into the curriculum a requirement that Tuskegee be used only as a primary training base with advanced training for graduates at other white-controlled bases. It would be there, it was believed, that the black pilots would be summarily washed out. Lewis knew of this intent, and he did his utmost to make sure it would not happen.

As Director of Training, he named C. Alfred Anderson as the Chief Instructor. Consequently, Alfred Anderson picked up the nickname "Chief" for the rest of his life. Jackson shared with Anderson his goals and objectives for the Tuskegee Flying School. They gathered a cadre of excellent pilots for program that were also excellent trainers. With the best trainers available, Lewis set standards far in excess of what was expected by SEACTC. If the washout rate was high, it would be better that Jackson and Anderson did the scrubbing rather than officials at the advanced training bases.

The training regimen was rigorous and, the students felt the pressure. They sensed that they were special and were being trained accordingly. Many initial washouts occurred, but those who made it were remained for combat flight.

There was no laxness in discipline or military behavior at Tuskegee, either. Jackson expected model officers from his command. Not everyone can function well in a military environment, those who would matriculate to advanced- training would be the very best flyers and excellent officers.

Chappie Jones came on board with Lewis Jackson early on. He was aware of the white establishment's intent. Chappie brought with him a mental fervor to further fuel the student's desire to excel. Jones hated the barriers and racist attitude. He became a perfect conduit between Jackson's desire to beat the white commanders at the game they devised, and the men who were called upon to do battle.

As one might expect, the flight candidates quickly began to sense that they were being specially prepared. Only the best within them was acceptable, whether as officers, combat pilots, and leaders of men or as black representatives of the United States Army officers' corps. This was the black man's opportunity. This was their chance to prove themselves equal to white counterparts. Actually, more than equal was the goal. Breaking even wouldn't do. Under Jackson's regime being 'just as good' wasn't good enough. They had to be the best. The difference had to be substantial and obvious. The students responded with extraordinary effort.

As a result, time and again, Tuskegee graduating classes not only ranked high relative to the other 22 schools in the country but placed first on a several occasions. No small feat this! One member of the first class of 1939. In his written flight examination, Charlie Fox, who was in the first class of 1939 achieved a near perfect score. Charlie became a flight instructor at Tuskegee and went on to write about his experiences in his book "Segregated Skies."

Results in actual combat were also encouraging. Volumes have been written about Tuskegee Airman's accomplishments. The real final examination pitted the skill. It would be the skill of the Tuskegee airmen against the warriors of the Third Reich. In terms of medals, their all-black famous 99th Fighter Squadron earned an impressive array of hardware including 150 Distinguished Flying

Crosses, 744 Air Medals, 8 Purple Hearts and 14 Bronze Stars. The distinctive red painted tails on their P-51 Mustangs were familiar and welcome sights to Allied bomber crews. The "Red Tail Angels" were justifiably pound of their reputation of never lost a plane they escorted into combat.

Thanks for all your help, Bennie! I couldn't have done it without you.

#580 Dayton, Ohio   Wright Brothers Airport
August 14, 2004   Type: Paved Identifier: MGY

#581 Cynthiana, Indiana   Hepler Field (Private)
Type: Grass   Identifier: IN43   September 8th, 2004

LOST AGAIN! THIS TIME IT IS NOT MY FAULT!

KOCH FIELD, ABOUT seven or eight miles west of Evansville, is a grass strip had just recently been added to the list of public access fields in Indiana. It was not in my GPS data base yet, so I stopped at Mount Carmel airport in Illinois, and got my bearing for a pilotage route. Koch is immediately adjacent to the Evansville Class C boundary and I did not want to violate their airspace.

The route looked easy - a straight shot on a 184-degree heading for about 24 miles. A key marker would be a cooling pond for a power generating station right on the vector between Mount Carmel and Koch. After passing on the east side of the lake, Koch Field should be in sight,

However, the manager at Mount Carmel cautioned that it would not be easy to find this field by sight, since the N-S and E-W section lines with which I am familiar up north do not exist in this region. He suggested that I contact Approach Control at

Evansville; they're nice guys and like to help. That sounded like a good idea.

The trip went exactly as planned. I was directly over the east side of the lake and had the little Cherokee aimed at a 184 heading. For a bit of insurance, I called Evansville Approach and told them my intentions. They were more than happy to help. I got a squawk code and they went to plot a course. After helping a few other planes, the controller came back and told me to turn left to a course of 158 degrees.

This isn't what I expected but I rolled over to the assigned course and within a minute or two, Evansville came back and told me Koch was at 2.5 miles and 11 o'clock. I thanked them for their friendly help. How could I have been so wrong? The field, just as Approach said, was just to the left of the airplane's nose and I was on an extended left base for landing.

My suspicion grew when I lined up on final with a heading of 90 degrees. It was a grass runway, alright, but I was anticipating a 4 and 22 degree runway, not this 90 and 270 degree wonderment beneath my nose.

At the east end of the runway was a country road and an open hangar with their airplanes inside (one was a Maule). The hangar was open and there were three airplanes inside including a Maule. From the right wing of the Cherokee, I shouted to a gentleman alongside the Maule, "This isn't Koch airport, is it?" The man smiled and said, "No, but welcome to Hepler Field!"

I thought back about the controller at Evansville and how I have taxed his patience, tested his good nature and stretched his forbearance with my amateurish ways in aviation. Sure, I was directed to the wrong airport, something I've done on my own, without outside help! No one's perfect, however. All in all, I owe traffic controllers a large debt.

#582 Carmi, Illinois   Carmi Municipal Airport
Type: Paved Identifier: CUL September 8th, 2004

#583 Sturgis, Kentucky Sturgis Municipal Airport
Type: Paved Identifier: I05 September 8th, 2004

#584 Providence, Kentucky   Providence - Webster County
Type: Paved   Identifier: 8M9   September 8th, 2004

#585 Princeton, Kentucky   Princeton - Caldwell County
Type: Paved   Identifier: 2M0   September 8th, 2004

A HORSE NAMED ERASTUS

DROPPING INTO LOW-TRAFFIC airports offers a good chance of finding a personable, witty and charming man such as Dewayne Orban Howton. Dewayne owns a civil construction company and operates heavy equipment in Dawson Springs. He also has a 1960 Cessna 210 (N9537T) hangared at Princeton-Caldwell.

Dewayne is an engaging young man who apparently enjoys life to its fullest. As a teenager, he raced motorcycles professionally and flirted with death. Of course, he saw the thrill in flying and promptly bought an airplane as soon as he obtained his pilot's license. His sweet wife Candy (who is also a joy to talk with) told me that his first time on horseback was in a rodeo on a bucking bronco. The story goes like this:

Candy is an avid horse enthusiast who rarely misses a horse show or a rodeo. Dewayne, being a good husband, caters to her hobby willingly. It was at a rodeo that Dewayne, who had never ridden a horse, decided to try riding a bronco. He believed that if he could ride motorcycles at breakneck speed, he could surely hold onto a horse bouncing around in one spot for a couple of seconds.

Candy told rodeo officials that Dewayne Howton, a widely respected motorcycle racer, was about to try his hand at bronco riding. The handlers knew a rookie when they saw one, they set him upon the wildest horse in the arena. If I recall correctly, the horse's name was Dynamite. Just before opening the gate, they shot the horse with a cattle prod. The horse bolted out furiously, and Dewayne had the ride of his life. The horse couldn't shake him - and vice versa - because Dewayne's hand was caught in the tie-down device. He had to be cut loose and was carried off by a couple of mounted cowboys.

Following the rodeo tale, I soon became spellbound by Dewayne's flying stories, one of which had to do with a horse named Erastus.

In Dewayne's Kentucky, a lot of families own horses; they are prolific in rural areas. Dewayne is no exception and one of them, Erastus, taught Dewayne a lesson he would never forget.

One day Dewayne took off in his Cessna 150 Aerobat with nowhere to go in particular, so he lollygagged around his home grounds. That is when he spotted Erastus in the pasture. Erastus was as wild as Dewayne and equally strong willed. With a giggle, Dewayne buzzed the horse so low that Erastus became frightened. Dewayne buzzed him again, only lower and Erastus was now running to escape to another corner of the pasture. I'm not sure how many times Dewayne dove down on Erastus but Dewayne came up with another idea. Dewayne decided to land the little Aerobat in the pasture and see how Erastus reacted.

Once on the ground with the engine stopped, Dewayne remained motionless in the plane. Erastus had no idea that his master was in this instrument of the devil, but the plane remaining quiet and motionless was too much for the horse to ignore.

The animal moved cautiously toward the plane with his head bobbing nervously. He circled the plane, drawing closer. Within minutes Erastus was next to the airplane. He would not go under the wing or approach the fuselage. He did stick out his nose out to sniff the horizontal stabilizer. He was getting braver. Dewayne had one more trick up his sleeve. With the horse standing alongside the tail, Dewayne stomped his right foot onto the rudder pedal, slamming the rudder against the stop next to the horse.

The horse reared up in fear. Dewayne thought he had turned to run but that was not the case. Erastus turned his backside to the plane but then he shot out back his two hind feet and instead, kicked at the tail assembly. He followed with a few more well-aimed strikes in rapid succession until the horizontal stab was seriously bent and ready to fall off the airplane. Dewayne bailed out of the plane to calm down the horse, but his sudden presence confounded the animal even more and Erastus ran toward safety.

Installation of a new tail assembly cost Dewayne a pretty penny. More importantly, he never pulled that trick again. I don't know what happened to Erastus.

#586 Dawson Springs, KY   Tradewater Airport
Type: Grass   Identifier: 8M7   September 8th, 2004

#587 Madisonville, Kentucky   Madisonville Municipal
Type: Paved   Identifier: 2I0   September 8th, 2004

#588 Greenville, Kentucky   Muhlenberg County Airport
Type: Paved   Identifier: M21   September 8th, 2004

#589 Hartford, Kentucky   Ohio County Airport
Type: Paved   Identifier: 7K4   September 8th, 2004

#590 Owensboro, Kentucky   Owensboro - Daviess County
Type: Class D Identifier: OWB   September 8th, 2004

#591 Henderson, Kentucky   Henderson Airport
Type: Paved   Identifier: HER   September 9th, 2004

NO VISIBILITY BELOW

MOST PILOTS LOG a lot of" hangar flying" time. Low ceilings, high winds and storms will stop pilots from flying but it will not keep them from the airport but it will keep them out of the air. When pilots venture forth, the weather they fear is fast-forming, low (or no visibility) weather beneath them. They may be flying in clear air at altitude, but they have to descend into the muck sooner or later. A case in point is Henderson, Kentucky.

I arrived at Owensboro-Daviess County airport shortly before sunup. The air was crisp, cool and clear. It is a pleasure to pre-flight with the low level of activity that an early AM departure provides. The weather forecast was for clear skies, with a warning of high moisture content due to the passing of Hurricane Frances. Her main impact would be on eastern Kentucky and Ohio. My route would be to westward and then northward, coming home. Just before chocks away, I could see forever.

Henderson is less than 20 minutes away. Dropping down to pattern altitude, I saw a well-defined line of clouds forming over the Ohio River. They were so small, the line was almost negligible, but it remained over the warm water. Coming into my downwind leg, I flew through some of them I could see through them.

The coffee was hot and the conversation with Nancy, who was on duty that morning, was excellent. We talked about many things. Within 30 or 45 minutes, I was back on my way to Cairo, Illinois. With no appreciable wind, take-off to the west was an advantage. Right at 150' AGL, I passed through a thin wisp of moisture. When level at 3,000 feet AGL, I could see the beauty of the sunrise from my back on the wing tops. The sky was remarkably blue that morning. Then fear grabbed my heart. I was on top of a cloud layer. That little thin section at 150' to 300' was history. It was 100% cloud cover and I was "VFR On Top"; flying on Visual Flight Rules but only at altitude above the weather. Any attempt to land would have to be with Ground Control assistance.

While cantankerous weather is serious, I really thought that, being as far north as I was, this was really a weak, left hook from Frances to the south of me. Fuel management and a northern objective were prudent, at least for an hour. I climbed to 3,500 feet which is the lowest altitude that Lycoming recommends for leaning and leaned the engine aggressively with a reduced power setting. There would be at least 4 hours plus in the tanks. I should get out of trouble with that. North and west looked better than south and west so Cairo was out of the question and Mount Vernon looked like a better bet.

While this trip, as they all are, was planned to be VFR for the whole trip including the run home, I still had IFR plates and Low Level Enroute Charts on hand. Evansville was a short distance behind me and there were many "outs" ahead in the St. Louis Class B. I would give it one hour before I changed the flight objective.

I was angry at myself for getting into this fix. Under my breath I muttered an apology to all of those whom I previously damned for getting caught on top. Indeed, it was easy. In fact, it was insidious and entrapping. Even if I recognized it during climb out from Henderson City, I still could not have done anything about it. It still would have been a below minimum approach. A landing coming out of a take-off climb would be equally dangerous. It did sneak up without warning.

Finally I spotted a substantial break in the clouds near the Mount Vernon area proved to be valid. We augured on, 69 Whiskey and me, to clear skies only eight or nine miles away. Now I knew firsthand what it like to be "caught on top" and how great it felt to be free.

#592 Mount Vernon, Illinois
Type: Paved   Identifier: MVN

Mount Vernon Municipal
September 9th, 2004

#593 Harrisburg, Illinois
Type: Paved   Identifier: HSB

Harrisburg - Raleigh Airport
September 9th, 2004

#594 Benton, Illinois
Type: Paved   Identifier: H96

Benton Municipal Airport
September 9th, 2004

#595 Pickneyville, Illinois
Type: Paved   Identifier: PJY

Pickneyville - Du Quoin A/P
September 9th, 2004

#596 Sparta, Illinois
Type: Paved   Identifier: SAR

Sparta - Hunter Airport
September 9th, 2004

THE "CITY OF CHICAGO"

SPARTA IS THE home of a very special flying household. The Hunter family, 4 brothers and 2 sisters, were always very excited about gas powered vehicles, especially their motorcycles. In short they ran the wheels off of their 'cycles. Every so often, the boys would take a ride to nearby St. Louis to the 'cycle dealer for repairs. In 1923, brothers John and Kenneth came into St. Louis for such a trade but instead, ambled over to Robertson Aviation at Lambert Field to watch the planes take off and land. Before long, Robertson talked them into trading their bikes for a plane, a Stinson SM-1B; NC5189. The boys were given 90 minutes of instruction and then they were flown over their home to Sparta. This was so they would learn how to get home. They were to use their newly acquired extensive knowledge of aviation to train their brothers how to fly.

The Hunter boys would hop over to Robertson Aviation frequently and became acquainted with the dozens of pilots that frequented the field. It was during one of these visits that Albert and his wife met with an adventurous young air mail pilot named Charles Lindberg. They had their 10 week old son with them at the time. The baby's name was Hershel and Lindberg loved to rock the youngster to sleep in his lap. It was Hershel who told me this story.

It was the afterglow of the roaring 20s widespread poverty of the depression that prompted folks to do everything and anything to make money. The Hunter boys, armed with their youth, their love of speed and things mechanical got an idea for a flying endurance record.

They would modify the SM-1B with a 132 gallon fuselage tank in addition to the two standard 45 gallon wing tanks, cat walks along the fuselage sides to aid in repairs and servicing and the frame was structurally strengthened to accept the extra weight. John, the oldest, and Kenneth would be the pilots. Walter and Albert would fly the supply plane. Service would be very frequent so Sister Irene would spell the brothers matching their flying hour for hour. Mabel, the remaining sibling, was bedridden with tuberculosis during this attempt and could not take part in the adventure.

The heavily loaded airplane broke ground at Chicago's Sky

Harbor airport (near the future site of O'Hare Field) on June 11th, 1930. The aircraft finally returned to the ground on July 4th. The flight lasted for a total of 533 hours and 45 minutes. That interprets to 23 days, 2 hours and 45 minutes.

The pilots were racked with exhaustion and fatigue. It was told that Kenneth went into the air with a painful toothache. Walter, Albert and Irene went into the air constantly with food, water, fuel and supplies. Keep in mind that weather could not interrupt any of these flights. I cannot imagine how I could snuggle a plane under the belly of a supply plane after flying for over 500 hours and maneuvering for the time it takes to complete the transfer of fuel and such. These are great pilots with enormous trust in their flying abilities.

John continued flying with a mail run between Evansville, IN and Chicago, IL. He was killed at age 26 on June 28, 1932 at Rosedale, Mississippi by a prop strike while attempting to untie an amphibian plane from the dock. Albert worked in trucking, farming and moving houses and heavy equipment. The third oldest, Walter, became a pilot with American Airways. Kenneth, the fourth oldest, won a WWII contract to fly aircraft to England, but instead went to work for Lockheed as a test pilot. Kenneth was badly burned in an accident at Lockheed, and then went with Kerr-McGee as a corporate pilot. He was killed in crash in 1975 when the Saber liner he was flying suffered a flameout during a landing approach. All four brothers were inducted into the Illinois Aviation Hall of fame in 1996.

Their record, like all records must fall and theirs has been eclipsed many times. The standing record was flown late 1958 and early '59 in a Cessna 172. Pilots Robert Timm and John Cook remained aloft over the Mojave Desert for 64 days, 22 hours, 19 minutes, 5 seconds. Food, water and supplies were hoisted in by a hook on a rope. They refueled by hoisting a hose up from a fuel truck. The flight ended at 1,558 hours continuous running; they could no longer climb away from the fuel truck. The Cessna 172 hangs from the ceiling at McCarran Airport in Las Vegas.

#597 Vandalia, Illinois   Vandalia Municipal Airport
Type: Paved   Identifier: VLA   September 9th, 2004

IS THIS THE BEGINNING OF THE END?

I COULD SEE THE end of my flying days on the horizon. You see, I have always had little medical issue. Occasionally, my heart would, of its own accord, suddenly beat at a very rapid pace. It would continue for 10 to 20 minutes, stop, not to be heard from again for several months.

One day, while on a stress test in the hospital, the little nerve condition came back and my heart rate went from 125 to 225 in one beat. Doctor Nichols, the cardiologist attending the test, became very concerned. Was I dizzy? No. Was I seeing red? No. Was I nauseous? No. He stopped the test and stretched me out on a gurney. Doctor Nichols injected a dose of medication nick-named the Mike Ditka medicine. The Bear's coach had recently had a heart attack and pioneered the use of this medication. It didn't slow my heart rate. The doctor ordered another dose and then another until he had injected me with several doses. Still nothing changed. I told him that it would stop on its own volition in a few minutes. He wasn't buying that opinion at all. He continued to work feverishly over me for about 20 minutes. Then, the strange heart beat stopped as quickly as it started. Still plugged into the data recording machine, I saw my heart beat drop from 225 to 85. The tension in the test lab remained very high.

I was now firmly in the hands of Cardiology Specialists; a, widely known and respected team of doctors. I was under the care of Dr. Brad Suprenant for an Electro Procedure. He was very kind, and realized that I was not too well versed in medical issues. He told me that the nerves around my heart (and there are a billion of them) appear to be short circuited in some way. He wanted to do the "EP" and find out (a) where they were malfunctioning and (b) could they be physically corrected. If not corrected, I would be put on medication to prevent a re-occurrence of the rapid heartbeat. In a few days, I checked into the hospital. For almost 4 hours, he ran little TV cameras up my large veins: two in my neck and two large (I believe they are called 'femur arteries') in my legs. With electrical stimulus, he could encourage all sorts of reactions. He could awaken me and put me to sleep. I could feel my temperature go up and down and a myriad of other little sensations. For hours they mapped out my insides and finally concluded they found the nerves which were electrically shorting. The most important conclusion was it could be fixed, on the spot.

It was explained to me in very understandable terms. The cameras were removed; an audio speaker was inserted into my arteries and directed to the area of the problematic nerves. They blasted the area with sound and, because they wanted scar tissue to develop between the nerves, the vibration had to cause some trauma between them. It seemed simple and straightforward; at least that is how I understand it.

Because all of this was taking place on the surface of my heart, there was danger of my heart wall inverting to the point where the insides of the walls would abrade against each other. So they put me into intensive care for the evening but nothing untoward happened.

Everything was coming up 'Aces!' We were achieving absolutely great results with an equally great prognosis. There would be no after effects or hindrances to my lifestyle. No medication was necessary. There would be no recurrences of my arrhythmic heart. The good doctors still insisted that I need to lose 15 to 20 pounds. Other than that, everything went my way.

That is, of course, until it came time for my next physical!

A question in the physical report asks if the applicant has been in the hospital in the last 3 years. I always thought this was an odd question in that Class B physicals are only good for two years. But then, who am I to call the FAA odd? Being a good citizen and never trying to hold anything from my government, I wrote 'yes.' Reviewing my application, the examining doctor asked why the hospitalization was needed. I tried to explain to him circumstances of my little nerve problem, but held his attention only until the word "heart" was mentioned. He readily confessed that he had no idea what I was talking about and that he would need some sort of help in this matter. Since the entire Cardio Specialists team was officed directly across the street from the examiner, he could have easily contacted Doctor Suprenant or his staff with a local phone call. Instead, he packaged up the whole application and sent it to the FAA in Oklahoma City.

The bureaucrats in "Oke City" advised me that they would not approve a physical until they knew more about it. That led to weeks and weeks of bothering doctors, writing letters, fielding phone calls and another stress test to boot. No one on this end had any idea why many of these questions were being asked and demands were being made. They simply complied. The FAA finally approved my application but cautioned that I had to report any change in my health immediately to them.

The next physical exam year, the FAA required a sheaf of letters from my personal doctors, a stress test for their benefit only and imposed special requirements upon the examining doctor. This time, I bypassed the original examining doctor and secured one who was a pilot as well. He agreed that the doctor who started all this mess should have handled the issue locally.

The new doctor and I each started a file which was updated throughout the two-year period between physicals. He would send letters to the FAA if a prescription changed. And if I caught a cold or anything, he would close his report with " ...there was no adverse effect on patient's ability to perform as a command pilot." For the first time in my flying life, preparation for the Class B physical started 3 months prior to showing up in front of the doctor. Flying was not fun anymore. I continued to fly for several months but the specter of the FAA hovering overhead and the potential of being physically disqualified from flying made it all seem hopelessly discouraging. I felt no verve anymore. I tried to become excited about getting into the airplane only to be flooded with thoughts that my precious friend could be taken away from me at any time.

I had set an exciting goal when I started this adventure so I decided set one more: I was only a handful of visits from a total of 600 airports so I plodded forward. This was good but still I couldn't shake the ultimate disgrace of losing my medical. Overwhelm it, Bob, do something to perk up, man. Finally there were less than 20 airports to 600. The three day trip could cover most of them; probably leaving only three or four to go.

And I wanted to go out with a flourish. Make those last airports three that could not be overlooked. Spit in the eye of the FAA and refuse to let them interfere with my life. While making the soiree through Kentucky, I formed the flight plan for a wondrous, remarkable end.

Airport number 598 would be Columbus, Ohio. It is run by Ohio University and every arriving aircraft is greeted with Welcome to Ohio State University's airport, "We are glad to have you with us!" It would be a good, positive story. I would re-fuel and then head east to the little airport near New Lexington, Ohio: Perry County airport. How cool it would it be to land on an airport that is built over a railroad! I would be combining my two careers, aviation and rail car manufacturing. Yes! Now what about number 600? What would be worthy? Not O'Hare or any of those big brutes. It would be the quintessential airport of all airports: Kitty Hawk, South Carolina. I am going to Kitty Hawk where flight began.

But alas, on the job demands including a lot of travel started to physically wear on me. It came time to face the inevitable. There weren't enough hours in the day except for those needed to put bread on the table and I certainly did not have the stamina to prepare for the Class B physical or to play more games with the FAA. Playtime in the sky was ending and there was no getting around it; N8369W had to go on the block.

Griffith traffic.
Cherokee eight three six niner whiskey is 10 West and coming home.... Forever!

EPITAPH

So it is done. A 15-year odyssey that captured my very soul and remained within me as a driving source of energy and a solid sense of direction was over. The airplane is gone. No other plane has taken the place of 8369W; none ever will. But somewhere inside lives a spirit that seeks new horizons and yearns to discover new things, be they people, vistas or little known-facts and stories. The spirit possesses strength and power which is persistent and demanding. Where to next?

Well, it was one of those lovely nights out with my wife that we both enjoy so much. We were at in our favorite restaurant, seated at a darkish, secluded table. As usual, we were chatting about a number of light and casual subjects. Somewhere between the first and second cocktail, I touched her hand and whispered, "Honey, I bought a boat."

SOME HELP WITH THE "PILOT TALK."

ABBREVIATIONS ARE USED in the text: My apology for any confusion or distress that may have been caused by excess 'pilot talk' or flying verbiage and mostly our inane use of abbreviations. To help, some common references are defined below. I hope this will help you enjoy the stories.

ADF	Instrument, Automatic Direction Finder
AGL	Value, Altitude above Ground Level
AH	Instrument, Artificial Horizon
ALT	Instrument, Altimeter
ASI	Instrument, Air Speed Indicator
ATC	Function, Air Traffic Control
ATIS	Recorded current status, Automatic Terminal Information Service
CATF	Common Air Traffic Advisory
CAVU	Visibility condition, Clear and Unlimited Visibility
CFI	Instructor, Certified Flight Instructor
CFII	Instructor, Certified Flight and Instrument Instructor
COM	Radio, Communication
DG	Instrument, Directional Gyro
DME	Distance Measuring Equipment; 1 DME = 1 mile
EGT	Instrument, Exhaust Gas Temperature
FAA	Function, Federal Aviation Agency
FBO	Airport function, Fixed Base Operation
IFR	Type, rating or status of flight, Instrument Flight Rating
ILS	Instrument Landing System, everything needed to land by instruments in the aircraft and on the ground.
Loran	Long Ranging navigation system, now obsolete.
MP	Manifold pressure; provides a manner of engine output
MSL	Value, altitude value at sea level atmospheric value

MVFR	Value, Marginal Visibility flight Plan
NOTAM	Information, Notices to Airmen
OAT	Value, Outside Air Temperature
RON	Remain Over Night
RPM	Value, (Engine) Revolutions per Minute
STOL	Short take-off and landing
T & B	Instrument, Turn and Bank Indicator
VFR	Type, rating or status of flight; visual ability only
VOR	Navigation Instrument, Omnidirectional Radio Range
VSI	Instrument, Vertical speed Indicator

APPENDIX

THE BEST WAY to understand my quest is to provide a summary. Total number of states visited was eleven. The number of airports by state is presented in the chart below. They need some explanation

State	Airports
Indiana	135
Iowa	93
Illinois	106
Kentucky	9
Michigan	112
Minnesota	8
Missouri	5
Ohio	53
Pennsylvania	1
West Virginia	1
Wisconsin	74
Total	597

My initial objective was to visit all of the airports in Indiana. I sought out private fields to be as inclusive as possible. For state acceptance as a public access airfield, minimum standards must be met. Standards set by the state are much higher than needed for a plane such as mine. Each private field had to be studied very carefully to make sure that it would be safe for me to land and take-off considering my abilities and the capabilities of the plane. Many private fields, however, are built and maintained for use by ultra-light aircraft, without due consideration for full-size, single engine aircraft. By statute, ultra-lights may not weigh more than 254 pounds. Typically, they require about 150 feet of field length for either take-off or landing. In contrast, a Piper Cherokee grosses at 2,400 pounds and needs over 700 feet for take-offs and landings. The hotter and more humid the day, the longer the runway must be. The end of the strip is also critical. Trees, power lines, barns and smoke stacks present special problems. I set my runway minimum at 2,000 feet to allow for whatever surprises may arise at the ends. This personal operational standard applies to both turf and paved fields.

There is no denying that I am a warm weather pilot as is evidenced by the per-month summary. Most of my flying was done from June through September. The days are relatively long and is nicer flying. In winter, we are often grounded by high winds and snow storms. Icing is also a threat here in northern Indiana. Moreover, the jet stream comes southward and is present at a very low altitude.

In one instance, a safety pilot and I were practicing VOR approaches into my home airport. On the surface, the winds were light and variable. It was very light with nothing above 5 knots. Airborne was a different story. At 3,000 feet above sea level or 2,400 above the ground, we encountered 68 knot winds out of the west. An approach with any sort of discipline and accuracy was out of the question. We were bounced around severely, but there was never a serious question of safety. We were wrung out from our experience, and yet managed to laugh at the winds on the surface which remained at 5 knots and variable!

Month	Airports
January	2
February	36
March	43
April	16
May	34
June	65
July	65
August	117
September	131

October	42
November	32
December	14
Total	597

The seasonal breakdown reveals a similar cold weather vs. warm weather discrepancy.

Season		Airports
Winter	(Dec., Jan., Feb.)	52
Spring	(Mar., Apr., May)	93
Summer	(Jun., Jul., Aug.)	247
Autumn	(Sept., Oct., Nov.)	205
Total		597

By year, the story unwinds a little more definitively. In 1992 and '93, having met my original objective, I played around close to home before embarking upon my expanded quest.

Year	Airports
1990	88
1991	26
1992	3
1993	None
1994	82
1995	79
1996	133
1997	68
1998	15
1999	4
2000	29
2001	2
2002	2
2003	41
2004	25
Total	597

THE AIRPORTS

LISTING THE TYPES of airports visited provides a virtual inventory of fields in the Midwest. The number of each type of field upon which I landed upon is shown here.

Type of Field	Number Visited
Class C	17
Class D	26
Military	2
Paved (non- controlled)	396
Grass (non- controlled)	156
Total	597

I visited no Class B airports, such as Chicago O'Hare, Los Angeles International and Washington National for two reasons. First of all, traffic controllers at these heavily trafficked airports don't want people like me flying in with our slow, general aviation aircraft. They maintain a tempo that is essential to the safe handling of their high flow of traffic. General aviation airplanes in the system would disrupt that rhythm. These points of entry also charge heavy landing fees to dissuade sport pilots like me.

Secondly, I don't like flying into such traffic. The best my little Cherokee can do is about 140 miles per hour with full power. The approach speed of most Boeing, Lockheed and McDonnell-Douglas built airplanes is substantially above that. While there is no rear view mirror or back window in a Piper Cherokee, I can feel the hot breath of 757s on the back of my neck any time we are lined up for landing. Early on in my flying career, Tampa tower positioned me between a Douglas DC-8-63 taking off Boeing 727-200 landing. Of course, they also repeatedly requested me to expedite my landing and departure from the runway. Recalling that afternoon long ago still raises goose bumps on the back of my neck. Call it fear if you like, I simply don't like to be in that kind of position. The Cherokee and I are simply out of our element in such company.

Class C airports are also high-traffic airports, but at a substantially lower level than Class B fields. Yet they offer many of the same equipment and staffing advantages as Class B airports. Class C airports have radar surveillance, but the service range is limited to 25 miles. Regardless, this radar is extremely beneficial to general aviation flyers once they enter Class C airspace. Class C fields have air traffic controllers in addition to tower operators. Most Class C fields have multiple approach segments, which means, planes flying in from the west would contact a different controller on a radio frequency different from the controller handling traffic coming in from the east. In such situations, controllers accept much more of the burden of coordination leaving pilots more time to fly assigned routes and keep an eye out for close-in traffic.

Most Midwestern airports are paved and self-controlled. Airplanes are easy to land on pavement. Maintenance of these strips is much easier, also. Rain does not make them soggy and groundhogs can't dig holes in them. Snow removal is a snap on asphalt and concrete while grass runways typically have to wait for warm weather to clear the snow. A pilot can depend upon a paved strip being there from one year to the next. They are established members of the community and life with them has become (more or less) one of peaceful co-existence.

Nevertheless, grass strips are my favorite. From the beginning, I have loved them. I learned early on that no matter what the crosswind component was, the landing would be smoothed out by the grass. If I crabbed the plane into the wind to accommodate a crosswind, the three wheels would be landing in a skewed orientation. Grass, being much more slippery than pavement, allows the wheels to slide a little and instantly align themselves with the forward direction of the plane. Grass made a beginner or an awkward pilot look good.

While some pilots may conclude that grass strips are poor relatives of other airports is inappropriate and undeserved. Several up-scale housing developments are built around grass strips. Skyway Estates at East Lansing, Michigan is a good example. Not only is the runway wide and long, it is as smooth and level as a pool table. It is a real showpiece. Furthermore, the grass runway at Lowell, Indiana is further distinguished by its Instrument Approach - probably the only grass field so equipped. Such approaches are typically limited to Class D airports (or above) with paved runways. Most importantly, grass airports exude the charm of aviation. I equate grass strips with grass-roots. This is where sport aviation is most at home. Time slows down and deeper friendships are more easily made at grass strips. No fuel trucks run around the ramp at grass fields; pilots must pull up the pump for service. With each cutting of the field, the rich, homey aroma of nature fills the nostrils.

Often I flew only to grass strips on a given day. If a paved field may have snuck in, it would only have been for fuel availability. Somehow, I feel General Aviation airplanes are at home on grass.

Then there are the private fields I visited, which became islands of warmth and fond memories. At these airports I spent the longest periods of time. If I have done my work correctly, the affection I have for the owners of these fields and the tenderness with which I speak of them should come through clearly. From time to time, I return to these fields, to those people, their smiles and good will. They are good folks and we share a love for grass-roots flying.

RECORD

ESTABLISHING A RECORD of any sort was never my intent and I claim none. No doubt, I have visited more airports than many flyers. I am equally certain that many pilots have visited more airports than I – probably by a factor of four, five or more. But I am not in the business of flying. My work is railroading. The only flying I enjoy is sport aviation. Weekends and holidays are usually the only days when I fly.

During discussions about my quest with several airline pilots, they quickly admit that they have not been to more than a couple of hundred airports. Several are of these pilots have logged upwards to 30,000 and 35,000 hours. That they spend a lot of time in the air. While they spend the whole day flying, they visit the same 25 airports.

The owner of my home airport is Paul Goldsmith. Paul is in his 70s and has been a pilot most of his life. At first, he flew about the country in support of his car racing career. Stock car racing buffs will remember one of the sport's greatest moments in stock car racing when, in 1964, Plymouth unleashed its 426 cubic inch Hemi engines at the Daytona 500. (By the way, Paul Goldsmith was instrumental in the design of that race track.) All previous speed records were blown away that year by the MOPAR team in their Plymouth Belvederes. The historic finish found Richard Petty, Jimmy Pardue and Paul Goldsmith coming in 1, 2 and 3.

Paul retired from racing to concentrate on aviation. He has a log book with well over 20,000 hours, and also owns the Griffith Airport and G & N Engine Overhaul, one of the premier aviation engine re-builders in the world. He has been to many more airports than I and probably more than most airline pilots. He is gone almost daily, picking up and delivering customer's airplanes and engines to support his business. He visits every type of airport imaginable.

Of course, he frequents smaller and out-of- the-way fields, as do I. Often people I meet at small grass strips will connect my home base with G & N Aviation and ask about Paul. Paul Goldsmith has acquaintances at hundreds, if not thousands of airports around the country. What I have done pales in comparison to his record.

My sport aviation hobby started in the early 1960s in California. With several interruptions, I finally got my license in 1972. As a matter of business travel, I flew extensively in Florida on business, all in rental airplanes. When we bought N8369W, the pride of ownership overwhelmed me to the point of setting such an immense goal of flying to all the airports in Indiana. The crusade began with the purchase of our own Cherokee.

At one time, I intended to flatter myself by working toward getting my name added to the National Aeronautical Association. The National Aeronautical Association is a smallish, non-profit organization that is in constant need of cash to keep its operation going. The reason that I thought of them as a means of getting my feat recognized is because they are known for the sale of records. A pilot can buy a record and get his name in their record book. Here's how it works.

Any pilot can get into any airplane and fly to any airport. If no other pilot has submitted a speed claim between the two airports specified by the submitting pilot, the pilot can claim a speed record between those two sites. That's it! No special airplane is required nor is any particular preparation needed. There is no competition or organization. A J-3 Cub in a casual flight can set a speed record! The NAA does not identify the airport pairs or give its sanction to any attempt. Just fly your little airplane somewhere and ask for recognition. Then just pay the National Aeronautical Association fee. The NAA is there waiting for your claim and a check. The fee in my case was just under $1,000.00.

While there are a lot of people that do this sort of thing, it has the stigma of being meaningless, cheap and without substance. While I entertained the idea for a while, it became painfully obvious that there were better things that could be done with the thousand dollars. I left the on-demand record setting for others.

THE VERIFICATION

N O ONE AT our airport had ever done what I was doing. The idea seemed unique and formidable. It was apparent that some form of documentation was required, and it had to fit a wide variety of situations. It would have been nice to get someone's signature at each airport. But at most fields, I was the only person there. Fuel purchases were ruled out, since fewer and fewer airports have fuel for sale to the public. A series of witnesses would be nice but many of my trips were solo. Then I hit upon the idea of a photograph of the Cherokee at each field. Of course, the picture had to include something recognizable and unique to the airport.

This proved to be not only a viable solution to the documentation question but also it became a source of enjoyment for Nancy and me. We would get the film developed by a 24 hour service. We made small identifying labels to be pasted onto the pictures. Once they were identified and sorted, we pored through them and Nancy selected one that would represent the airport in our special album. Typically, she would select the best photograph with someone from the airport in it. The remaining photos were put into a separate book.

Non-pilots view these albums as boring. Five hundred and ninety seven pictures of the same red and white low wing airplane parked at an airport. Pilots, of course, do not see it that way. They leaf through the book page by page and comment on this picture or that one because they spot something unique or familiar, or something that brings back a personal memory of theirs. They really do study every photograph.

I cherish it!

INDEX OF AIRPORTS

Indiana

Iowa

Kentucky

Tradewater A/P, 294

Michigan

Wyncoop A/P, 142

Pennsylvania

Erie International A/P, 77

West Virginia

Ohio County, 220

Wisconsin

Adams County, 173
Austen-Staubel A/P, 224
Beloit Municipal, 165
Blackhawk Field, 170
Black River Falls A/P, 222
Bloyer Field, 222
Boscobel Municipal, 137
Brodhead A/P, 166
Burlington Municipal, 165
Cassville Municipal, 137
Central Wisconsin A/P, 244
Clintonville Municipal, 224
Dane County, 169
Dodge County, 222
Dornink A/P, 172
East Troy Municipal, 163
Ephraim-Fish Creek A/P, 224
Fond du Lac Skyport, 223
Fort Atkinson Municipal, 168
Fox River A/P, 164
Grant County, 137
Gutzmer's Twin Oaks, 168
Hartford Municipal, 215
Iowa County, 136
Jana A/P, 168
Kenosha Regional, 214
Kettle Moraine A/P, 224
LaCrosse International, 200
Lake Geneva Estates, 215
Lake Geneva Private, 163
Lake Lawn Resort, 168

Lancaster A/P, 192
Langlade County, 244
Lawrence J. Timmerman A/P, 235
Manitowoc County, 216
Marshfield Municipal, 240
Mauston-New Lisbon Union, 173
McHenry Farm, 163
Mitchell International, 237
Monroe Municipal, 136
Morey A/P, 170
Necedah A/P, 222
New Holstein Municipal, 218
Oconto Municipal, 224
Oneida County, 244
Outgamie County, 216
Palmyra A/P, 168
Portage Municipal, 173
Prairie du Chien Municipal, 137
Reedsburg Municipal, 138
Richland A/P, 171
Robert H. Batten Field, 214
Rock County, 166
Sauk Praire A/P, 171
Shawano Municipal, 224
Sheboygan County, 216
Sparta-Camp McCoy Field, 222
S & S Ranch, 172
Stevens Point Municipal, 239
Steve Wittman Field, 224
Sturgeon Municipal, 224
Sylvania A/P, 214
Three Castles A/P, 173
Tri-Co Regional, 136
Viroqua Municipal, 173
Wag-Aero Private, 214
Watertown Municipal, 173
Waukesha County, 215
Waunakee A/P, 170
Waupaca Municipal, 224
Wautoma Municipal, 173
Westosha A/P, 163
Wisconsin Dells A/P, 222